THE ART OF COMPARISON
HOW NOVELS AND CRITICS COMPARE

LEGENDA

LEGENDA, founded in 1995 by the European Humanities Research Centre of the University of Oxford, is now a joint imprint of the Modern Humanities Research Association and Maney Publishing. Titles range from medieval texts to contemporary cinema and form a widely comparative view of the modern humanities, including works on Arabic, Catalan, English, French, German, Greek, Italian, Portuguese, Russian, Spanish, and Yiddish literature. An Editorial Board of distinguished academic specialists works in collaboration with leading scholarly bodies such as the Society for French Studies and the British Comparative Literature Association.

MHRA

The Modern Humanities Research Association (MHRA) encourages and promotes advanced study and research in the field of the modern humanities, especially modern European languages and literature, including English, and also cinema. It also aims to break down the barriers between scholars working in different disciplines and to maintain the unity of humanistic scholarship in the face of increasing specialization. The Association fulfils this purpose primarily through the publication of journals, bibliographies, monographs and other aids to research.

Maney Publishing is one of the few remaining independent British academic publishers. Founded in 1900 the company has offices both in the UK, in Leeds and London, and in North America, in Boston. Since 1945 Maney Publishing has worked closely with learned societies, their editors, authors, and members, in publishing academic books and journals to the highest traditional standards of materials and production.

STUDIES IN COMPARATIVE LITERATURE

Editorial Committee
Professor Stephen Bann, University of Bristol (Chairman)
Professor Duncan Large, University of Swansea
Dr Elinor Shaffer, School of Advanced Study, London

Studies in Comparative Literature are produced in close collaboration with the British Comparative Literature Association, and range widely across comparative and theoretical topics in literary and translation studies, accommodating research at the interface between different artistic media and between the humanities and the sciences.

PUBLISHED IN THIS SERIES

The Art of Comparison

How Novels and Critics Compare

Catherine Brown

Studies in Comparative Literature 23
Modern Humanities Research Association and Maney Publishing
2011

Published by the
Modern Humanities Research Association and Maney Publishing
1 Carlton House Terrace
London SW1Y 5AF
United Kingdom

LEGENDA is an imprint of the
Modern Humanities Research Association and Maney Publishing

Maney Publishing is the trading name of W. S. Maney & Son Ltd,
whose registered office is at Suite 1C, Joseph's Well, Hanover Walk, Leeds LS3 1AB

ISBN 978-1-906540-81-4

First published 2011

Printed in Great Britain

Cover: 875 Design

Copy-Editor: Nigel Hope

CONTENTS

To David Brown and Ursula Brown (geb. Heß)
for their ongoing teaching

ACKNOWLEDGEMENTS

I acknowledge the generous encouragement and advice of my editor Professor Elinor Shaffer, my series editor Dr Graham Nelson, and my copy-editor Nigel Hope, my PhD supervisor Professor Adrian Poole, and my PhD examiners Dr Rod Mengham and Professor Michael Bell. The Ludwig Fund of New College, Oxford, has provided support. Alexander Mercouris and Haukur Heimisson have illumined my life throughout the writing. Mr Jeremy Prynne, at Gonville and Caius College, Cambridge, has instructed mind and soul.

CONVENTIONS

Non-English words and phrases are given in the original language followed by an English translation, with three categories of exception. The names of well-known places are given in English translation (e.g. *Moscow*). Russian personal names and lesser-known places are given in English transliteration (e.g. *Lev Tolstoi, Vozdvizhenskoe*). The titles of well-known texts are given first in Russian and in future references in English (e.g. *Война и мир, War and Peace*). Where no reference is given to translations, they are my own.

The chapters of *Women in Love* and *Daniel Deronda* as first published were numbered consecutively; those of *Anna Karenina* were numbered within parts. Chapters in all three novels were originally headed by roman numerals, but I will refer to them with Arabic numerals. *Daniel Deronda* is divided into eight *books*, and *Anna Karenina* is divided into eight **части** or parts. The books had roman numerals, which I have retained. The **части** were referred to as **Часть первая** etc. [*Part the First*], but I refer to them by roman numerals.

The 1989 second edition of the *Oxford English Dictionary*, the King James Authorized translation of the Bible, and the 1986 Oxford University Press Shakespeare are quoted without bibliographical references. Other references are given in the text using the author-date system supplemented by the abbreviations which follow.

ABBREVIATIONS

AK VIII, IX   Лев Толстой, *Анна Каренина: роман в восьми частях* in *Л. Н. Толстой, Собрание сочинении в четырнадсати томах* (Москва: Государственное издательство художественнои литературы, 1952), VIII, IX

AK D   *Anna Karénina*, trans. by Nathan Haskell Dole (London: Walter Scott, 1896)

AK E   *Anna Karenin*, trans. by Rosemary Edmonds (London: Penguin, 1956)

AK G   *Anna Karenina*, trans. by Constance Garnett, 2 vols (New York: Random House, 1939), I, 3–520; II, 523–969

AK MM   *Anna Karenina*, trans. by Louise and Aylmer Maude (Hertfordshire: Wordsworth Editions, 1995)

AK PV   *Anna Karenina*, trans. by Richard Pevear and Larissa Volokhonsky (London: Penguin, 2000)

DD   George Eliot, *Daniel Deronda*, ed. by Graham Handley (Oxford: Oxford University Press, 1984)

EL   *The George Eliot Letters (1871–1881)*, ed. by Gordon S. Haight, 9 vols (London: Oxford University Press and New Haven: Yale University Press, 1954–78)

LL   *The Cambridge Edition of the Letters of D. H. Lawrence*, General Editor James T. Boulton, 8 vols (Cambridge: Cambridge University Press, 1979–2000)

M   George Eliot, *Middlemarch*, ed. by David Carroll (Oxford: Clarendon Press, 1986)

PUFU   D. H. Lawrence, *Psychoanalysis and the Unconscious and Fantasia of the Unconscious*, ed. by Bruce Steele (Cambridge: Cambridge University Press, 2004)

R   D. H. Lawrence, *The Rainbow*, ed. by Mark Kinkead-Weekes (Cambridge: Cambridge University Press, 1989)

RDP   D. H. Lawrence, *Reflections on the Death of a Porcupine and Other Essays*, ed. by Michael Herbert (Cambridge: Cambridge University Press, 1988)

SCAL   D. H. Lawrence, *Studies in Classic American Literature*, ed. by Ezra Greenspan, Lindeth Vasey, and John Worthen (Cambridge: Cambridge University Press, 2003)

STH   D. H. Lawrence, *Study of Thomas Hardy and Other Essays*, ed. by Bruce Steele (Cambridge: Cambridge University Press, 1985)

TL   *Tolstoy's Letters*, trans. and ed. by R. F. Christian, 2 vols (London: The Athlone Press, 1978)

WIA Лев Толстой, *Что такое искусство?*, ed. by Militsa Greene (Bradda: Letchworth, 1963)

WL D. H. Lawrence, *Women in Love*, ed. by David Farmer, Lindeth Vasey, and John Worthen (Cambridge: Cambridge University Press, 1987)

1WL D. H. Lawrence, *The First 'Women in Love'*, ed. by John Worthen and Lindeth Vasey (Cambridge: Cambridge University Press, 2002)

WP Лев Толстой, *Война и мир,* in *Л. Н. Толстои, Собрание сочинении в четырнадсати томах* (Москва: Государственное издательство художественной литературы, 1952), IV–VII

NOTE ON THE TEXT OF *ANNA KARENINA*

Russian text. The Russian edition of *Anna Karenina* to which my page numbers refer forms volumes VIII and IX of a fourteen-volume edition of Lev Tolstoi's works published by the State Publishers of Artistic Literature in Moscow in 1952. This edition differs slightly both from a more recent scholarly Russian edition and from the edition which Constance Garnett and the Maudes translated into English, which itself differs from the edition which was serialized. After *Anna Karenina* was published in *Русский вестник* [*Russian Messenger*], Tolstoi and his friend Nikolai Strakhov spent the summer of 1877 making revisions for the 1878 single-volume edition. The 1920s and 1930s ninety-volume *Юбилей* [*Jubilee*] edition of Tolstoi, and the 1970 *Литературные памятники* [*Literary Monuments*] edition of V. A. Zhdanov and E. E. Zaidenshnur, corrected misprints and progressively removed Strakhov's, and some of Sofiia's and other copyists', amendments. The latter edition contains hundreds of changes from the Jubilee edition on which my own is based. Turner notes that 'Few of the new readings are of more than minimal significance' (1993: 55). The variations between source texts slightly qualify the validity of the comparison of translations which appears below.

D. H. Lawrence and English translations. Lawrence did not know Russian (although he made several attempts to learn it), and read *Anna Karenina* in English translation. By the time that he first read the novel, some time between 1905 and 1907, two English translations were available. The first, by the American translator and author Nathan Haskell Dole, was published in 1886 in America, and by Heinemann in England in 1889 (Birdwood-Hedger 2006: 71; R. Garnett [1923–] 1991: 107). The second translation was Constance Garnett's, published by Heinemann in 1901. The following inferences are based on Lawrence's spellings of Tolstoi's name and the novel's title, since he left no record of which translations he read (a possible indication that the issue did not greatly concern him). Lawrence almost certainly read Dole's translation first, and had been introduced to it in the extract from the novel which appears in volume XIX of the 1899 twenty-volume *The International Library of Famous Literature*, by Richard Garnett [1835–1906], which Lawrence's family possessed. To avoid confusion it should be noted here that this Richard Garnett is the father of Lawrence's friend Edward Garnett (the husband of the translator Constance Garnett), grandfather of Lawrence's other friend David Garnett, and great-grandfather of Richard Garnett [1923–], biographer of his grandmother Constance. Dole's was considered an acceptable translation, even after the publication of Garnett's (Birdwood-Hedger 2006: 75). Dole worked with the assistance of a French translation, and correspondingly referred to Tolstoi as *Lyof N. Tolstoï*, and to the novel as *Anna Karénina*. Garnett referred to the author as *Leo*

Tolstoy, and to the novel as *Anna Karenin*. Jessie Chambers recorded that for her twenty-first birthday, in 1907, Lawrence gave her 'his own copy of Tolstoi's *Anna Karénina*' (1965: 114). That December, Lawrence told Louie Burrows that he was sending her 'these few words of Tolstoï' (LL 1: 127). In his earliest extant reference to the novel, in 1909, Lawrence wrote of '*Anna Karénina*', and in 1910 he referred to the character of 'Anna Karénin' (LL 1: 191).

However, even though he never adopted Garnett's spelling of *Tolstoy* (from 1908 onwards he replaced the *ï* of *Tolstoï* with an *i*) Lawrence also almost certainly read Garnett's translation. During his elopement in 1912 he and Frieda were thinking about, and probably reading, the novel. By then Garnett had a reputation in England as the leading translator of Russian literature into English. Lawrence had become friends with Edward Garnett in the summer of 1911, and with David Garnett in the year following (Garnett [1923] 1991: 270). Both men would have mentioned Constance's translations to Lawrence, although he did not meet her until 1913. In May 1912 he referred to *Anna Karenina*, without Dole's acute accent (LL 1: 412). That November he wrote to Edward Garnett about *Anna Karenin* (LL 1: 463). It is unlikely that he did so merely out of deference to the Garnetts; in an interview of 1925 he described Constance as 'turning out reams of her marvelous translations [. . .] all magical' (Garnett [1923] 1991: 133). On the assumption that Lawrence had read Garnett's translation by November 1912, this was probably the translation which Lawrence had most recently read when beginning *The Sisters* in March 1913. He was sufficiently intimate with the Garnetts during 1913 and 1914 for Constance to read the second draft of *The Sisters*, and to give him her (negative) comments on it in February 1914 (Garnett [1923] 1991: 281). Constance probably dissuaded him from rereading Dole's translation, which she had read before writing her own, and claimed to find 'so exceptionally bad that it gives hardly any idea of the original' (Garnett [1923] 1991: 191). Lawrence may have read Louise and Aylmer Maude's translation, which appeared as a rival to Garnett's in 1918, but he could not have read this before completing most of *Women in Love*, and there is no record that he read *Anna Karenina* in 1918 or 1919. He continued to use Garnett's *Karenin* form for the rest of his life. The fact that he never adopted her *Tolstoy* form (which was also that of David Garnett, Virginia Woolf, the Maudes, and several other critics of Tolstoi whom Lawrence read) may easily be accounted for. Only after Lawrence's death did *Tolstoy* become the English standard. *Tolstoi* was the spelling in which he had first encountered the author, since this rather than Dole's *Tolstoï* appeared in Garnett's *International Library*. It was also the spelling used by Matthew Arnold, Edward Garnett, S.S. Kotelianskii (with whom he collaborated), and any German author whom Lawrence may have read on the author.

In order to give a sense of the translation with which Lawrence was most familiar, I have compared sections of Garnett's translation with corresponding passages in four other English translations: those of Dole, the Maudes, Rosemary Edmonds (1956), and Richard Pevear and Larissa Volokhonsky (2000).[1] The freest translation is Dole's. He states in his Preface to the American edition that he has omitted certain scenes in deference to the 'Puritan taste' of America; he omits for example most of Part II, Chapter 11, which contains the scene after Anna and Vronskii have had sex for the first time (Birdwood-Hedger 2006: 74). Oblonskii is described as merely 'too attentive' to the French governess (AK D: 5). He eliminates mundane details, and alters certain words in favour of clarity of meaning: at the end of the novel Levin feels that the moments of his life will be full of 'deep meaning', rather than of 'смысл добра' [meaning of goodness] (AK D: 769; AK IX: 404). He alters Tolstoi's paragraph and sentence structures, and makes some mistakes, giving for example 'For such work my brother was beaten once' for 'За это нашего брата по горбу бывало', which is closer to Garnett's 'For such work us fellows would catch it!' (AK D: 263; AK VIII: 266; AK G: 300). With the exception of the exoticisms noted below, his American English is fluent.

On the scale of free versus literal translation Garnett's is more literal that the Maudes' and Edmonds's, but considerably less so than Pevear and Volokhonsky's. She exercises occasional freedom, such as 'right and wrong' for 'добра' [right], and makes certain mistakes (AK G: 967; AK IX: 402). She translates the novel into the intellectual atmosphere of her own time, which was that in which the teenaged Lawrence started reading — as is particularly apparent in her translation of terms referring to mental states into terms with stronger scientific and psychoanalytic connotations. She translates by 'to be conscious of' not only *сознавать* but also *чувствовать* [to feel], *заметить* [to notice], and *испытать* [to experience]. Anna at the ball has 'deliberate grace' according to Garnett, whereas Pevear and Volokhonsky, more accurately, render 'отчётливую грацию' as 'precise grace'; at this stage in the novel, Anna's attractiveness to Vronskii and others is precisely not 'deliberate' (AK G: 97; AK VIII: 89; AK PV: 81). Garnett was an intermediary figure, born thirty-three years after Tolstoi and twenty-four years before Lawrence. She published her translation at a time (1901) when theories of consciousness were both being more rapidly developed, and were more widely known, than in Russia at the time of *Anna Karenina*. The Maudes too were intermediaries: Aylmer knew Tolstoi and was a prominent English Tolstoyan; his and Louise's translation and *Women in Love* are exactly contemporary.

Garnett's English is generally fluent, congruent with Lawrence's observation that she covered sheet after sheet with her translations with hardly a pause (Garnett [1923] 1991: 133). Henry Gifford finds her English more fluent than the Maudes' (Gifford 1978). However, sometimes her conversation is clumsy, as in Vronskii's question to Anna: 'Anna, what is it for, why will you?' for *Анна зачем, зачем?* ['Anna, why, why?] (AK G: 838; AK IX: 287). Gifford praised her 'refusal to tamper with Tolstoy's syntax' because 'she would accept the angularities and not shrink from his repetitions [. . .] She has reproduced his mannerism, and yet contrives to write an English that does not seem uncouth or defiant, as a literal translation without her modest harmonies probably would' (Garnett [1923] 1991: 205; Gifford 1978: 22). Garnett herself thought that she was improving on Tolstoi's style; she wrote to her husband in 1901: 'I really think the English version of Anna is clearer and more free from glaring defects of style than the Russian original. So at least Fanny Stepniak has often declared when we have been reading my translation together' (Garnett [1923] 1991: 205). However, she remains closer to the original structures, and frequent naivety or coarseness of Tolstoi's tone, than the Maudes and Edmonds, and is less prudish than either. The latter's translations are more formal; Edmonds in particular makes alterations in favour of elegance, giving: 'Swath followed swath' for 'Прошли ещё и ещё ряд' [They went through another and another row] (AK E: 271; AK VIII: 268).

Pevear and Volokhonsky's is the most literally precise of the five translations: it follows Tolstoi's word order, sentence, and paragraph structures the most closely, and gives the best sense of the coarseness of the original, which was mildly censored for obscenity in Soviet editions. The translators describe the mowing peasants as 'sweaty' ['потные'] rather than 'perspiring' (Maudes and Edmonds) or 'hot' (Garnett) — although Dole does give 'covered with sweat' (AK PV: 249; AK VIII: 266; AK MM: 246; AK E: 270; AK G: 29; AK D: 262). Nonetheless, in common with the other translations, they fail to re-enact Tolstoi's occasional choice of old-fashioned or highly formal words. They also make mistakes, giving for example 'look at the hired men!' for 'виш, подряде-то!' (peasant dialect for, literally, 'look! His swaths dip in the middle'), which is closer to Dole's 'but look at his row!' (AK PV: 250; AK VIII: 266; AK D: 263). In common with many source-language-biased translations, Pevear and Volokhonsky's English is often stilted.

Cultural transplantation is most favoured by the Maudes and Edmonds. The Maudes nativize certain of the proper nouns (for example 'Стива' to 'Steve'), and Latinize the peasant 'Тит' to 'Titus'. Dole is the most exotic. He gives many Russian nouns and idiomatic expressions in the text (for example '*Nu*' [well now] and '*barin*' [master]), glossing some immediately afterwards, and listing all in a glossary. Pevear and Volokhonsky do the same to a far smaller extent, giving for example '*muzhiks*' for 'peasants'. In this respect Garnett occupies a position between the Maudes and Edmonds, and Dole and Pevear and Volokhonsky. Garnett does not anglicize the names, nor does she render affectionate names. After his death Levin refers to Nikolay as '*Nikolenka*' (as given by Pevear and Volokhonsky), which indicates great affection — whereas Garnett gives 'Nikolay' (AK IX: 136; AK G: 668; AK PV: 559; Birdwood-Hedger 1986: 128–29). Dole, Garnett, and Edmonds all attempt to render Russian peasant dialect by an equivalent English (although the former was further removed from educated Russian than was the equivalent from educated English). They give respectively ''Tention!', 'Mind'ee', and 'Mind'ee' for 'Мотри', a corruption of 'Смотри' [Look] for which the Maudes give 'Mind!' and Pevear and Volokhonsky, most stiltedly, give 'Watch out now' (AK D: 262; AK G: 299; AK E: 270; AK VIII: 266; AK MM: 246; AK PV: 249). Garnett, and Pevear and Volokhonsky, both aim to use diction correspondent to the period in which the original was written. Garnett claims that:

> I have always tried to translate the Russians into the language of the period in which they wrote, which is of course possible with Russian literature, since it is all relatively modern. [. . .] One's aim should always be to translate into the language of the corresponding life. (Birdwood-Hedger 2006: 81)

Richard Pevear claims that 'in fact, one of our principles has been to use no English words that were not current in Tolstoy's time' (Birdwood-Hedger 2006: 98). For Garnett, who wrote within Tolstoi's lifetime, this principle was relatively easy to follow.

In summary, the translation of *Anna Karenina* which Lawrence had in mind at the time of writing *Women in Love* is more source-language-biased than Dole's, the Maudes', or Edmonds's, more target-language-biased than Pevear and Volokhonsky's and (other aspects of) Dole's, and with regard to cultural transplantation has the advantage of relative temporal proximity to the original. It had Tolstoi's approval: according to Richard Garnett, when Constance met Tolstoi in 1893 'She must have reassured him that she had proved a fit translator, for he pressed on her another book of his' (Garnett [1923] 1991: 122). In fact, he had also authorized Dole's and Aylmer Maude's translations, and was an imperfect judge of English. Nonetheless, Lawrence read a translation of the novel which is rightly still read today. Its peculiarities will where relevant be noted in my discussion of Lawrence's responses to Tolstoi.

Note

1. *Anna Karénina*, trans. by Nathan Haskell Dole (1896). This is the one-volume second British edition, which it is most likely that Lawrence read. *Anna Karenina*, trans. by Constance Garnett, 2 vols (1939); *Anna Karenin*, trans. by Rosemary Edmonds (1956); *Anna Karenina*, trans. by Louise and Aylmer Maude (1995); *Anna Karenina*, trans. by Richard Pevear and Larissa Volokhonsky (2000). For a full discussion of English translations of *Anna Karenina* see Birdwood-Hedger 2006.

I put here on the table a green vase, and beside it a yellow orange. Now, those two things affect each other. Side by side, they produce a reaction which neither of them will produce alone. [. . .] I want the reader to see the orange and the vase — beyond that, *I* am out of it.

WILLA CATHER in an interview with Latrobe Carroll,
3 May 1921; Bohlke 1986: 24

You cannot compare apples and oranges

ENGLISH IDIOM

CHAPTER 1

Introduction

What is Comparative Literature?

Aims of the Book

> Every act of the reception of significant form, in language, in art, in music, is comparative.
>
> GEORGE STEINER 1996: 157

This book considers a practice which is involved in all reading, yet is rarely the explicit subject of literary theory. Comparison, in the broadest sense of term, is the mental process which enables the perception of similarity and difference. As such it is intrinsic to thought. Sights, sounds, smells, touches, tastes, and concepts cannot be distinguished without a perception of their similarities and differences to others. Will cannot be exercised without a comparison of options; *to choose* comes from *gusto*, and involves *tasting the difference*; Anna yields to Vronskii after a comparison of Vronskii with Karenin. Unfamiliarity is mediated by comparison of the less with the more familiar; an orange is likened to an apple, and distinguished from it as Chinese (Icelandic *appelsína*, Russian *апельсин*). Words used to describe comparison are either highly abstract, or metaphoric and therefore comparative: broad, narrow, strict, loose, reflecting, shedding light. This book frequently uses the terms which it is describing, in describing them. Criticism involves judging the difference between things.[1] A reader will describe a literary work as *mimetic* only after comparing it with both life and other works. A reader of Heinrich Heine's 'Die schlesischen Weber' will unconsciously compare this experience with all of the other experiences that she or he has had. Assuming appropriate prior experience on her part, this will allow her to determine that she is reading a mid-nineteenth-century German poem in trochaic-cum-dactylic tetrameter which ventriloquizes the rage of exploited machine-weavers. In order to establish these characteristics, and having established them, she will compare the poem with her general sense or detailed memory of any of the other things which share any of them. Matthew Arnold, who coined the term *comparative literature* as a translation of *literature comparée*, claimed in his inaugural lecture at Oxford University in 1857 that 'Everywhere there is connection, everywhere there is illustration. No single event, no single literature is adequately comprehended except in relation to other events, to other literature' (quoted in Bassnett-McGuire 1993: 1). In our own century, Richard Rorty wrote: 'Good criticism is a matter of bouncing some of the books you have read off the rest of the books you have read' (2006: 64). He might have added that good reading of criticism involves bouncing the criticism you are reading off the rest of the criticism which you have read.

Such bouncing, even if unconscious, involves a narrower focus and greater mental effort than the comparison which is involved in any act of cognition. Yet it is not comparison in the narrowest sense of the term. The latter involves paying a similar quantity and quality of attention to a discrete number of things in order to determine their similarities and differences with regard to possession, lack, or degree of possession of a particular quality. A minority of literary criticism is of this kind — both the international, inter-lingual, and inter-artistic criticism which is often considered to be *comparative literature*, and the criticism which includes none of these divisions. The minority may be larger in the first case, but it is still a minority. A comparison of George Eliot with George Sand on a given topic may have the interest, but also the complication, of involving linguistic and cultural variables which are not directly related to the topic concerned. A comparison of George Eliot with Elizabeth Gaskell, which involves fewer circumstantial variables, may be more cleanly comparative, and in this sense *more* comparative. But only relatively; any two writers have differences of circumstance, and any comparison must be performed against a ground which is to some degree abstract, like the flat table surface and block background of *Bright Pear* (on this book's cover), which presents three fruits for comparison.

Describing the *relations* which obtain among things is a broader, more complex process than comparison itself. First, whereas the latter involves comparing things in relation to the same quality, the former may involve characterizing their different qualities. Second, the relations of things include not just the percept but the significance of their similarities and differences, understood in their separate and shared contexts. Third, relations may be described in terms of the comparer's responses to things as juxtaposed: for example, the relationship of *Shamela* to *Pamela*, or of the poems of Thomas Hood to those of Alfred Tennyson, may be felt to make certain features of the latter of each pair appear ridiculous. Fourth, relations may be described in terms of influence: that is, the similarities and differences of objects may be coordinated with historical and biographical information which at least allows the possibility that the creator of one knew something of the other object. Unlike comparison strictly defined, influence studies analyse relationships in an asymmetric manner, describing the presence and absence of the qualities of the earlier work in the later (the Japanese verb for comparison, *hikaku suru*, can be translated by *to do metaphor* — to describe one thing in terms of something else). However, asymmetric comparison does not necessarily imply that the comparer is more interested in either the one or the other. One might identify characteristics of Charles Dickens's writing in those of Franz Kafka out of a greater interest in Dickens or Kafka or out of equal interest in both. In Latin one may distinguish the *primum comparandum*, one's primary interest, from the *secundum comparatum*, what one compares it to, and the *tertium comparationis*, which is their similarity. This book, however, will use *comparandum/a* as a generic term for any patient of comparison. Asymmetric comparison has strong similarities with criticism which is not usually considered comparative. For example, studying the influence of Miguel de Cervantes's *El ingenioso hidalgo don Quixote de la Mancha* on Nikos Kazantsakis's Βίος και Πολιτεία του Αλέξη Ζορμπά [*Life and Adventures of Alexis Zorbas*] has much in common with studying the representation of attitudes towards sex in rural 1930s Greece in the latter novel. In both cases the critic is looking for features of one complex entity (a novel, and an aspect of a culture) in another; the discussion of any topic in literature involves a comparison of the form *looking for X in Y*.

Types and theories of literary criticism assert the importance of comparative practices to varying degrees. Plato contrasted artistic representations with the objects they represented and with the ideal Forms. Vladimir Propp — to say nothing of the intervening millennia — pursued detailed comparisons in order to reach the conclusion of Морфология сказки [*Morphology of the Folk Tale*] that folk tales are structurally similar. New Critics, and F. R. Leavis, emphasized the singularity of texts, but used comparisons rhetorically to point to differences in their quality: 'Adam Bede is good — but compare him with Caleb Garth' (Leavis 1948: 37). Leavis and T. S. Eliot each traced a literary tradition according to their perception of works' affinities to a perpetually evolving structure. The Czech structuralist Jan Mukařovský thought that the most acclaimed works of literature violated the aesthetic norms established collectively by previous works. Explicitly ideological theorists advocate comparisons according to the categories in which they are interested: writings by women and by men, by colonials and colonizers, by monologists and heteroglots, by those who accurately depict society in its historical evolution and those who do not. Comparison in its broadest sense is embedded in structuralist and post-structuralist theory, with their shared emphasis on difference as intrinsic to meaning.

Nonetheless, comparison in its narrower senses has received little explicit attention. In the sixth yearbook of the British Comparative Literary Association's *Comparative Criticism* Elinor Shaffer commented: 'Conducting a retrospective inquiry into specifically comparative modes of close analysis, we find that a very few comparative literary handbooks offered some direct discussion of comparative analysis of texts' (1984: xiv). The position of comparison as a topic in philosophy is also undeservedly obscure. No English-language reference work of philosophy of which I am aware has an entry for the term, despite the facts that comparison is as important a method to philosophy as to literary criticism, and that it is philosophically complex. Harry Levin recounted the dream of a student's wife, in which two men in overalls (Levin and Renato Poggioli) arrived at their house late at night, claiming to have come 'to compare the literature' (1972: 76). The anecdote's humour relies on the apparent meaninglessness of their claim, in contrast to for example the claim of having come to mend the pipes. However, this book argues that to compare literature does mean something, that all literary criticism is comparative in a broad sense whereas much criticism called comparative is not comparative in the strictest sense, and that an analysis of these distinct senses can contribute to several debates in literary criticism.

This chapter and Chapter 5 will consider comparison *per se*, how it is used in literary criticism and this book, and how these issues relate to comparative literature. The three central chapters are case studies, which will discuss George

Eliot's *Daniel Deronda* (1874–76), Lev Tolstoi's *Анна Каренина* (hereafter *Anna Karenina*) (1873–77), and D. H. Lawrence's *Women in Love* (1915–19). These have been chosen as novels containing two plots focused on two couples, one of which ends with the death of a partner and misery of the survivor, and the other of which ends in relative happiness. These novels invite the reader to pay comparative attention to the similar literary objects — stories — which they contain. Chapter 5 will then compare how the novels compare their stories, and reflect on what can be learned about the comparison of literature from comparisons within literature itself. This two-way traffic between criticism and meta-criticism justifies the puns of the book's title and subtitle: *The Art of Comparison* refers both to art which is inherently comparative, and to the process of comparing; *How Novels and Critics Compare* refers both to the comparisons which novels and critics severally construct, and to how these may be compared with each other. That is, not only how *Daniel Deronda*, *Anna Karenina*, and *Women in Love* are similar and different with regard to the comparisons which they invite, but how the comparison of objects juxtaposed by the choice of an artist (the stories of Gwendolen Harleth and Daniel Deronda) resembles and differs from the comparison of objects juxtaposed by the choice of a critic (*Daniel Deronda* and *Anna Karenina*). This book therefore joins other studies which draw, and advocate drawing, meta-critical conclusions from the intensive close reading of literary texts, including Vladimir E. Alexandrov's 2004 *Limits to Interpretation*, K. M. Newton's 1986 *In Defence of Literary Interpretation: Theory and Practice*, and John Bayley's 1960 *The Characters of Love*. The first of these resembles this book in its combination of meta-criticism with close critical attention to *Anna Karenina*, which in Alexandrov's case furnishes a case study for the neo-formalist, quasi-structuralist approach for which he argues. Bayley's book resembles this one by basing a meta-critical statement on the scrutiny of one topic in three major works (*Troilus and Criseyde*, *Othello*, and *The Golden Bowl*). In this book the central chapters are semi-independent: they may be read on their own, but Chapter 2 lays out terms in which all three novels are discussed, and Chapters 3 and 4 make comparative reference to previous discussions.

The three novels are not only intensively compared on the topic of double-plotting, but are briefly related to the Bible, Shakespeare, Goethe, and Germany. The Bible's religion covers the entire geographical region marked out by the countries in which the novels were produced. Shakespeare was native to one of those countries but was well known in the other (for example through Nikolai Gerbel's translation of 1865). References are made to Shakespeare's work in each of the novels: Gwendolen acts the part of Hermione in *The Winter's Tale*, Levin listens to a *Fantasia of King Lear*, and the Fräulein at Breadalby suggests acting the Three Witches from *Macbeth*. Moreover, Shakespeare was keenly concerned with the attractions and dangers of comparison as an intellectual and rhetorical strategy; the growing acquaintance of Goethe's Wilhelm Meister with Shakespeare himself is emblematic of his openness to the practice of comparison, as well as to foreign influences. Goethe and his country lie between England and Russia, and mediate between them; Germany's cultural influence had been particularly strong in Russia since the time of Ekaterina II Velikaia [Catherine the Great], and in Britain since the accession of the House of Hanover; German families connected the monarchies of Britain and Russia. Goethe popularized (although he did not coin) the concept of *Weltliteratur* [world literature], by which he meant literature which could mediate between peoples. His own works served this function, and drew the temporary or lasting admiration of Eliot, Tolstoi, and Lawrence, all three of whom knew German, and had read *Die Wahlverwandschaften*, which itself contrasts two couples. The novels will be compared in their attitudes towards contrast, comparison, nationhood, and mediation. The novels examined in this book all contain crucial episodes set in Germanic resorts at which people from across Europe are brought together. For such reasons Germany, and its early advocate of *vergleichende Literatur* [comparative literature], are well-placed to support the novels' comparison.

Issues in Comparative Literature

> The comparative method, precisely because it is a mere method of research, cannot suffice to delimit a field of study.
>
> Benedetto Croce quoted in Saussy 2006: 12

The academic subject *comparative literature*, it is commented with a frequency which has tamed it into a reassuring truism, is *anxiogenic*.[2] The academic subject *English literature* has some of the same problems of self-definition, but in its case they are less acute and currently pose little threat to the survival of departments which bear its name. Comparative literature is not easily defined by either method or matter. Saussy comments that:

> Most disciplines are founded on successful reifications. Not to reify is to settle for a weak hypothesis about the identity of the thing one is describing [. . .] Comparative literature in the contextualizing mode finds itself once more an adverb among earthshaking nouns. (Saussy 2006: 20–21)

And this adverb was, by the very breadth of its applicability, a weak one for the purposes of definition. In 1936 Frank Chandler noted that Columbia University's comparative literature department, which had existed when he was a student, had been merged into the 'Department of English and Comparative Literature'. He put this down to a recognition that 'all literary study is now regarded as more or less comparative' (Chandler 1936: 137). Four decades later Robert Clements commented that 'Comparative Literature sometimes figures in university curricula, but very few people know what they mean by the term', and the last two decennial reports of the American Comparative Literature Association defined themselves as concerned with the state (and therefore also the nature) of the discipline, rather than, as previously, on the standard of what was performed within it (Clements 1978: 1; Bernheimer 1995; Saussy 2006). In 2006 Robert Weninger claimed that 'nothing is written or published *in comparative*', and pointed out that the Bernheimer report had dropped the proud initial capital letters from the discipline (Weninger 2006: xii). Even this, it seemed, was too bold a move, and the Saussy report oscillated between *comparative literature* and *Comparative Literature*. As early as 1972 Levin thought that this anxiety had gone too far, and urged comparatists to 'cease to preoccupy themselves with the trivia of Paracomparatism' and get on with 'comparing the literature' (Levin 1972: 89). In response I would observe that 'Paracomparatism' is partly connected to 'comparing the literature', and that in the next chapter I will be getting on with both.

The problem of defining the subject by method is that much of what is done under its remit is not comparative in the narrower sense denoted by Earl Miner when he wrote that 'comparative literature is seldom comparative' (Miner 1987: 123). The bibliography of the British Comparative Literature Association's first (1979) *Yearbook of Comparative and General Literature* contained sections for works concerning 'Literary Genres, Types and Forms', 'Bible, Classical Antiquity', 'Individual Countries', 'Individual Authors', and 'Comparative, World and General Literature'. The three terms of the last category are often imprecisely distinguished — as *общая литература*, *Allgemeinliteratur*, *littérature générale*, and *literatura universal* are from the equivalents of *comparative literature* in their own languages. In 1947 R. A. Jelliffe complained that the teaching of World Literature too often resembled conducting a student through one room of a museum after another, each gallery restricted to works of its own time and place. He considered that this was preferable to confining the student to the American wing alone, but that it was not the same as the practice of comparative literature, and that one room of the museum should be set aside for comparative exhibitions (Jelliffe 1947: 85).

Failing comparison as a unifying factor, some critics have argued that comparative literature is the natural home of literary theory, and that it has served as such particularly since the 1970s (when comparative literature departments did much to raise awareness of French structuralism and post-structuralism in the United States (Bernheimer 1995: 40; Saussy 2003: 337)). There are several reasons for this: much theory is, or claims to be, applicable to literature in many or any languages; polyglots can transmit theory across linguistic boundaries; and theory provides a common core of teaching for students on comparative literature courses. In 1985 Shaffer considered that 'the overview of literary theory which [comparative literature] affords makes it possible to equal and cope with the supranational character of philosophy' (Shaffer 1985: xvii). However, despite the fact that comparative literature itself involves particular theoretical issues, very little theory specifically on comparison is written, or taught as the theoretical component of comparative literature courses.

The question then arises whether comparative literature should simply be called, and become, the study of literature. Brunel, Pichois, and Rousseau, in their 1983 *Qu'est-ce que la littérature comparée?*, defined comparative literature as:

> *description analytique, comparaison méthodique et différentielle, interpretation synthétique des phénomenes littéraires interlinguistiques ou interculturels, par l'histoires, la critique et la philosophie,* afin de mieux comprendre la Littérature comme fonction spécifique de l'esprit humain [*analytic description, methodic and differential comparison, synthetic interpretation of interlinguistic or intercultural literary phenomena, through history, criticism, and philosophy,* in order to better understand literature as a specific function of the human spirit] (151; roman font used by me for emphasis in an originally italic text)

Proponents of departments of literature include René Wellek and Austin Warren, who in 1949 argued in *Theory of Literature* against the idea of national literatures: 'There's just literature' (Wellek and Warren 1949: 49). Fourteen years later Wellek wished that 'we could simply speak of the study of literature [. . .] and that there were, as Albert Thibaudet proposed, professors of literature just as there are professors of philosophy and of history' (1963: 290). In 1988 Lowry Nelson, Jr. wrote: 'In the simplest and best formulation, Comparative Literature is nothing other than the study of literature' (Koelb 1988: 37). And in 2006 Jonathan Culler argued against Charles Bernheimer that: 'The turn to culture makes sense for national literature departments: the division of literature by national or linguistic boundaries was always rather dubious, but such divisions as these are a very reasonable way of organizing the study of culture'; this would leave comparative literature with the distinctive role of studying literature: 'As the site of the study of literature in general, comparative literature would provide a home for poetics' (240). Objections to such a plan come from those who consider that literature should always be related to culture in its broadest sense, and to other art forms. In 1972 Levin, and in 1995 Bernheimer, argued that comparative literature did not and should not concern literature alone (Levin 1972: 74; Bernheimer 1995: 45). It is also objected that the general study of literature in practice rarely fulfils that remit, consisting largely in the study of European literature and its nearest relatives. Clearly, *European literature*, not *general*, *world*, or *comparative literature*, should be the title of courses if that is what is studied. However, Anthony Appiah rightly urged in response to the criticisms of eurocentrism made in the 1995 ACLA report: 'Study these interconnected European literatures, I say. They make sense together. They were made for each other' (Bernheimer 1995: 51–57). The introduction of so-called postcolonial literature into national literature departments had on the one hand the effect of reinforcing these departments' linguistic exclusivity, and on the other of increasing the amount of comparison carried out within them; the very label points towards the comparative framework in which postcolonial theory typically demands that such literature be analysed.

Both parts of the title *comparative literature*, then, imperfectly denote the subject's *de facto* remit. I would like to make a proposal which cuts through the Gordian knot of most of the problems of definition discussed above. Since these questions impinge on other subjects also, the proposal involves rearranging all university subjects. If one were to conceive of academic departments as a city which has developed haphazardly from Antiquity onwards, then I, a zealous town-planner, propose to raze the city to the ground and rebuild it on a grid-plan. Although these proposals may have no immediate or eventual effect, they at least illustrate my conception of comparative literature as an academic subject.

Excursus on the Idea of a University

> As to the other Faculties, the subject-matter which they profess is intelligible, as soon as named, and beyond all dispute. We know what Science is, what Medicine, what Law, and what Theology; but we have not so much ease in determining what is meant by Philosophy and Letters.
>
> NEWMAN 1976: 226

Each university should have two types of structure, to be called for example *faculties* and *divisions*. The *faculties* would be named after disciplines, or objects of study which clearly indicate a correspondent discipline: history (the discipline of historiography), archaeology, sociology, anthropology, politics (political science), linguistics, literature (literary criticism), music (musicology), art (criticism of visual art), philosophy, theology, politics (political science), law (jurisprudence), economics, mathematics, engineering, architecture, physics, chemistry, biology, and so on. The *divisions* would correspond to categories of subject matter. For the arts and humanities these categories could be either regional or temporal, but since collocation has historically permitted greater cultural interaction and continuity than has contemporaneity, the former principle of classification will here be pursued. India, Russia, and Britain, for example, might have their own divisions. Any regional or state name has historical and ideological implications, and either conceptual consistency, or familiarity and ease of use, could be favoured in the choice of divisional names. Divisions could also have subdivisions. All teachers and students would be obliged to belong to at least one, and rarely more than two, faculties *and* divisions. The present author, for example, would belong to the faculty of literature and to the British and Russian divisions. Someone working on Tolstoi's relationship to Repin might belong to the faculties of literature and art, and to the Russian division. Someone else, researching English Common Law, might belong to the law faculty and the British division. Certain academics and students would feel most at home in their faculty, whilst others (for example historically orientated critics of music) would feel most at home in their division. The creation of visual, verbal, and sonic art, and the performance of music and drama, would be taught in the corresponding faculties. Languages would be taught by the relevant divisions; the French division would be responsible for teaching metropolitan French, and the Caribbean division (or whichever division was responsible for that area) would be responsible for teaching French-Caribbean Creoles. The divisions would encourage multi- and inter-disciplinary collaboration through informal personal interaction, seminars, and conferences. Selected divisions could collaborate with each other in the study of particular periods (for example eighth-century Europe). Degrees would bear compound titles made up of the relevant faculty/ies and division/s, and students could give a shortened version of this title in order to indicate where they felt their allegiance primarily to lie.

Such a warp and weft of discipline and subject matter would encourage both disciplinarity and inter-disciplinarity. Since all academics other than pure mathematicians would be obliged to belong to a division, lawyers and philosophers (for example) would be obliged to identify and be conscious of the culture from which the objects of their thought arose and arise. Conversely, students of what is now called area studies would be obliged to select, and develop their skills in, one or more disciplines. Students studying what is now called modern foreign languages would be able to choose in which discipline or disciplines to specialize, and would be under no obligation to study either literature or linguistics. If a student at the University of Istanbul, for example, wished to study German history, then she could study in the university's history faculty and German division. This would give her a better grounding for becoming a historian of Germany than either students of German, or of history, currently attain. Likewise, students studying what is now called Classics would belong to the Greek and Italian divisions, and would be able to choose from the faculties of archaeology, history, politics, philosophy, theology, law, literature, and art. They might alternatively choose to belong to for example the Greek and Iranian, Italian and North African, or Italian and German divisions.

Certain anomalies which currently exist would be abolished, such as that a European wishing to study Polish history will study history, whereas someone wishing to study Bahraini history may be obliged to study area studies, with the implication that Poland but not Bahrain has extension in time. The Palestinian division would provide a forum for collaborative work on a region, the ancient history of which is at present unhelpfully divided between theology, Biblical studies, Jewish studies, Hebrew studies, Arabic studies, and archaeology, in a manner which tends to discourage the involvement of *soi-disant* historians. The renaming of the discipline of *art history* as *art* would place it on the same footing in relation to its subject matter as literary criticism to literature. Cultural studies and critical theory would be taught in the faculty of anthropology. Literary theory would be taught in the faculty of literature using examples from different languages, thereby demonstrating the breadth of applicability of the theories, and avoiding the current replication of teaching between language faculties. G. C. Spivak, in her 2000 Wellek Library Lectures in Critical Theory, complained that 'without a transformed Area Studies, Comparative Literature remains imprisoned within the borders it will not cross' (2003: 7). She claimed that since area studies was conservative, rigorous, and polyglot, whereas Cultural Studies was on the radical fringes of national language departments, monoglot, non–rigorous, and transparently based on foregone conclusions, both disciplines might be improved by rapprochement (Spivak 2003: 8). My scheme would facilitate this, since anyone in cultural studies would be attached to one or more divisions. Comparative literature and area studies would also be brought closer together, as Spivak advocates (2003: 20). In 2006 Emily Apter pointed out that the contemporary methodology of comparative study was inadvertently perpetuating

> neocolonial geopolitics in carrying over the imperial carve–up of linguistic fields. So, for example, in the case of the Caribbean: Haiti, Martinique, and Guadeloupe are placed under the rubric of Francophone studies, Cuba falls under the purview of Spanish and Latin American studies, and Jamaica remains sequestered in Anglophone fields. (Apter 2006: 87)

Under my proposals this objection would be met, since region would be the primary principle of division.

Someone currently belonging to a comparative literature department would belong to one or more divisions, and either to the literature faculty alone, or also to the history, sociology, philosophy, theology, art, or music faculties. The theory of literary comparison would be taught in the literature faculty. Survey courses of world or general literature could be taught with the collaboration of teachers from the relevant divisions. The phrase *comparative literature* would be reserved to describe criticism which compared (in a strict to middling sense) literary works with each other. Those who, as Peter Brooks claimed of himself as a graduate student, are not '*comparing* literature, just working in more than one' would consider themselves to be working not in comparative literature, but literature (1995: 53). Those working in inter-artistic or literary-philosophical study would describe themselves as doing precisely that. As a result the anxiety surrounding the phrase *comparative literature* would be much diminished. As Wellek wrote in 'The Crisis of Comparative Literature':

> These related disciplines have been much wiser: there are musicologists, art historians, historians of philosophy, and they do not pretend that there are special disciplines such as comparative painting, music, or philosophy. (Wellek 1963: 283–84)

Individual institutions would decide the distribution of resources between each type of department, and would build up reputations for excellence in particular ones. The teaching of literature could be organized by either the literature faculty or the relevant division, provided that the same kind of department taught literature of all languages. The present structure of literature departments unconsciously disposes their members to think in nationalist terms; David Damrosch rightly pointed out that, in contrast to the time 'when Auerbach and Wellek came to the United States',

> Much recent literary study has taken a dim view of nationalist ideologies and their imperial projections, and yet in an odd way the critique of nationalism has turned out to coexist quite comfortably with a continuing nationalism in academic practice. (2003: 285)

National literature departments throw the onus of self-justification onto critics who do not consider the nation to be an inevitable, or inevitably important, category of literary interpretation — as opposed to the *ethnie*, period, or genre.[3] Indeed, comparative (or, more indicatively, contrastive) literature itself arose in the context of early nineteenth-century European ethnic and linguistic Romanticism — hence Guérard's comments in 1958 that 'we [comparatists] are needed so long as the nationalistic heresy has not been extirpated', and 'Comparative Literature will disappear in its very victory; just as "foreign trade" between France and Germany will disappear in the Common Market' (Guérard 1958 5, 4). By contrast, post-Second World War American comparative (or, more indicatively, general) literature 'did not take it for granted, as did the departments of English, French, Spanish, Italian, Chinese, that a national literature in its historical evolution was the natural and appropriate unit of literary study' (Culler 2006: 237). Under my proposals this perspective would find a more secure and prestigious home, in literature faculties. In this book Tolstoi displaces the obvious co-national mediator between Eliot and Lawrence — Thomas Hardy — as himself, more than as a Russian.

On the other hand, the freedom of individual academics to have more contact with their faculty or their division would reflect the obvious importance of both perspectives to literary study. It is partly, and only partly, true that 'the difference between the study of influences occurring within a national literature, and that of influences which transcend linguistic boundaries is not a qualitative and hence a methodological one', and that 'There is no fundamental difference between methods of research in national literature and comparative literature, between, for example, a comparison of Racine with Corneille and of Racine with Goethe' (Weisstein and Riggan 1973: 29; Remak 1961: 10). Spivak's claim that 'The verbal text is jealous of its linguistic signature but impatient of national identity' is far from equally true of all texts (2003: 9). Nationalism may, as Freud claimed, involve 'Narzißmus der kleinen Differenzen' [narcissism in respect of minor differences], but ethnic distinctions pre-exist the development of the nationalist movements which seize on, manipulate, and exaggerate them (1930: 85). In addition people of certain cultures and periods are consciously and unconsciously affected by nationalist ideology. Consciously, they are aware of the concept of a national literature, may seek to create their own place within it, and may promote its rivalry with other national literatures. Unconsciously, they are affected by what Michael Billig terms 'banal nationalism', according to which 'the community and its place are not so much imagined, but their absence becomes unimaginable' (1995: 77). Such cultures tend to prioritize the reading and teaching of writers of their own nation over others. For all of these reasons a reader should take Virginia Woolf's caution, expressed in 'The Russian Point of View', that 'the mind takes its bias from the place of its birth, and no doubt, when it strikes upon a literature so alien as the Russian, flies off at a tangent far from the truth' (1957: 231).

Nation and Language

> Jedenfalls aber ist unsere philologische Heimat die Erde; die Nation kann es nicht mehr sein. [But in any case, our philological home is the Earth; it can't be the nation any more.]
>
> AUERBACH 1967: 310

Although the period from the 1870s to the 1910s was one of high and growing nationalism (the bloody culmination of which haunts *Women in Love*) it was also one of growing supranationalism. Goethe's concept of *Weltliteratur*, in referring to the mediation of nations, itself mediates between nationalism and supranationalism. In 1848 *Das kommunistische Manifest* [*The Communist Manifesto*] had asserted that as economic self-sufficiency gave way to international commerce, the equivalent occurred in the intellectual production of nations:

> Die geistigen Ezeugnisse der einzelnen Nationen weden Gemeingut. Die nationale Einseitigkeit und Beschränktheit wird mehr und mehr unmöglich, und aus den vielen nationalen und lokalen Literaturen bildet sich eine Welt-literatur

[National one-sidedness and narrow-mindedness become more and more impossible, and from the numerous national and local literatures, there arises a world literature] (Marx and Engels [1848] 1918: 29)

Hugo Meltzl de Lomnitz founded the *Zeitschrift für Vergleichende Literatur* in the year that *Anna Karenina* was completed; this aimed to be transnational rather than romantically inter-ethnic (Saussy 2006: 6). The three authors with whom this book is concerned embraced this principle to varying degrees.

Eliot, who was as broad as Tolstoi in her reading, had more sympathy than him with ethnic nationalism, and was more inclined than him to conceive of literature in its national context; she described French, English, and German literatures as the three best, and distinguished Heine as an honourable exception to the lack of humour and satire which typified the last (Pinney 1968: 390, 222). On the other hand, as will be discussed in the next chapter, she had considerable (if implicit) sympathy with Goethe's concept of *Weltliteratur*, and her attitude towards nationalism itself was ambivalent. Although Daniel Deronda's final project is to achieve a state for his people, Eliot distrusted revolution, distanced herself from the nationalism of Mazzini, and discouraged Lewes's son Thornie from going to fight for the Poles against the Russians in 1863. The narrator of *Daniel Deronda* questions the possibility of 'pure English blood', which is one of the bases of ethnic nationalism; Eliot's narrators make generalizations on humanity in general (DD: 446).

Tolstoi had only a mild interest in national character. He thought of English authors in the context of England, listing in 1890 those English authors who had made the greatest impression on him; his character Levin generalizes about the Russian peasantry (Gareth Jones 1995: 49). But, like Eliot, he felt distanced from the nationalist revolts of Eastern Europe. He studied Turkic and Caucasian languages at the University of Kazan' in the 1840s, thirty years before the Veselovskii brothers (initiators of Russian comparative literature) became influential, and his later writings show little trace of their influence. *Что такое искусство?* [*What is Art?*] (1898) makes such horizontal class generalizations as 'Так что вследствие безверия и исключительности жизни богатых классов искусство этих классов обеднело содержанием' [Thus because of the lack of belief and exceptional lifestyle of the wealthy classes, the art of those classes became impoverished in its content], but is loftily supranational, giving as examples of real art Genesis, Vedic hymns, the *Iliad*, Vogul drama of North-Central Siberia, and *Adam Bede* (WIA: 98, 125, 200)

Lawrence was more inclined than Tolstoi or Eliot to attribute spiritual essence to nations and other cultural groupings. In his non-fiction, and in particular his travel writings, he generalized in confident tones on the Sicilians, the Etruscans, the English, the Jews, and the Russians. The physiological psychology which he developed from *Study of Thomas Hardy* through to *Fantasia of the Unconscious*, on the other hand, is pan-human. His interpretation of literature was cross-hatched, veering between vertical division according to such groupings, and Tolstoyan pan-humanism. In *Study of Thomas Hardy* the Gospels, Genesis, and Exodus are classified as great novels (STH: 179, 181). There is no comparatist's self-consciousness in his claim that in Shakespeare and Sophocles the greater morality is transgressed, whereas in Hardy and Tolstoi it is the lesser (STH: 30). Nation-based comparative literary theory had little hold on English universities in Lawrence's time. His comments on nineteenth-century Russian literature make little reference to Russia, and *Study of Thomas Hardy* and Lawrence's mid-1920s essays on the novel make no more reference to nationality than does the *What is Art?* to which Lawrence responded. On the other hand, the subjects of *Studies in Classic American Literature* are interpreted partly with reference to the United States ('American art-speech reveals what the American plain speech almost deliberately conceals') (SCAL: 168).

It is because national context was of some conscious and great unconscious importance to all three authors that the last part of this chapter will place Tolstoi's reaction to Eliot in the context of the English craze of later nineteenth-century Russia, and Lawrence's reaction to Tolstoi in the context of the Russian craze of First World War England. It should be added that neither the embrace nor the rejection of the nation as a category of literary interpretation determines that a critic will work comparatively. A supranationally minded critic, freed from the obligation to generalize, can concentrate on the close comparative study of specific works. A nationally minded critic may write about Lawrence's responses to Russian literature without being comparative in a narrow sense.

Thus far my discussion has excluded languages, since they and nations do not necessarily coincide. Tolstoi attributed no more of a *Volksgeist* to Russian than did Eliot or Lawrence to the English language; neither language had ever been a strong focus for ethno-linguistic nationalism (in contrast to, say, Bulgarian or Gaelic), in part because they were exported across multi-ethnic empires. For the same reason and to the same extent that literature written in different languages can usefully be compared, translation can usefully be performed. Since comparison is heavily involved in translation, translation theory is also of relevance to comparative literature (and vice versa). As Shaffer says, 'Translation comes to the fore in comparative literary studies as the characteristic mode of "close analysis" of texts' (1985: xiv). If one aims to transplant one's source text culturally, then one must compare the relations of a source word, phrase, or passage — and those of the proposed target word, phrase, or passage — to the hypothesized non-verbal meaning signified by the source, and try to make the two relationships as similar as possible. If, on the other hand, one aims for exoticism — palpably to assert the connection between the source text and its non-verbal signified — then one must make the relations dissimilar. Any translator must frequently compare the usefulness of competing words and phrases in forming relationships of precisely the degree of symmetry or asymmetry desired. Translations may be supplemented by commentary comparing the translation with the source text. In his 1968 *Littérature Générale et Littérature Comparée* Simon Jeune pointed out that free translations or imitations and their source texts required separate analyses (*explications de texte*) before the two were compared, whereas close translations could be commented upon by a form of asymmetric literary comparison which he called *explication comparative* (Jeune 1968: 99–102). However, another type of *explication comparative* could be thought to be involved in reading one work in terms of its similarities to and deviations from a different text, since this can involve imagining what the first work would be were it to resemble the other more, and in detailing the discrepancies from the hypothetically translated work. For example, it could be imagined what *Daniel Deronda* would be were it set in roughly 1915 — and how this differs from what *Women in Love* is. These two issues — divergence of text, and divergence of language — come together in the comparison of texts written in different languages. If one of the works is translated, then one is impelled to two stages of comparison — of the source with its translation, and of the translation with the other text. If not then, just as one uses non-verbal concepts as intermediaries in the process of translation (one finds собака as a translation of *dog* via the putative non-verbal concept of what in English is denoted by *dog* and in Russian by собака), one compares texts of different languages via a non-verbal understanding (in a broad sense of the latter term) of each text. The belief that such an understanding is possible justifies the provision of translations of extracts of *Anna Karenina* in this book.

However, unless the comparer belongs equally to the two cultures which produced the texts — and this applies whether the texts are in different languages or not — then he or she inevitably to some extent translates the text from the less into the more familiar culture. This is the process which Damrosch describes as occurring to texts which he describes as world literature — although it occurs to some degree to any text. According to him, works become

> world literature by being received *into* the space of a foreign culture, a space defined in many ways by the host culture's national tradition and the present needs of its own writers [. . .] World literature is thus always as much about the host culture's values and needs as it is about a work's source culture; hence it is a double refraction, one that can be described through the figure of the ellipse, with the source and host cultures providing the two foci that generate the elliptical space within which a work lives as world literature, connected to both cultures, circumscribed by neither alone. (Damrosch 2003: 283)

Of course, the exact shape of the ellipse will depend not only on the interrelations of the two cultures concerned, but on the work itself and the peculiarities of each reader. To extend the analogy, when a reader compares works of two different cultures, then the comparison takes place in the intersection of the spaces in which each work is understood by that reader. In the central chapters of this book, this intersection is determined by my own position as someone more familiar with English than Russian culture. English also predominates as the language of the book's expression. This is not inappropriate to the authors concerned: Tolstoi read Eliot, and Lawrence read Tolstoi, in English (a possible exception is *Middlemarch*, which in Tolstoi's library is a Berlin edition, probably E. Lehmann's German translation of 1872–73; Tolstoi may also have read Eliot in the Russian translations of which his niece made several). My approach to Tolstoi therefore resembles Tolstoi's to Eliot: I have greater familiarity with the writers and language of my own country, but am able to read without translation — except in Damrosch's analogical sense.

Nonetheless, it remains an issue that practitioners of comparative literature have limited expertise compared to that of the specialists concerned with the same works: this is 'the spectre of amateurism' which 'haunts comparative literature' (Damrosch 2003: 284). Of course, this phenomenon is connected not to comparativism *per se* but to generalism. Still, the more different the cultural origins of the works compared, the weaker the comparatist's probable position in comparison to that of at least one of the relevant experts. This point has been made repeatedly, and the solution has been repeatedly proposed that comparatists should use the work of specialists. Texte considered that the general study of literature would only be possible when 'l'histoire des littératures nationales ait étée suffisament etudiée pour qu'on puisse songer maintenant à de tels travaux' [the history of national literatures has been sufficiently studied for one to be able to start thinking about such studies] (1900: xix). In 1986 Remak remarked that:

> The number of creative, historical and critical works to be absorbed by a scholar before he can hope to portray adequately even a limited period or aspect of *one* literature has become so enormous that we cannot expect the same scholar to take on one or more additional literatures [. . .] A third group of scholars is therefore needed to pull together the findings of national literature and comparative literature and merge them into general literature. (Remak and Riesz 1986: 17)

Seventeen years later Spivak used the analogy of *Médecins sans Frontiers*, whose doctors cannot learn all the local languages of the places where they are required to work, but instead use interpreters: 'Hegemonic Comparative Literature would continue the analogy', and should cultivate 'the role of the interpreter' (2003: 38). In the same year Damrosch advocated 'collaborative work' which could 'help bridge the divide between amateurism and specialization, mitigating both the global generalist's besetting hubris and the national specialist's deeply ingrained caution' (and, one might add, the reverse) (2003: 286). Finally, in 2005 Moretti made a plea for a worldwide collaborative process in which specialists would perform *extensive reading* of thousands of texts, and comparatists would perform *distant reading* using their findings, in order to reach their conclusions (Moretti 2007: 4–5).

Remak warned that in such a case 'Comparative-literature and general-literature scholars would have to be content with organizing the findings of others [. . .] an assignment bound to expose them to loss of contact with the literary text, and carrying the seeds of mechanization, superficialization and dehumanization of literature' (Remak and Riesz 1986: 17). Moretti confronts this issue directly, specifying that distant reading should only be done with data 'which are ideally independent from any individual researcher', and that 'the reality of the text undergoes a process of deliberate reduction and abstraction' and quantification (2007: 5, 1). Such work is an important corrective to an understanding of canonical works in relation on the one hand only to other canonical works, and on the other to culture in its broadest sense, since the middle ground constituted by the majority of literary works is often overlooked. It also rightly asserts the usefulness of quantitative methods in literary study, and sets an example of empiricism which, however complicated its application to arts subjects, is currently under-valued. Moretti's approach is aware of its own limitations, and does not seek to prohibit other kinds of criticism. Damrosch maintains that:

> world literature is not an immense body of material that must somehow, impossibly, be mastered; it is a mode of reading that can be experienced

intensively with a few works just as effectively as it can be explored *extensively* with a large number. (2003: 299)

Still, it is important to have the benefit of both, and both can be combined in a further study. It should also be noted that different modes of close reading, as of translation, are characteristic of different places (universities, states, and linguistic areas), and that collaborative work of the kind which Damrosch proposes, and which could take place in literature faculties, would allow the comparison of these modes. This book does not directly follow the proposals of Damrosch, Spivak, or Moretti: it performs close readings, is collaborative only in the loose sense of reliance on historical and critical works, and reads Russian literature in a manner influenced by English modes of criticism. In doing so it represents a well-established mode of comparative literature which it considers worth practising and reflecting upon, but one which is far from uniquely useful, and the results of which may properly be used in further, more synthetic, studies.

Comparison *per se*

> not only the colourless propositions of logic, even the highest and most brilliant flights of oratorical eloquence or poetic fancy are sustained by this rudimentary structure of comparison and difference, this primary scaffolding, as we may call it, of human thought.
>
> POSNETT 1886: 73

Some of the issues necessarily (as opposed to institutionally) faced by comparative literature may be explored by returning in more detail to the nature of comparison. The transitive verb *to compare* can mean 'to mark or point out the similarities and differences of (two or more things); to bring or place together (actually or mentally) for the purpose of noting the similarities and differences' (OED, first cited 1509). But *a comparison* is both an action and its outcome, and *making a comparison* can refer both to the process of comparing and to the description of this process and its result (one cannot be described without the other). For example, were someone to say that a given historian compares Hitler and Stalin, she might mean that the historian tries to discover the similarities and differences between these men, or that he draws attention to such similarities and differences as he has found them to possess. This is an important ambiguity; although in this book both *a comparison* and *making a comparison* are most often used in the former sense, there is an indefinite distinction between the performance and results of comparison, between the discovery of results and their dissemination, and therefore between empiricism and rhetoric.

Language is not necessary to the performance of comparison, but it is to its description, in which it can prove limited. In English the language of comparison tends to imply one of three positions, which may be approximated to similarity, difference, and neutrality. One compares something *and*, *with*, or *to* something else; *and* is neutral, *with* suggests the expectation of similarity, and *to* suggests the expectation of difference. Something is the same *as* something, but different *to*, *from*, or *than* it. Apart from the fact that *to* is more common in British English, and *from* and *than*, in North American English, *to* implies orientation towards the differing other, *from* implies departure from it, and *than* implies an alternative to and possible displacement of it. The comparer should compare and choose her words with care.

In contrast to *to contrast* (*contra-stare*, to stand against), *to compare* also means 'to regard or represent as analogous or similar', and, intransitively, 'to be of the same or similar quality or value [as in]: *gin compares with rum in alcoholic content*' — hence the implied contrast of examination questions beginning 'compare and contrast' (*Collins English Dictionary*). Posnett implies identity by *comparison* when he asserts that 'The most colourless proposition of the logician is either the assertion of a comparison, A is B, or the denial of a comparison, A is not B' (1886: 73). Correspondingly, a *compare* is an analogy, equal, or rival of something else. Many terms for comparison stress likeness over difference: to *com-pare* is to bring together parities, *vergleichen* makes *gleich* [the same], and *сравнить'* makes *равный* [equal]; a *сравнение* is a simile as well as a comparison.[4] The ancient Greek παραβολή [from παρα plus βολή, a casting, throwing, or putting] is a placing side by side, or an analogy. In a parable, as in an allegory, something is made to stand for something else on the basis of similarity or translation; παραβολή was borrowed in the Latin *parabola*, or comparison, and in post-classical Latin it is an allegory, proverb, discourse, or speech — an expansion of meaning which acknowledges the importance of comparison to rhetoric. The Latin *comparare* also meant to place together, couple, unite, pit against, treat as equal. By contrast, the modern Greek term for comparison, συγκρίνω [to judge together] avoids the prejudgement of results which pertain to both *compare* and *contrast*. Whereas the Latin instruction *cp.* in practice often invites contrast, *cf.* invites open-minded comparison.

Of course, no two things are identical or absolutely different; they attract comparative investigation because they are felt to be a *metaphor* in Todorov's sense (constituted by the tension of difference and resemblance, separateness and communication). (1978: 226). That is, an initial comparison will have suggested either that the *comparanda* are *different* (an adjective used rhetorically to indicate that they are more different than might be expected) or, more often, that they are *similar* (that is, more similar than might be expected). In my own case, differences between my novels are the assumed basis, and one of the ends, of the investigation: the background of temporal and spatial divergence against which the similarities which suggest the comparison appear, and the finer points which appear against those similarities. The most obvious differences between the works must either be ignored, or made to serve their analysis. The idea of an initial comparison preceding further comparison indicates another ambiguity in *comparison*, which can refer not just to a methodical process, but to the unexamined impression which prompts it.

One condition of a methodical comparison being considered worthy of pursuit on grounds of usefulness or interest is that the things concerned are considered *comparable*. Comparability involves a degree of similarity in the *comparanda*; this is the sense expressed in Paul Masson-Oursel's argument that 'whites' and 'the primitive' should not be understood in terms of each other, but in terms of 'intermediate types of mankind [. . .] Thus, although comparative philosophy ought to be universal, we have the right and the duty [. . .] to restrict it for the present to the study of those peoples already dowered with a history', such as the Indians, the Chinese, and the Europeans (1926: 36). Of course, anything can be compared with anything else, and *comparable* resembles *similar* and *different* in being a relative, not an absolute, term, the applicability of which rests on a comparison. The same is true of *non-* and *in-comparable*.

Certain adjectives, such as *pregnant* or *perfect*, are considered (by non-descriptive grammarians) to be absolute and not to allow of the relative or superlative form. Yet these conventions change over time; in Shakespeare's period several adjectives were comparable which are no longer so, for example *chief* (Shakespeare has *chiefest*), *due* (he has *duer*), and *rather* (he has *ratherest*). Charges of non-comparability rhetorically assert that lack of interest, tactlessness, unfairness, or some other wrong would be involved in pursuing the comparison. That is, they are statements of value. The assertion that any one thing, rather than an assembly of things, is *non-comparable*, *beyond compare*, or *incomparable* implies that the qualities which it has in common with the other things most similar to it are inconsequential in comparison to its distinguishing characteristic/s, and that the pursuance of comparison would involve paying insufficient attention to those characteristics, rendering the comparison either trivial or invalid. The assertion 'you can't compare Salieri to Mozart' implicitly argues that their similarities are unimportant compared to their differences, that the latter could be explained only in terms of the difference in their levels of talent, and that to do so would at best be uninteresting and at worst be insulting to Mozart. Similarly, Orsino tells Viola: 'Make no compare | Between that love a woman can bear me | And that I owe Olivia' (*Twelfth Night*, II. 4. 100). People describe a work of art as *incomparable* in order to express admiration for the work and distaste for considering other similar works alongside it, and sometimes also to express the perception that it is in the nature of the work's excellence to determine a mode in which it alone should be explored, and which is always by far the most valuable mode in which to explore it. This is also what is meant by claims of uniqueness. The most extreme version of this argument is that the work's own terms are the *only* terms on which it can be understood. The implication (rarely embraced) is that the work uses a private language in Wittgenstein's sense, and is therefore incomprehensible — comparison and comprehension being inextricably connected. It will be evident that I do not consider the novels discussed in this book to be incomparable any more than I consider them to be untranslatable. Peter Szondi asserted that 'Kein Kunstwerk behauptet, daß es unvergleichbar ist (das behauptet allenfalls der Künstler oder den Kritiker), wohl aber verlangt es, daß es nicht verglichen werde' [No work of art declares that it is incomparable (at most it is the artist or critic who claims that), but every work of art demands that it not be compared] (1967: 21). Yet certain works do ask to be compared with others: James Joyce's *Ulysses* and Derek Walcott's *Omeros* to the Ὀδύσσεια [*Odyssey*] of Homer for example. The three novels which I have chosen do not clamour for mutual comparison anywhere near as loudly, but nor do they resist it on the terms which I have chosen.

One entity of which incomprehensibility as well as incomparability is sometimes asserted is God — a claim made by several kinds of theism. The same compound assertion is made in order to express or advocate a sense of quasi-religious awe in relation to non-divine subjects — for example, since the later 1960s, to the Holocaust (Finkelstein 2003: 16, 41–48). Such an assertion implies both fact and value: that the Holocaust cannot be compared or understood, and that one should not attempt to do so, firstly because the results of the failed attempt would misrepresent a subject which it is immoral to misrepresent, and secondly because the ambition to compare or understand it would indicate insufficient respect for it. Of course, not only are such assertions based on a preliminary comparison of the Holocaust to other similar events, but they are often deployed to contrastive effect — for example, a prohibition on comparing Israel's treatment of Palestinians to the Holocaust implicitly asserts a comparison of the phenomena which finds them to be of very different qualities and the latter of far greater magnitude. The intended effect is both positive and negative — to foster a sense of awe in relation to the Holocaust, and to prohibit any comparative method which finds significant similarities between the phenomena. The first would rule out any comparison; the second, certain results of comparison; the first encompasses the second, but a wish to assert the second can be an incentive for asserting the first. Shakespeare's Sonnet 18 implicitly answers its opening question 'Shall I compare thee to a summer's day?' in the negative, by contrasting its addressee to such a day.

Assertions of non-comparability as applied to combinations of objects are often based on a sense that the way in which they are most likely to be compared will not generate true, fair, or *valid* results (the last here meaning either true or fair). Neither apples nor oranges are proverbially asserted to be intrinsically incomparable, but they are asserted to be mutually non-comparable — presumably because their similarities of size and use generate the risk that they will be judged according to the same criteria, and because the particular qualities for which either fruit is most valued would be undesirable if found in the other (in this sense the idiom may be contrasted with *chalk and cheese*). An orange would be unfairly criticized as less crisp than an apple. Hazlitt stated that: 'Comparisons are [. . .] impertinent, and lead only to the discovery of defects by making one thing the standard of another which has no relation to it' (1998: 92). Similarities should therefore not be allowed to obscure differences which affect comparability; this is perhaps the sense behind the perfect rhyme in the roughly equivalent Serbian phrase *поредити бабе и жабе* [to compare grandmothers and toads]. The charge of incommensurability denies that a certain type of measure can be applied to all of the proposed *comparanda*. For example, Spanish has an idiom which disparages *sumar peras con manzanas* [adding pears and apples].[5] It is certainly possible to count *pieces of fruit*, but the specific category of *pear-or-apple* is, the idiom implies, of little usefulness. The Russian idiom *сравнивать тёплое с мягким* prohibits the comparison of the warm with the soft, since no single measure can be made of warmth and softness. Finally, certain qualities are differently perceived by different people. The Hungarian idiom *ízlések és pofonok* [tastes and smacks] suggests that the relative value of different objects cannot be absolutely decided if they are judged on qualities which are differently perceived by individuals, rather as two smacks in the face cannot be compared if they are received by different people. Mirah's comparison of Gwendolen to the

Princess of Eboli in *Don Carlos* is 'a riddle for me', to Mrs Meyrick, because Mirah 'was pursuing an association in her own mind not intelligible to her hearers — an association with a certain actress as well as the part she represented' (DD: 562). It is also the case that *any* comparison must be performed by one person, and in a single moment. Non-subjective qualities can be determined as belonging to different objects by different people, and the objects can be compared by a third person making use of their descriptions, but for a comparison to take place the *comparanda* must be apprehended by one mind. Relative unity of physical or conceptual place assists the equally important unity of time (which is why Jacob Cohen holds 'two knives in his palms' and bends 'over them in meditative comparison') (DD: 229). Systematic comparisons require a succession of mental movements between wholes and parts in order to select the *comparanda*, to decide on the quality on which to compare them, and to determine the correspondent qualities of each of the *comparanda*. However, the end result of comparison is generated in an instant in which the qualities are simultaneously present to the comparer's mind.

Comparison in Comparative Literature

> The comparative method of acquiring or communicating knowledge is in one sense as old as thought itself, in another the peculiar glory of our nineteenth century.
>
> POSNETT 1886: 73

> Nous croyons plutôt a la pérennité du comparatiste comme 'spécialiste' des généralités. [We believe, rather, in the persistence of the comparatist as a 'specialist' of generalities.]
>
> BRUNEL, PICHOIS, and ROUSSEAU 1983: 151

In the first article of *Modern Language Review* G. Gregory Smith remarked that:

> It is perhaps worth noting that academic criticism was, in its earlier stages, strictly comparative. The evidence of Greece and Rome is clear on this point; and sixteenth-century Italy, the birthplace of the new criticism, worked by this method and passed on the lesson to the rest of Europe. Example and Comparison were of course essential to Classicism, with its doctrine of the Model, the Ancients, etc. (1905: 4)

George Steiner concurred:

> Plutarch's 'pairings' of a Greek and a Roman statesman, legislator or man of war are exemplary of a comparative method also used in the study of writers and rhetoricians. Soon centuries of clerics and of schoolboys were to toil over the comparison of Cicero with Demosthenes, of Virgil with Theocritus. (1996: 159)

In addition, one of the concerns of the seventeenth- and eighteenth-century 'Moderns' was precisely to compare themselves with the 'Ancients'. The Irish New Zealander Posnett commented in his 1886 *Comparative Literature*:

> When Dante wrote *De Eloquia Vulgaria* he marked the starting-point of our modern comparative science [. . .] The Latin, followed at an interval by the

> Greek, Renaissance laid the foundations of comparative reflection in the mind
> of modern Europe.

He added, 'Meanwhile the rise of European nationalities was creating new stand-points, new materials, for comparison', and that 'The discovery of the New World' was a further source of comparison (Posnett 1886: 74–75). Since his time of writing, critics from European countries and the countries then colonized by them have engaged in comparative criticism of the literature they have severally produced.

Comparison and literary criticism were connected in a more systematic way when, in the later nineteenth century, the evolving discipline of literary study being annotated on the evolving scientific disciplines. Shaffer notes that 'literary theory, and specifically comparative literary theory, arose in [an] attempt to come to terms with the methods of the emerging social sciences' (1980: xii). The attempt was apparent in the German term *Literaturwissenschaft*, which is modelled, like *Geisteswissenschaft*, on the analogy of *Naturwissenschaft* [natural science]. Posnett was by training a lawyer and an economist, and before publishing *Comparative Literature* had written *The Historical Method in Ethics, Jurisprudence, and Political Economy* (1882). His *Comparative Literature* was published in London in 1886 as Volume LV of *The International Scientific Series*, which also included 'Forms of Water' (I), 'Physics and Politics' (II), and volumes concerning biology, psychology, economics, and engineering. Fifteen years later he wrote an article entitled 'The Science of Comparative Literature'. Specifically, comparative literature was modelled on other subjects with *comparative* in their titles, such as philology, biology, and philosophy. Rachel Polonsky considers that in Russia comparative literature 'emerged as a product of the comparatism that governed the human and natural sciences in the mid nineteenth century' (1998: 16). Posnett noted, more broadly, that since the late eighteenth century:

> the method of comparison has been applied to many subjects besides philology, and many new influences have combined to make the mind of Europe more ready to compare and to contrast than it ever was before. The steam-engine, telegraph, daily press, now bring the local and central, the popular and the cultured, life of each European country and the general actions of the entire world face to face; and habits of comparison have arisen such as never before prevailed so widely and so vigorously. (Posnett 1886: 76)

Science proceeds inductively through comparison; experiments analyse a *comparandum* in relation to an isolated variable, and observe deviations from the *secundum comparatum* or *control*. In his introduction to Masson-Oursel's 1926 *Comparative Philosophy*, F. G. Crookshank connected comparison to objectivity in his observation that: 'M. Masson-Oursel's method is one which may be said [. . .] to be designed to attain the positive by way of the comparative, for he would secure objectivity by the due appreciation of relativity', and noted that 'even now, literary and artistic studies are also seeking how to provide themselves with a method that is at once rigorous and comparative' (Masson-Oursel 1926: 2; 42). Comparative philology operated by observing similarities in languages which had been hitherto assumed to be unconnected, and then by both using historical information to explain the connection, and by inducing historical hypotheses from the connection.

The comparison involved was asymmetric: European philologists noticed and then looked for features of European languages in non-European languages; the eighteenth-century English philologist William Jones noticed features of Greek and Latin in Sanskrit, then moved inductively to the idea of a proto-Indo-European language from which other languages branched out.

The results of such comparisons were sometimes explained with the use of a tree metaphor. Haun Saussy observed that:

> Comparative religion, comparative law, and the other comparative disciplines that arose in the nineteenth century under the strange dual patronage of comparative anatomy and comparative philology all began as what one might call tree-shaped disciplines, organizing historical and typological diversity into a common historical narrative with many parallel branches. Difference became *differentiation*, the subject of a historical-developmental account. Through that account, morphology became readable as genesis. (2003: 337)

He goes on to argue that whereas 'tree-shaped comparativism' proved of enduring use in biology, linguistics, mythology, and 'manuscript filiation', 'In comparative literature, the typological tree of written culture was never more than a vestige anyway' (Saussy 2003: 338). On the other hand, as he observes, as late as 1948 E. R. Curtius's *Europäische Literatur und lateinisches Mittelalter* [*European Literature and the Latin Middle Ages*] pointed to Latin literature as the basis of all European literatures. In fact, 'tree-shaped comparativism' has shown considerable durability in literary study, where it has tended either to point to similar social conditions generating similar literary phenomena, or to posit direct influence between phenomena. Posnett tended to the first in his comparisons of clan, town, national, and world literature: '"Comparative" for him meant keeping "the varying relations of social development to literary growth steadily in view"' (Shaffer 1979: Introduction n.p.). Socio-historical context has also been important in Russian comparative literature; Aleksandr Veselovksii, first holder of the Saint Petersburg Chair of General Literature, explained parallels between literatures of different cultures by postulates pertaining to stages in human development, an idea which he developed as *stadialism* (Weisstein and Riggan 1973: 247). Once he had formed his first hypotheses through asymmetric comparison, he refined them through more strictly symmetric comparisons of literature which had emerged from similar conditions. More recently, Franco Moretti described the history of British nineteenth-century detective fiction in evolutionary terms, showing the results of his symmetric comparisons of novels in tree diagrams which showed the divergence and convergence over time of what he denoted as different genres (2007: 73, 75)

The study of influence, which has proved a stronger and more enduring vein of criticism than social comparison, is necessarily asymmetric. Aleksei Veselovskii, brother of Aleksandr and co-founder of the Department of World Literature at Moscow University with Nikolai Storozhenko in 1873, stated at the beginning of his 1881 Западное влияние в русской литературе [*The Western Influence in Russian Literature*] that 'The exchange of ideas, images, fables, artistic forms between the tribes and peoples of the civilized world is one of the most important things studied by the still-young science of literary history' (quoted in Polonsky 1998: 18). In 1961

Henry Remak criticized French criticism for its emphasis on influence studies rather than comparison in the strictest sense, arguing that '*Purely* comparative subjects constitute an inexhaustible reservoir hardly tapped by contemporary scholars who seem to have forgotten that the name of our discipline is "comparative literature" not "influential literature"' (Remak 1961: 5).

The scientific model for comparative literature came under attack from early on. G. Gregory Smith, in his 1905 'Some Notes on the Comparative Study of Literature', expressed scepticism about the analogy of literary study with the natural sciences, and distinguished the scientific from the comparative method. Whereas 'an exaggerated delight in scientific classification' gave rise to 'mere Darwinism', the comparative method was 'not concerned with the statement of so-called literary "laws": indeed it tends to disprove the analogies' (5). He also argued that influence study could be considered a form of literary Darwinism: 'a greater or less reciprocity [of influence] is not the major premises, and *may* be quite immaterial' (6). Instead, he called for a focus on the 'connexion and development of critical ideas' (4). In 1993 Claudio Guillén distinguished three supranational bases for literary comparison: influence, socio-historic conditions, and critical methodology; Smith implicitly asserts the importance of the last of these bases (Guillén 1993: 69–70). Of course, some critical methodology is necessary to the observation of those similarities and differences which may then be explained in terms of socio-historical conditions or influence; in this sense, Guillén's third basis is the only 'basis', and the other two are contexts used to explain the results found thereon. For example, Moretti classified and compared detective novels according to the kinds of clues which they gave to the reader, and explained the survival and extinction of genres in terms of the literary marketplace (2007: 75). Nonetheless, the intention to explain similarities and differences in terms extrinsic to the literature can affect the modes of comparison used, and results generated. In this sense, the central chapters of this book are written in the empirical spirit of Smith and Moretti: possible direct and indirect influence between the authors is noted, but my findings are as tentatively correlated to the novels' authors, languages, times, and places as is warranted by the size of the sample taken of each of these categories.

Culler argued that 'World literature courses that bring together the great books from around the world seem to base comparability on a notion of excellence, so that comparison — the principle of comparability — rather than opening new possibilities for cultural value, more often than not restricts and totalizes it' (2006: 242). However, courses of world and general literature do not necessarily assert the comparability of the works of literature they select, any more than they demand their comparison; indeed, they may purport to select on the criterion of incomparability. When comparison is required, it will not be the comparison of excellence (the excellence of a work of literature being connected to its uniqueness), but will have reference to 'specific intellectual norms or models — generic, thematic, historical' which, Culler himself argues, 'are subject to investigation and argument in ways that the vacuous bureaucratic norms are not' (244).

In the phrase *comparative literature*, *comparative* is the attribute of *literature*. Yet it is almost never understood in this way, the semantic meaning having drifted apart from the compositional meaning. The same is true of *vergleichende Literatur* and *сравнительная литература*, although not of *literature comparée*, in which the literature is the passive object of comparison. Clements noted that the equivalent

> East Asian terms are a compound essentially of two substantives. The Chinese *pi-chiao wên-hsüeh*, the Japanese *hikaku bungaku*, and the Korean *pigyo munhak* consist of 'comparison' plus 'literature'. The terms thus denote [. . .] the scientific comparison of two or more literatures without inclusion of adjectival modifiers. Perhaps if we followed suit and adopted the simple 'literature comparison' we might eliminate a great deal of discussion. (1978: 11)

Wellek, on the other hand, considered that 'There is little use in deploring the grammar of the term and to insist that it should be called "the comparative study of literature", since everybody understands the elliptic usage' (1963: 290). Yet the phrase *comparative literature* does have a potential meaning which corresponds with its compositional sense: literature which invites the performance of internal comparison, or which, to put it another way, *contains comparisons*. This is to use the noun *comparison* in a sense distinct from the two discussed above, a process and its result. In this sense a comparison is a quality or set of qualities which may obviously or easily be interestingly compared with another quality or qualities in the same literary work. The work which contains them may not be well understood without the performance of this comparison. *Waiting for Godot* is comparative between its first and second halves; *Daniel Deronda*, *Anna Karenina*, and *Women in Love* are comparative between their two stories. This might be the most useful possible application of the term *comparative literature*. All degrees are possible, however; all works contain rhymes, and might be thought to invite comparison of those words which are rhymed.

A comparison of novels as comparative works of literature is a second-order comparison similar to the comparison of ratios. This kind of comparison has the advantage of confessing the variable of context. To say that 'Daniel's relationship to Gwendolen is the equivalent in *Daniel Deronda* of Levin's relationship to Anna in *Anna Karenina*' is less problematic than claiming 'Daniel is like Levin', or even 'Gwendolen is like Alcharisi'. According to Crookshank 'The comparability of two facts is a function of the comparability of their contexts', and 'scrupulous criticism' 'forbids the possibly fortuitous resemblance between two several data detached from their circumstances being taken as significant' (Masson-Oursel 1926: 7, 50). In the comparative methodology of science or philosophy, the

> guiding principle will be analogy, reasoning in accordance with what in mathematics is called a proportion, that is to say, the equality between two ratios: A is to B as Y is to Z. Such an equivalence is compatible with no matter how great an heterogeneity between A and Y, B and Z. [. . .] Confucius was in China that which Socrates was in Greece. (Masson-Oursel 1926: 44)

It is more important 'to establish some kind of a positive ratio between the two variables than, following a will-o'-the-wisp, to give a positive value to one variable in terms of an assumed positive value of another' (Masson-Oursel 1926: 3). Fluellen, when trying to prove the resemblance of Henry V to Alexander of Macedon, claims:

> I speak but in the figures, and comparisons of it: as Alexander kild his friend
> Clytus, being in his Ales and his Cuppes; so also Harry Monmouth being in
> his right wittes, and his good iudgements, turn'd away the fat Knight with the
> great belly doublet. (*Henry V*, IV. 7. 42–46)

Despite its comic aspect this is one of Fluellen's stronger comparisons, precisely
because it involves a ratio (the fact that Henry indirectly causes Falstaff's death
retrospectively gives the comment a darker cast). Internal literary comparisons
likewise involve differences of context, and all assertions of the similarities of
Gwendolen and Alcharisi should be contextualized by the two women's very
different family circumstances, native countries, and musical talents. A simile
might run: 'Gwendolen is to her circumstances as Alcharisi is to hers'. Indeed,
any comparison of components of complex objects is, implicitly or otherwise,
a comparison of ratios. One is reminded that *ratio* is the etymological ancestor
of *reason*, *pace* René Étiemble's claim that 'comparaison n'est pas raison' (1963).
Comparing the comparisons of two stories in three novels of two times and two
countries makes this fact particularly clear. Of course, the questions remain of the
relationship of China to Greece, of Hellenistic Macedon to late medieval England,
of *Anna Karenina* to *Daniel Deronda*, and of Russian to English. Gwendolen and
Alcharisi are *comparable* in a way in which Gwendolen and Anna are not, simply
because they are parts of the same work of art. This book takes the New Critical
assumption of the mutual coherence of all parts of a work of art as a hypothesis; it
does not assume that such coherence will be found, but does consider that its absence
is qualitatively different from the disparateness of qualities between different works
of art. In this sense the two levels of comparison — within, and between, works of
art — are importantly different.

Comparison is an unusual topic of comparison. Most comparisons have one
or both of two motives: the desire to compare the *comparanda*, and the desire to
explore the topic or topics on which they are being compared. In the latter case
the *comparanda* will be chosen according to the topic, and will not necessarily
be compared directly with each other. In the former case, topics of comparison
will be suggested by the *comparanda*. The three fruits of *Bright Pear*, for example,
may be compared with regard to dimensions, shininess, the presence or absence
of a stalk, the casting or bearing of shadow, and the completeness or otherwise
of representation. The two tangerines may further be compared with relation to
shades of red and orange, and the right-hand tangerine and pear with regard to the
presence or absence of a leaf on their stalks. The interestingly comparable qualities
are limited, however, whereas the non-delimited comparison of works of literature
generates potentially infinite results which are of interest. A full description of an
act of literary comparison therefore contains an adverbial phrase: 'I compare A and
B *with regard to C* (and D and E)'. Steiner posited an axis from literal translation
of texts, through imitation, to what he called the *interanimation* of texts within a
national, linguistic, or broader cultural region (1975: 436). This *interanimation* may
be observed in relation to particular topics or qualities, on which they might be said
to *compare notes*. The novels with which this book is concerned could interestingly
be compared with regard to double-plotting, love, lust, married life, tragedy,

comedy, art, politics, intellectualism, cosmopolitanism, children, Schopenhauer, death, misanthropy, God, satire, horses, railways, symbolism, kitsch — amongst many others. Complex topics of comparison generate a field of comparison — a nexus of subject matter and methodologies within which the novels are compared on the possession of simpler qualities. For example, a consideration of the ways in which novels are realist or otherwise would require their description with regard to a range of literary qualities. A comparison of the novels as double-plotted is also made up of more delimited comparisons.

Erich Auerbach rightly observed that 'Schon die Auffindung des Ansatzpunktes [. . .] ist Intuition' (even the discovery of the starting point is a matter of intuition) (1967: 306). A comparative topic may be intuited as the highest common factor of interest of all of the *comparanda*: a comparison of race-horses which have nothing else in common might well concern their ability to race against other horses. The category *later-nineteenth early-twentieth century European novel*, however, is too large to bring novels of which this is the highest common factor into direct comparative contact. The smallest common category is likely to expand the more *comparanda* are involved; any two of the novels discussed in this book could be compared on certain topics which would exclude the third. However, all three of them are members of a much smaller category than *later-nineteenth early-twentieth century European novel*. *Double-plotted novels* is a small enough category to determine a topic, even though it lacks sufficient recognition to constitute a genre. As Martin Swales observes,

> One could, presumably, envisage the novel of adultery, the novel of business, the novel of bankruptcy, and so on. Such a model of a genre would have no pretensions to historical status: it would simply be a heuristic tool, a grid which allows the critic to select a number of novels for analytical and comparative purposes. (Swales 1979: 92)

Wayne C. Booth classified the questions which may be asked of a text into those which it invites, those to which it responds, and those by which it is violated (1988: 89). His personification of texts may be adapted to describe my approach: I have aimed to bring together works which are capable of conducting with each other an exploratory conversation, on a single topic, which is worth overhearing. The topic is not necessarily the topic about which each one individually has most to say — but all have plenty to say on it when questioned.

The concept of a *topic* may be replaced by any one of several metaphors, each of which implies a slightly different comparative method. An *axis* of comparison implies a quality according to the degree of possession of which the *comparanda* are placed along a single axis. A *fulcrum* implies asymmetric comparison, the idea being that performing comparison is like magnifying the force of a *secundum comparatum* through a lever resting on a *tertium comparationis* in order to lift the *primum comparandum* into clearer view or onto the same level as the *secundum comparatum*. For example, one could lift *Frankenstein* into clearer view by applying the force of *Paradise Lost* through a lever resting on the fulcrum of the Fall, or lift Birkin into closer view by applying the force of Levin through a lever resting on the fulcrum of the idea of God. Auerbach uses *Ansatzpunkt* to denote a point of vantage from which different cultural objects may be simultaneously viewed. The *Ansatz* (start) should be a 'zugleich fest umgrenzten, übersehbaren und zentralen Phänomen [. . .] nämlich der rhetorischen Überlieferung, and insbesondere der Topoi' [simultaneously a clearly defined, assessable, and central phenomenon [. . .] namely of the rhetorical tradition, and in particular the *topoi*]. 'Die Eigentümlichkeit des guten Ansatzes liegt einerseits in seiner Konkretheit und Prägnanz, andererseits in seiner potentiellen Strahlkraft' [The peculiarity of a good start lies in the one hand in its concreteness and concision, and on the other in its potential radiant energy] (Auerbach 1967: 308–09). Comparisons of quantity (for example, *amount of reference to God*) can to some extent be distinguished from comparisons of quality (for example, *conception of God*). However, this distinction, which is apparently one of kind, could also be expressed as one of degree, just as distinctions of degree can also be expressed as distinctions of kind. In the next chapters three novels will be compared, for example, on the *degree* to which they scapegoat their central characters, and as different *kinds* of tragicomedy — but the distinction between these modes of comparison is blurred.

Clearer is the distinction between comparisons which do, and do not, employ a standard external to the objects being compared. For example, Iasnaia Poliana and Saint Petersburg can be compared in terms of their proximity to the fixed third point which is Moscow. In this case, the objects, having been measured against the standard (Moscow), can be precisely compared on the single axis of distance. In more complex comparisons the resultant comparison is more ostensive. Leavis compares Eliot and Lawrence on sex as follows: 'the point may be made by saying that they are not only equally unlike Maupassant in their attitudes towards sex; they are unlike in the same way' (which is like saying that Tula and Iasnaia Poliana both lie in roughly the same direction from Moscow) (Leavis 1955: 107). Masaki Hirai in *Sisters in Literature* compares the relationships of the two sisters of Eliot's *Middlemarch*, E. M. Forster's *Howard's End*, and *Women in Love* to those of Antigone and Ismene in Sophocles' *Antigone*, on the analogy of describing musical variations upon a theme (1998: 8, 25). No conversion to a single axis is possible here, and nor was it when R. A. Jelliffe attempted to foster comparativism by teaching a course on tragedy: 'constant reference was made [. . .] both to the governing idea of the course, the idea of tragedy, and to the substance and the treatment of one of these plays compared with another' (1947: 86). The relations of *Вишнёвый сад* [*The Cherry Orchard*] and *Happy Days* to 'the idea of tragedy' cannot be placed on an axis, but both plays can be raised to view on the fulcrum of tragedy, or viewed from the tragic high ground.

Alternatively, *comparanda* may be compared in relation to qualities which are generated by their very comparison. This may be illustrated by analogy with Anna's reaction to Karenin on her return from Moscow. Anna has frequent social contacts with many men, but after meeting Vronskii she does not compare him and Karenin in relation to a real or imagined standard, but judges each largely on possession of the quality *attractiveness to Anna when the comparison is between Karenin and Vronskii*. Of course, this quality has as much reference to Anna as to those men. Critics comparing literature, unlike women comparing men, should seek to exclude intrinsically personal reactions as far as possible. However, comparisons of complex objects inevitably generate qualities which are peculiar to that comparison; to some extent, therefore, *Women in Love* will be compared to *Daniel Deronda* and *Anna Karenina* on qualities which inhere only in that constellation. In this sense the novels can be thought of as involved in a mutual process, as suggested by the reflexive Russian verb *соотноситься* [to correspond with or compare oneself] which, unlike *сравнивать/сравнить*, exists only in the imperfective aspect, and so is a process rather than a finite action. Saussy observed that 'the model texts of comparative literature link together sets of examples whose mutual coherence is not obvious in advance of their combination. It is as if the reader who asks "What do X, Y, and Z have to do with one another" could only get the answer, "Nothing — up to now"' (2003: 339). He adds: 'The willingness to tolerate readings that produce, rather than discover, meanings brings a risky, experimental quality to comparative literature and shows why its virtues are inseparable from its questionable legitimacy' (Saussy 2003: 339).

Fluellen attempts to demonstrate the likeness of 'Macedon and Monmouth' as follows:

> if you look in the maps of the world, I warrant you shall find, in the comparisons between Macedon and Monmouth, that the situations, look you, is both alike. There is a river in Macedon, and there is also moreover a river at Monmouth. It is called Wye at Monmouth, but it is out of my prains what is the name of the other river; but 'tis all one, 'tis alike as my fingers is to my fingers, and there is salmons in both. (*Henry V*, IV. 7. 21–31)

The significance of the results of his comparison is on Fluellen's own terms clear: similarities of places imply the similarities of their rulers, and the similarities of their rulers support his King's claim to France. Literary comparatists, by contrast, sometimes face the question about their efforts: *cui bono?* *Women in Love* resembles and differs from *Anna Karenina* in certain ways. What follows? The comparatist can respond in one or both of two ways. He or she can try to establish the *reasons* for the results (in terms of space, time, or influence), and he can try to establish the results' *significance*. The latter, which might be related to the reasons, could lie in an improved understanding of the texts and of their genres, of the authors' lives, oeuvres, countries, and languages, of cultural modes, and of human beings ('What does comparative literature discover? The most obvious, and usually untheorized, candidate' 'is simply the universality of human experience') (Saussy 2006: 13).

The fact that this book uses both two and three *comparanda* (stories and novels respectively) allows two types of comparison to be compared. The results of the comparison of two *comparanda* are more likely to be conceivable on a single axis, of which they may involuntarily be considered to mark out opposite ends. Modern English does not employ superlatives unless at least three *comparanda* are alluded to, but that does not prevent the illusion that the *comparandum* out of two which possesses *more* of a given quality, is *most* in possession of it. Leavis exemplifies and embraces the exaggeration to which such comparison can give rise in literary criticism: 'Lawrence sees what the needs are, and understands their nature, so much better than George Eliot. In the comparison, in fact, we have to judge that George

Eliot doesn't understand them at all' (Leavis 1955: 115–16). The addition of a third *comparandum* makes it more likely that the results will be conceived on a two-dimensional field, and can also dilute the generalizations which may be suggested by a comparison of two: a Russian and an English novel may appear less strongly representative of their respective countries if read in comparison with a German, Czech, or American novel. Sometimes one of three *comparanda* will present itself as a standpoint from which to compare the other two, or as a synthesis of them: 'As in surveying, every completion of a triangle makes measurement, and thus conclusive knowledge, possible' (Saussy 2006: 13). However, Saussy is more disposed to see the literary third *comparandum* as a disruptive factor. With reference to the third language, which used to be required of many comparatists in the United States, he wrote: 'the third language, like an uninvited guest, points to the things that a two-language pattern leaves out'; 'the apex of the triangle just determined is also a point from which a new angle opens up for measurement' (Saussy 2003: 336, 340). Certainly, Fluellen might have had greater difficulty in demonstrating that King Henry was a second Alexander had a third point of comparison been involved.

David Ferris celebrates comparisons which do not generate coherent results in the bluntly paradoxical assertion: 'We compare what cannot be compared' (2006: 91). Like any assertion of incomparability, this is either a relative statement or untrue; it indicates a desire to reveal quiddity through comparison with alterity. Bernheimer celebrates comparison for revealing external presences within works: 'the voice of comparative literature is "unhomely" and that this very quality of dispossession — a kind of haunting by otherness — is that voice's great strength' (1995: 12). However, there is an important distinction to be made between a consideration of both of two works of literature from the standpoint of each other but not from a third point, and the attempt to apprehend the quiddity of two objects (whether contradictory or not) at the same time. The latter can correspond to what F. Scott Fitzgerald called 'The Crack-up': 'The test of a first-rate intelligence is the ability to hold two opposed ideas in the mind at the same time, and still retain the ability to function' (1965: 39). Both types of approach will be used in the comparison of stories in the chapters which follow. Willa Cather once likened her artistic practice to creating an image like that of *Bright Pear* — to putting

> on the table a green vase, and beside it a yellow orange. Now, those two things affect each other. Side by side, they produce a reaction which neither of them will produce alone. [. . .] I want the reader to see the orange and the vase — beyond that, *I* am out of it. (Bohlke 1986: 24)

Yet the following chapters do not consider the authors — let alone the implied authors — of the three novels concerned to be 'out of it', for which reason their mutual relations and contexts will first be summarized.

The Authors and their Countries

> The best introduction to astronomy is to think of the nightly heavens as a little
> lot of stars belonging to one's own homestead (DD: 16)

> Все удивительные заключения [. . .] основаны только на видимом
> движении светил вокруг неподвижной земли [All the amazing conclusions
> [. . .] are founded only on the apparent motions of the stars around a stationary
> earth] (AK IX: 403)

Eliot, Tolstoi, and Lawrence

Eliot, Tolstoi, and Lawrence invite comparison — and are comparable — on the
basis of certain similarities. They were self-confessed moralists who attracted disci-
ples, disappointed radicals, and scandalized conservatives by word and deed; wrote
novels, fables, and essays; were raised in Christian dogma, left the church, but retained
a lifelong interest in Christianity; were autodidactic polymaths with experience of
and interest in teaching; faced social, clerical, or governmental condemnation;
lived in different types of exile; matched their increasingly critical conceptions of
society by the radicalism of their proposed solutions; were indifferent or hostile to
democratization in general and to the female suffrage in particular; thought that
social change should be effected in individual souls; and failed wholly to practice what
they preached. They wrote literary criticism but, being overwhelmingly concerned
with art's ethical and spiritual effects, wrote relatively little on the distinguishing
features of verbal art *per se*: Eliot made no specifically aesthetic criticisms of 'Silly
Novels by Lady Novelists' (Ashton 1992: 296–321). Tolstoi approved, in *What
is Art?*, of that which makes emotion contagious in artistry, but beyond this he
rejected discernible techniques as adornment, with the same negative ethical value
as he considered to inhere to adornment on women: 'Настоящее искусство не
нуждается в украшениях, как жена любящего мужа. Поддельное искусство,
как проститутка, должно быть всегда изукрашено' [Real art doesn't need
adornment, like the wife of a loving husband. Counterfeit art, like a prostitute,
always needs to be adorned] (WIA: 227). Lawrence, in 'Art and the Individual',
referred vaguely to technique as 'mostly a question of pleasurable feeling', and his
confession that 'We can excellently well criticize what we call the "spirit" of the
thing [. . .] But we are not so well able to understand, or even to appreciate the
technique', applies to much of his subsequent literary criticism (STH: 227–28).
All three writers have been praised — particularly in their own time — for their
emotional content rather than for artistic form; French critics, for example, compared
Tolstoi and Eliot in these terms, in contrast to Flaubert and Zola (Eliot 1991: xxv).

Daniel Deronda, *Anna Karenina*, and *Women in Love* have certain similarities which
are underlined by their relationships with the novels which precede them in their
authors' *oeuvres*. *Middlemarch*, *Война и мир* [*War and Peace*], and *The Rainbow* have
social, abstract, and symbolic titles, begin with action set between three and ten
decades before the time of writing, contain multiple stories of similar importance,
and are soberly optimistic. The later novels, completed within four to seven years of

the earlier, have more personal titles, are set in or closer to the present, are shorter, concentrate on fewer central characters and stories, and are more critical of and less hopeful for the societies they describe. Each marked the end of a phase in its author's career: it was Eliot's last novel, Tolstoi's last novel for twenty years, and Lawrence's last published novel set in England for ten years.

A similar volume of work has been done on Tolstoi's relation to Eliot as on his relation to Lawrence. My triad of authors has rarely been constructed by critics, and my triad of novels, so far as I know, never; two English critics have referred to Eliot and Lawrence in their discussions of *Anna Karenina* (Barbara Hardy and F. R. Leavis), but comparative studies of these novelists tend not to focus on the novels I have chosen (Hardy 1971: 174–211; Leavis 1967: 9–32). Of Eliot's works, *Anna Karenina* is most often studied in relation to, and as possibly influenced by, *Middlemarch*, *The Mill on the Floss*, and *Adam Bede*.[6] Jill Felicity Durey compares *The Mill on the Floss*, *Middlemarch*, *War and Peace*, *Anna Karenina*, *Madame Bovary*, and *L'Education Sentimentale*, and Peter Jones juxtaposes studies of *Middlemarch*, *Anna Karenina*, *The Brothers Karamazov*, and *A La Rechèrche du Temps Perdu* (Durey 1993; Peter Jones 1975). Kenneth Newton (1998), however, considers *Daniel Deronda* in relation to *Anna Karenina* (and *Madame Bovary*). Of Lawrence's works, *Anna Karenina* has often been compared to *Lady Chatterley's Lover* and *The Rainbow* (Zytaruk 1971: 95–103). The most notable discussion in English of *Anna Karenina* in relation to *Women in Love* is by Raymond Williams (1963: 633–50; 1966).[7] *Daniel Deronda* stands at the right-angle of the triangle of time and space formed by my novels, but Tolstoi mediates temporally between the other authors; his life overlaps those of Eliot and Lawrence by fifty-seven and twenty-five years respectively. The forty-year-old Eliot and the twenty-five-year-old Lawrence could have visited Tolstoi at Iasnaia Poliana; Lawrence responded to Tolstoi, and Tolstoi to Eliot, as contemporaries.

Eliot and Tolstoi

Tolstoi and Eliot invite comparison as novelists, rationalists, and moralists with strong religious inclinations. Tolstoi earlier, and Eliot later, fervently embraced their national religions. When Tolstoi was around fourteen he became agnostic; at around the same age, Eliot became Evangelical. Between the ages of twenty and thirty she became atheist, as Tolstoi never did. He believed in a cosmic spiritual order, which she did not. Between the ages of twenty-four and forty-nine he grappled with Orthodoxy, after which he began to disentangle what he saw as the metaphysical dross of Christianity from its spiritual truth. Both he and Eliot came to understand Christianity as one among many religions through which ethical truth might be embraced. But whereas Tolstoi highlighted the contradictions he perceived between intellectual and ethical understanding, Eliot wished to believe that the two were interdependent. His major task was to establish in what form to accept religion; hers was how to live without it.

As writers, they researched their fiction widely and meticulously, were concerned for the accuracy of their texts (which they emended minutely), were highly sensitive to criticism, and were reliant upon their spouses as agents. They published with liberal and conservative publishers (*Daniel Deronda* and *Anna Karenina* were both published by conservatives). Both wrote historical fiction; there is some evidence from the *Pforzheimer* notebook that Eliot may have abandoned work on a spy novel set during the Napoleonic Wars in favour of *Daniel Deronda* with its near-contemporary setting; Tolstoi abandoned research on a novel set at the time of Peter the Great in order to set *Anna Karenina* in the present.

Eliot wrote the bulk of her non-fiction before starting on her fiction, whereas Tolstoi did the reverse. In January 1876 Eliot implied that her fiction validated her ethical formulae by clothing them 'in some human figure and individual experience, and perhaps that is a sign that if I help others to see at all it must be through that medium of art' (EL VI: 217). Tolstoi's turn to fables and non-fiction in the 1880s, by contrast, involved revulsion from the relative aesthetic autonomy and ethical flexibility of his earlier fiction, including *Anna Karenina*. In many respects this novel stands at a queasy moment of transition: retaining a modicum of the exuberance and rationalism of *War and Peace*, but also critical of reason; suading itself into an uneasy embrace of Orthodoxy, dictatorship, and economic inequality; straining towards certain aesthetic norms (such as the West European, particularly French, novel of adultery) but demonstrating limited confidence in art *per se*. *Daniel Deronda*, far from embracing Eliot's national religion, embraces the religion of another *ethnie*, is confident in its ethical and spiritual denunciations of the English aristocracy and gentry, and exults in its status as art (although it is less exuberant and rationalistic than *Middlemarch*). Both authors were acutely aware of death at the time of writing. Tolstoi and Eliot were bereaved shortly before or during writing, and Eliot was in poor health. They had read and been influenced by Schopenhauer in the interval since the publication of their more comedic, preceding, work. However, their familiarity with each other's works and national literatures was asymmetric.

English literature first arrived in Russia in French and German translations. In 1767 a department of translation was established under Catherine II in the Academy of Science: *Tom Jones* was translated into Russian in 1770–71, *Pamela* in 1787, and *A Sentimental Journey* in 1793 (Simmons 1935: 135, 143). The popularity of Defoe, Richardson, Fielding, and Sterne helped to stimulate the production of novels in Russia itself, and the first Chair of Russian literature was established in 1835 (Simmons 1935: 138; Emerson 2006: 203). The waning of neo-Classicism, and the Napoleonic Wars, led to the decline of France as a cultural influence, and to its partial replacement by England. English clubs were established in the major cities, one of Tatiana's favourite novels in *Eugene Onegin* (1823–31) is *Clarissa*, and Onegin's house has English furnishings fifty years before Vronskii's house does (Simmons 1935: 158, 239–41). Polonsky writes that:

> After the 'anglomania' of the 1830s, when Russian society had been smitten by a passion for Byron, Shakespeare and Walter Scott, the ability to read English literature in its original language had become not merely a sign of taste among educated Russians, but a measure of literacy. (1998: 24)

Dickens, Trollope, and Eliot became particularly popular; most of Eliot's novels were published in Russian in Moscow or Saint Petersburg between six months and one year of their first English publication. Three editions of *Adam Bede* appeared in

1859, five of *Middlemarch* appeared before 1875, and Lewes's *Problems of Life and Mind* was serialized as *Вопросы о жизни и духе* in Saint Petersburg whilst *Daniel Deronda* was being serialized in England (Haight 1968: 279). Knowledge of English increased further in the 1870s, and the 1890s saw a second wave of *anglomania* (Polonsky 1998: 24). Aleksei Veselovskii's *Западное влияние в русской литературе* [*The Western Influence in Russian Literature*] went through five editions between 1881 and 1916, indicating the level of Russian interest in the subject.

Tolstoi was a selective anglophile. His disapproval of certain characteristics of the English was expressed shortly after the Crimean War in his 1857 short story 'Люцерн' ['Luzern'], in which the English tourists are arrogant, smug, and callous. They procure the replacement of the Hofbrücke by a rectilinear row of buildings, converse in clichés, and are ungracious to an itinerant singer (Tolstoi 1921: 3–22; Gareth Jones 1995: 36). However, Tolstoi greatly admired English fiction, Evangelicalism, humanitarianism, civil liberties, and the healthy soldiers whom he had encountered in the war (Gareth Jones 1995: 2). He taught himself English, visited England in 1861 to investigate its educational practices, and in the year before starting *Anna Karenina* (1872), when he was held responsible for the death of a peasant gored by a bull on his estate, wrote in a pique that he planned to move with his family to southern England (Gareth Jones 1995: 1).

Although none of the characters of *Anna Karenina* visit England, they and the novel's form reach towards it. The novel was written with conscious reference to English literary models amongst others, and Anna imagines herself as several of the characters of the English novel which she reads on her journey to Saint Petersburg. She shows more interest in rearing an English girl than her own daughter, the Varenka of an early draft was an English evangelical (one imagines her as the teenaged Mary Ann Evans), and five of the central female characters — including the novel's exemplars of Russian womanhood — are nominally rendered as characters in an English novel. That is, Анна Вронская [Anna Vronskaia], Дарья Щербатская [Dar´ia Shcherbatskaia], Екатерина Щербатская [Ekaterina Shcherbatskaia], and Елизабета Тверская [Elizaveta Tverskaia] are called not by the standard familiar forms of Аня [Ania], Даша [Dasha], Катя [Katia], and Лиза [Liza], but by what Nabokov calls the 'new-fangled English diminutives' of Ани [Ani], Доли [Dolli], Кити [Kiti], and Бетси [Betsi] (Turner 1993: 21; Nabokov 1981: 225). Vronskii never calls his lover Аня but only Анна [Anna], and it is likely that he is calling her by an English, rather than the formal, version of her name. The novel's title, a name by which Anna is called only twice in the novel, conforms to West European naming practice by excluding Anna's patronymic, and therefore resembling such titles as *Jane Eyre*, *Agnes Grey*, and indeed *Daniel Deronda*. England is represented as having reached an enviable state of modernity, having satisfactorily resolved land questions and abolished duels (although the novel is agnostic whether, as in England, women should be able to choose their marriage partners). English enriches the characters' vocabularies with such casual, urbane phrases as 'blood that tells', 'pluck', 'not in my line', and 'small talk' (AK VIII: 194, 193, 143; IX: 246). It is Dolli teaching her children French, not English, which strikes Levin as 'неестественно и фальшиво' [unnatural and false] (AK VIII: 289).

However, English words are used only by the novel's Saint Petersburg characters. Prince Shtcherbatskii shuns anglicized names in his dispute with his wife about his daughters Катенька [Katen´ka] and Дашенка [Dashen´ka] (AK VIII: 63; Birdwood-Hedger 2006: 129). High society's anglophilia is negatively associated with luxury. The Saint Petersburg officers' English Club is debauched, Moscow's England Hotel and Betsi Tverskaia's English carriage are decadent, Annie's English nursery toys are merely extravagant, Betsi's croquet party and Vronskii and Anna's billiards and lawn tennis are scenes of amoral leisure, and altogether the estate of Vozdvizhenskoe gives Dolli a 'впечатление изобилия и щегольства и той новой европейской роскоши, про которые она читала только в английских романах' [impression of abundance and sumptuousness and of that modern European luxury of which she had only read in English novels] (AK IX: 195). It is fitting that the 1967 Mosfil'm adaptation makes Kord (Vronskii's English groom) an American, since it was made at a time when American luxury and technology were regarded with similar admiring disapproval by the Soviet government as were the English equivalents by Tolstoi a century before (*Анна Каренина*, dir. Alexandr Zarkhi, Mosfil'm, 1967). In the novel's final part, originally called an epilogue, Levin implicitly rejects European models of modernity, presaging the stage in Tolstoi's career when he would reject much of European art, including his own novels: 'ещё должен заметить, что свои художественные произведения я причисяю к области дурного искусство, за исключением рассказа «Бог правду видет», желающего принадлежать к первому роду, и «Кавкаского пленника», принадлежащего ко второму' [it should be added that I judge my own artistic productions to belong the category of bad art, with the exception of the story 'God Sees the Truth', which aspires to the first class, and 'Prisoner of the Caucasus', which belongs to the second] (WIA Footnote: 205–06). *What is Art?* was published two decades after *Anna Karenina*, but had been at least fifteen years in preparation.

Nonetheless, Tolstoi's fiction both before and after *Anna Karenina* was strongly influenced by English literature. He claimed that his 1850 reading of a translation of Sterne's *A Sentimental Journey* prompted him to spend his life on fiction, and to learn English (Gareth Jones 1995: 3). Sonia Tolstaia wrote in 1878: 'I happen to know, however, that when Lyovushka turns to English novels he is about to start writing himself' (quoted in Gareth Jones 1995: 5). He began his reading of Dickens with *David Copperfield* in 1852 and *Bleak House* in 1854, and admired Dickens throughout his life (making exceptions of *Martin Chuzzlewit* in 1905, and *Our Mutual Friend* in 1908). Towards Shakespeare, whom he first read in 1856, his attitude veered from admiration (for *Othello* in 1891 and Shakespeare in general in 1898) to strong criticism (of *Henry IV* in 1856, *Coriolanus* in 1884, and the whole *oeuvre* in *О Шекспире и о драме* [*On Shakespeare and Drama*] of 1903; in the last he accused Shakespeare of insincerity, filth, and derision of the masses). He admired Trollope, Thackeray, Mrs Wood (author of *East Lynne*), Goldsmith, and Ruskin, and disliked Kipling and Wells. In 1907 he thought that Shaw had more brains than were good for him, and in 1909 wrote to him a letter of advice to be more serious.

According to Haight, Tolstoi read many of Eliot's works in the same year in which they appeared in England (Haight 1968: 279). He first read *Scenes of Clerical Life* and *Adam Bede* in 1859, and strongly recommended the former to his Aunt Alexandra (Knapp 1983: 318; Gareth Jones 1995: 44). He found the latter tragic, but untrue, and too dominated by one thought. In *What is Art?* (1898) he classified both works, along with parables, gospels, psalms, and the works of Dostoevskii, as 'религиозное искусство' [religious art], exemplary of his *desideratum* that art should foster sympathy and bridge the distance between social classes (WIA: 200; Knapp 1983: 320–22). In 1885 he found *Felix Holt* excellent on rereading, and a year later completed a tract which shares its emphases on the dignity of labour and the vacuity of fine ladies — *What Then Must We Do?* (Knapp 1983: 323). Tolstoi's niece translated *Adam Bede*, *The Mill on the Floss*, and *Silas Marner*; Tolstoi owned and marginally annotated copies of *Adam Bede*, *Felix Holt*, *Romola*, and *Middlemarch* (Knapp 1983: 323). There is no extant evidence that he read *Daniel Deronda*, but his interest in Eliot makes it likely that he did so, in which case it would not be the only one of her works he read, on which his thoughts do not survive. In 1890 Tolstoi ranked his favourite English authors as Dickens followed by Thackeray and Trollope. When questioned about Eliot, he put her on a par with Dickens. A year later, in a note appended to a letter of October 1891, he specified that between the ages of thirty-five and fifty he was particularly influenced by Mrs Wood, Trollope, and 'George Elliot' (*sic*), although he listed their influence for these years only as great, rather than very great or enormous — as opposed to that of authors of other countries (Tolstoi 1978 II: 486).[8] *Anna Karenina* falls within this period.

Eliot represented much that Tolstoi at various times admired, and some of what he despised. The former included ethical earnestness, hostility to religious dogma, belief in the achievement of social through spiritual change, an understanding of the distinct gifts and roles of the sexes, and the demand that art should foster harmony between individuals: 'The greatest benefit we owe the artist [. . .] is the extension of our sympathies'; 'Задача христианского искусства осуществление братского единения людей' [The task of Christian art is to create the brotherly union of people] (Ashton 1992: 263; WIA: 251).[9] Although there is no record that he did so, it is highly likely that he disapproved of Eliot's adultery, atheism, and (from the perspective of the later Tolstoi) her professional and materialistic attitude towards writing.

The English were not only markedly slower to translate Russian literature than were the Russians to translate English literature, but slower than both the French and the Germans to translate Russian literature. For example Turgenev, who visited England regularly between 1847 and 1881, was read by the English in French for several decades (Phelps 1956: 45). Few English translations of Russian literature appeared before the 1850s: Pushkin's 'Queen of Spades' appeared in 1850, *The Captain's Daughter* in 1859, and an Englishman passed Turgenev's *Sportsman's Sketches* off as his own in 1855 (Brewster 1954: 78, 69). Vizetelly published *Crime and Punishment* in 1866, and extracts from Ostrovskii in 1868 (Brewster 1954: 79). However, the take-off decade for English translations did not occur until the 1880s: in 1881 *Eugene Onegin* appeared, and many of the works of Dostoevskii and Tolstoi followed (Brewster 1954: 173). By 1887 Matthew Arnold considered that the

Russian novel had inherited the vogue lost by the French novel, an Anglo-French debate had developed as to the relative merits of English, Russian, and French fiction, and Oxford University's Department of Lithu-Slavonic Languages had been established. In the following decade Constance Garnett and the Maudes began their translations, and in 1897 the comparative literature journal *Cosmopolis* added Russian to German, French, and English as one of its languages of publication, one year after its founding (Brewster 1954: 45; Phelps 1956: 38; Polonsky 1998: 27). In the 1870s, then as now, Russians' reading habits and linguistic knowledge were more cosmopolitan than were those of the English. The only works by Tolstoi which had appeared in English before 1880 were *Childhood and Youth* (1862, respectively ten and five years after their Russian publication), and *The Cossacks* (1878, fifteen years after Russian publication). In 1888 there was a sharp increase in English reviews of Tolstoi, and the first British visitors travelled to his Iasnaia Poliana estate (Gareth Jones 1995: 125). Five years later Constance Garnett met Tolstoi (Gareth Jones 1995: 198).

If Tolstoi was particularly interested in England by the standards of educated Russians, Eliot typified the educated English lack of interest in and distaste for Russia as uncivilized, brutal, and autocratic. Her reading of Russian literature consisted principally of Turgenev, whom Lewes met as a student in Berlin in 1839. On 7 January 1871 Turgenev paid the first of several visits to the Priory; in 1875 (during the writing of *Daniel Deronda*) Eliot and Lewes read aloud *Les Nouvelles Moscovites*, and in 1877 they read *Les Terres Vierges* (Karl 1995: 476). In the following year Turgenev, at a meal hosted by the Bullock-Halls at Six Mile Bottom, deflected to Eliot Lewes' compliment to him as the greatest living novelist (quoted in Haight 1968: 513). As far as I have been able to ascertain, Eliot never read Tolstoi in any language. The only Russian author who is known to have aroused her interest lived for much of his life in Western Europe, and wrote after West European models.

Whereas Russia's sole mention in Eliot's fiction up to and including *Middlemarch* is as a source of linseed in *The Mill on the Floss*, it plays a notable minor role in Eliot's most cosmopolitan novel, as a backwater of the Gentile world. Like England in *Anna Karenina*, it is negatively associated with wealth and luxury. Alcharisi's revelations to Daniel are presaged not only by Daniel's growing interest in Judaism, but in the narrative's unobtrusive references to the country of her present miserable, moneyed exile. Daniel stays in the Czarina Hotel in Leubronn, Gwendolen (in an inversion of Levin and Oblonskii's meal at the England) is reported to have dined several times at the Russie, and Grandcourt pauses on his way to Leubronn to win 'about two hundred' from 'some Russian acquaintances' (DD: 136). To Alcharisi Russia is a place of wealth, suspended animation, and literal and metaphorical exile, of which she speaks as little as of her 'husband and five children' (DD: 547).[10] Neither she nor the narrator mentions the fact that Russia was anti-Semitic by European standards. She would probably have remarried in the 1840s. According to a decree of Catherine the Great, not revoked until the Russian Revolution, Jewish subjects were required to live within the Pale of Settlement in the Western Empire. Exceptions were made for some wealthy Jews, and by the 1870s Oblonskii is humiliated at having to apply to two Jews for a position related to the railways.

It was commonplace for a Russian Prince to keep a foreign actress or singer as a mistress, but to marry her would have been unusual, and if she were Jewish it would have been scandalous. Halm-Eberstein makes an offer of marriage which was generous and suggested infatuation, as Alcharisi recognizes. In order to marry, Alcharisi would have converted to Orthodoxy and been confessed, like Levin, after which she and her children would have had official Christian status (since Judaism was defined by faith). As she says, 'I acted that part' of 'the wife of a Russian noble' (it may be remembered that around the same time Lola Montez successfully acted the part of a Spaniard in Russia) (DD: 548). Eliot and Alcharisi would have known about the condition of Jews in Russia, and the fact that neither mentions it is possibly an indication of Eliot's lack of interest in the country. This would almost certainly have changed had Eliot lived slightly longer. She died in the year before Alexander II's assassination led to state-sponsored anti-Semitic pogroms and provoked large-scale Russian-Jewish emigration to Palestine. The Russian Leo Pinsker (1821–91) was, with the Austrian Theodor Herzl, one of the founders of the Zionism which Mordecai forecasts. Simultaneously, the first wave of English translations of Russian literature began, and it became common for English authors to be acquainted with Tolstoi.

Tolstoi and Lawrence

In 1932 David Garnett, a friend of Lawrence whose mother had translated *Anna Karenina* and whose father had in 1914 written *Tolstoi: His Life and Writings*, compared Tolstoi and Lawrence as follows:

> Indeed both in their gifts, and in the limitation they seem wantonly to have put to their intelligences and their art, there is a curious resemblance between Tolstoy and Lawrence. In their vitality, their astonishing understanding of women, their attitude toward science and toward the greatest works of art and toward other artists, in their desire to change the world spiritually by founding small communities, in their hatred of their disciples, in their desire to change the world and to withdraw from it, in all these and many other ways there is a curious parallelism between them. And if Tolstoi was a great artist spoiled by ideas, by religious impulses, so was Lawrence, only spoiled much more. (R. Garnett [1923] 1991: 100–01)[11]

I would endorse Garnett's praise, but modify his criticisms, and qualify some of his assertions of similarity (their attitudes towards science differed significantly). However, Tolstoi and Lawrence certainly desired to withdraw from and change the world, and both lived largely apart from high society whilst writing *Anna Karenina* and *Women in Love*. These novels opposed the wars in which Russia and Britain were currently engaged, and encountered difficulties with publication partly because of this. Further similarities between the authors might be added: they had considerable experience of teaching and strong views on pedagogy, had turbulent marriages in which they performed their own housework, attributed society's degeneracy in part to industrialization and in part to the presence or absence of certain kinds of sex, and approved of humanity's existence only in proportion to its worth.

> What will die out is man the animal. What a terrible misfortune that would be!
> Just as the animals of prehistoric times died out, so, probably will the human
> animal. . . Let it die out. I am no more sorry for this two-legged animal than
> I am for the ichthyosaurs etc. What I care about is that the true life should not
> die out, the love of creatures that are able to love.
>
> If only man was swept off the face of the earth, creation would go on so
> marvellously, with a new start, non-human. Man is one of the mistakes of
> creation — like the ichthyosauri. — If only he were gone again, think what
> lovely things would come out of the liberated days.

The first is Tolstoi's response to Chertkov's objection in 1888 to *The Kreutzer Sonata*,
that total sexual abstinence would cause humanity to die out; the second is Birkin's
argument to Ursula on 'An Island' (Tolstoi quoted in introduction to Tolstoi 1983:
12; WL: 128).

Lawrence's works in general, and *The Rainbow* and *Women in Love* in particular,
have been more extensively explored in relation to German than Russian culture
— with reason.[12] The German influences apparent in *The Rainbow* (the dedication
of which, to his sister-in-law Else, Lawrence originally wished to be written in
German in Gothic script) undermined wartime support for the novel in some who
might otherwise have more strongly protested against its suppression on grounds
of obscenity (R: lxxiii). Lawrence's temperamental affinity with contemporary
Germany, which was as strong as George Eliot's, was strengthened by his
marriage.

Lawrence's interest in Russian culture is less pronounced. However, it is worth
considering his relationship to a culture which had for over two centuries been
far more strongly influenced than had English culture by German academia and
art. For example, Schelling deeply influenced the Slavophile movement with
which Tolstoi, through such friends as Pogodin, Samarin, and Tiutchev, was
connected (Berlin 1978: 241). Contrariwise, during Lawrence's lifetime Russian
culture influenced many of those aspects of German culture to which Lawrence
was most strongly attracted. In the late nineteenth and early twentieth centuries
Russian innovations and formulations of anti-Semitism, racial nationalism, anti-
intellectualism, spiritualism, theosophy, and the cult of the strong leader, fell on
fertile ground in Germany. Lawrence's relations to both Germany and Russia can
be understood in the context of the oscillating cultural relations between these
neighbours during his lifetime. Whereas Lawrence was largely resistant to the
escalation of English anti-German sentiment, he was affected by the escalation
of philo-Russian sentiment, and was well-placed to understand the connections
between the two cultures.

Lawrence also perceived the similarities of Russia with the United States —
allies which had expanded across their respective continents in the previous two
centuries, possessing tiny cultural elites who were conscious of, and in part sought
to reduce, their reliance on European culture. Lawrence was particularly attracted
to both countries between 1916 and 1923, for what he perceived as their youth
and promising futures (in contrast to Germany; he ended his 1913 *Blue Review*
article on Thomas Mann with the sentence: 'Germany does not feel very young
to me') (quoted in Armin Arnold 1961: 38). Although America ultimately attracted

him more, he planned to visit both countries, and made several attempts to learn Russian. After the suppression of *The Rainbow* and Pinker's failure to find a publisher for the 1916 version of *Women in Love*, Lawrence thought not only of the American but of the Russian market as a potential outlet for the latter. In England Lawrence came into contact with Russia's avant-garde art and its exiles, one of whom, David Maxim Litvinov, was a source for *Women in Love*'s Maxim Libidnikov. This character's nationality is repeatedly stressed in connection with his youth (he is nine times referred to as 'the young Russian') and civilization (in *The First Women in Love*, in particular, his body represents the beautiful, 'civilised human body') (WL: 69–76; *The First 'Women in Love'*: 67). 'The emotional, rather rootless life of the Russians appealed to' Gudrun and also, to a degree, to Lawrence (WL: 211). Whilst still making the final revisions to the typescript of *Women in Love* in the summer of 1919, he helped his friend Kotelianskii with his translation of Shestov's *Apofeoz Bespochvennosti* [*The Apotheosis of Groundlessness*]. Lawrence's replacement title (*All Things Are Possible*) and Preface are more optimistic than Shestov. The Preface predicts that when Russia frees itself from European influence, 'Russia will certainly inherit the future' (Lawrence 1961: 215). His interest in that country, as in others, subsequently diminished: in 1924 he condemned Lenin as a bullying Saint leading a revolution which does 'not cleanse' (RDP: 200). His interests in Russia's future, and in its nineteenth-century literature, follow similar bell curves; the latter precedes the former by about eight years.

By the time that Lawrence began reading literature in his teens, translations of Russian literature by Nathan Haskell Dole, Constance Garnett, and Louise and Aylmer Maude were widely available. He had read some of these before the rapid rise in the profile of Russian literature which coincided with his entry into English literary circles in 1909. In December 1908 he wrote to May Holbrook: 'Read, my dear, read Balzac and Ibsen and Tolstoi and think about them; don't take offence at them; they were great men, all, and who are we that we should curl our lips' (LL I: 96). He then became friends with several of the people who most assisted in the rise of the profile of Russian literature. Ford Madox Hueffer had close contacts with such Russian revolutionaries as Kropotkin, Stepniak, and Volkhonskii; his brother-in-law David Soskice had escaped from Siberian exile; and he published works by Tolstoi and Chekhov in the first editions of the *English Review* (LL I: 12). Between 1911 and 1913 Lawrence met the Garnetts. Then in 1914 he met Kotelianskii, a Ukrainian Jew who was to introduce him to contemporary Russian culture and to collaborate with him in translating Shestov, Bunin, and Gorkii — with the last of whom he strongly identified (Reinhold 2007: 188).

The First World War coincided both with the composition of most of *The Rainbow* and *Women in Love*, and with the peak of the Bloomsbury-centred Russian craze fostered by the political sympathies and wider cultural awareness which pertained to the war, an appetite for literary experimentation, and an interest in psychology and spiritualism (Brewster 1954: 162). The author on whom the peak of the Russian craze rested was Dostoevskii, whom Woolf, Mansfield, Bennett, and Murry particularly admired (Zytaruk 1971: 108–10).[13] Later, towards the weary end of the war, Dostoevskii was replaced by Chekhov as the focus of English admiration. Throughout Lawrence's life Tolstoi was less spectacularly but more consistently popular than either. Lawrence scarcely mentions the Russian craze in the novel written during its peak, *Women in Love* (of which the two references to Russian high culture, Turgenev's *Fathers and Sons* and 'the Russian Ballet of Pavlova and Nijinsky', remain unchanged between the 1916 and 1920 versions) (WL: 86, 91). However, he was consistently critical of the craze in general and the Dostoevskii cult in particular (Kaye 1999: 7). This was in part the result of his irritation with literary crazes of any kind. It was also an indication of the depth of his respect for and engagement with Russian writers, through argument with whom features of his own thought and writing had emerged. For example, Gifford thought that 'Lawrence came to self-realization, I think, in some part through wrestling with Tolstoi, whose "marvelous sensuous understanding" he rated highly, but whose "metaphysic" he thought "ignoble"' (quoted in Davie 1965: 148). His response to many of the writers whom he admired was characterized by strong approval followed by criticism at least as strong, as he sought to define himself against them. In a letter of June 1914 he defended *The Wedding Ring* to Edward Garnett, distinguishing his own artistry from that of certain Russians including Tolstoi:

> I don't think the psychology is wrong: it is only that I have a different attitude to my characters [. . .] that which is physic — non-human, in humanity, is more interesting to me than the old-fashioned human element — which causes one to conceive a character in a certain moral scheme and make him consistent. [. . .] In Turguenev, and in Tolstoi, and in Dostoievski, the moral scheme into which all the characters fit — and it is nearly the same scheme — is, whatever the extraordinariness of the characters themselves, dull, old, dead. (LL II: 182–83)

In November 1916 he commented to Catherine Carswell:

> It amazes me that we have bowed down and worshipped these foreigners [Turgenev, Tolstoi, Dostoevsky, Maupassant, Flaubert] as we have. Their art is clumsy, really, and clayey, compared with our own. [. . .] But it is characteristic of a highly-developed nation to bow down to that which is more gross and raw and affected. (LL III: 41)

By then his interest in Russian literature of the nineteenth century was being replaced by his interest in the twentieth-century literature which he was to help to translate, and in American literature. In his 1923 foreword to *Studies in Classic American Literature* he wrote: 'Two bodies of modern literature seem to me to have come to a real verge: the Russian and the American' (SCAL: 11–12). Those Russian writers of whom he read most in his lifetime were Tolstoi, Dostoevskii, Turgenev, Chekhov, Merezhkovskii, Sovoliev, Rozanov, Shestov, Bunin, and Gor'kii. Of Tolstoi's works, it is known that Lawrence read *Anna Karenina*, *War and Peace*, *Resurrection*, *What is Art?*, *The Kreutzer Sonata*, and a number of tales from the 1870s onwards, and that he saw an English production of *The Live Corpse*. He also read George Calderon's 1914 translation of *Count Ilya Tolstoy's Reminiscences of Tolstoy* and Edward Garnett's *Tolstoi: His Life and Writings* of the same year. He probably read Kotelianskii's translations of *The Autobiography of Countess Tolstoi* (with Virginia Woolf), *Tolstoi's Love Letters*, and A. B. Goldenveizer's *Talks with Tolstoi*. He may also have read *Leo Tolstoi* (a 1903 collection of essays by Edward Garnett, G. K. Chesterton, and G. H. Perris), Paul Birukoff's 1906 *Leo Tolstoy: His Life and Work*, and J. A. T. Lloyd's 1910 *Two Russian Reformers: Ivan Turgenev, Leo Tolstoi* (Zytaruk 1971: 19).

Unlike many contemporary and subsequent critics of Tolstoi, Lawrence did not describe Tolstoi in terms of periods: early (before *War and Peace*), middle (it and *Anna Karenina*), and late (subsequently). He makes no criticism of *War and Peace* or *Resurrection* that he does not also apply to *Anna Karenina*, although the reverse is not the case. He read *What is Art?*, and certain of Tolstoi's moral tales, at the same time as or soon after the two long novels, and it is likely that the explicit and categorical moral didacticism, vision of Christianity, condemnation of sexuality, and valorization of the Russian peasant, which he found in the later works, intensified his perception of these qualities in the earlier works. Lawrence's earliest written response to Tolstoi, which was also his own first statement of a philosophy of art, is a response to *What is Art?*: the paper 'Art and the Individual', delivered to a meeting of the Eastwood Debating Society in March 1908.

Lawrence commented most on *Anna Karenina*, followed by *War and Peace* and *Resurrection* (Zytaruk 1971: 81). His opinion of *Anna Karenina* fluctuated. In 1907 he told Jessie Chambers that it was 'the greatest novel in the world' (Chambers 1965: 114). May Chambers disapproved of his identification with Anna; to her 'The marital troubles of an aunt and uncle of his seemed far more important than the troubles of Anna Karenina with whom he sympathized to such a point of suffering that I accused him of being foolish' (quoted in Nehls III: 593). Half a year later, in May 1909, he wrote to Blanche Jennings urging her to read *Anna Karénina*, which she 'dare not fall out with' or else he will 'swear aloud' (LL I: 127). In a cheerfully polemic response to J. M. Robertson's and Jennings's opinion that *Crime and Punishment* was 'the finest book written', he called this novel 'a tract, a treatise, a pamphlet compared with Tolstoi's *Anna Karénina* or *War and Peace*', even before the Russian craze had given him a reason to distance himself from Dostoevskii (LL I: 126–27). In the following year he used Anna to describe Louie Burrows, who offered 'a fine, warm, healthy, natural love — not like Jane Eyre, who is Muriel, but like — say Rhoda Fleming or a commoner Anna Karénin' (LL I: 191). During his elopement in May 1912 he and Frieda thought of their situation in relation to the novel; in June he wrote to Jessie Chambers: 'I only know I love Frieda. . . I can think of nothing but of Anna Karenina' (LL I: 412). That November he wrote jovially to Edward Garnett: 'F. had carefully studied *Anna Karenin*, in a sort of "How to be happy though livanted" [*sic*] spirit' (LL I: 463). Frieda was probably particularly interested in Anna's remorse over her son. In the following year Lawrence wrote that he had a horror of Frieda 'stopping her son as he comes from school, and seeing him so', an imagined scene which resembles Anna's clandestine visit to Seriozha (LL I: 542). He may not have wished to discuss in writing this aspect of the novel, which invoked a subject of great contention between them.

As his relationship with Frieda developed, Lawrence became increasingly critical of the novel (Preston 1988: 112). This is apparent in his *Study of Thomas Hardy*, which was typed up by Kotelianskii in late 1914, and developed ideas with reference to Hardy and Tolstoi which affected what became *The Rainbow* and *Women in Love* (R: xxxii). In the *Study* he criticized '*Anna Karenin*' as a tragedy in which 'the mechanical system is actively transgressed, and holds, and punishes the protagonist, whilst the greater morality is only passively, negatively transgressed'. In this respect Tolstoi resembles Hardy, and both fail to resemble Shakespeare and Sophocles, in whom 'the greater morality' is transgressed. 'Anna, Eustacia, Tess or Sue — what was there in their position that was necessarily tragic? Necessarily painful it was, but they were not at war with God, only with Society [. . .] the judgment of man killed them' (STH: 30). Of Anna and Vronskii he wrote that:

> Their real tragedy is that they are unfaithful to the greater unwritten morality, which would have bidden Anna Karenin be patient and wait until she, by virtue of greater right, could take what she needed from society; would have bidden Vronsky detach himself from the system, become an individual, creating a new colony of morality with Anna. (STH: 29–30)

Study of Thomas Hardy also criticized Tolstoi, with implicit reference to his later works, for repudiating his own nature. This he defined as belonging to 'the father' — the physical, sensual, feminine, inert, non-intellectual, unified, soul, and the Law.

> Probably because of profligacy in his youth [. . .] Tolstoi, in his metaphysic, renounced the flesh altogether [. . .] He had a marvelous sensuous understanding, and very little clarity of mind [. . .] Reading the reminiscences of Tolstoi, one can only feel shame at the way Tolstoi denied all that was great in him [. . .] he said there was no difficulty in it, because it came naturally to him. (STH: 92)[14]

Lawrence's charge of Tolstoi's betrayal of the gifts of his spirit was echoed in form by Murry's charge against Lawrence at the end of *Son of Woman*: 'You were richly endowed with spirit and love, and denied both' (1931: 144–45). Murry likened Lawrence-as-man to Jesus and Lawrence-as-artist to Judas. On the other hand, both men were accused *as men* of betraying their artistic selves, as represented in *Sons and Lovers*, *War and Peace*, and *Anna Karenina*. In 1928 Lawrence claimed that: 'It was only as a moralist and a personal being that Tolstoi was perverse. As a true artist, he worshipped, as Verga did, every manifestation of pure, spontaneous, passionate life' (Verga 1928: 18–19). True artistry, here, is freighted with Lawrence's spiritual normativity: this is not the 'talent' 'necessary for the transmission of feeling' of which he spoke in 'Art and the Individual', and which he found absent from 'Tolstoi and his simple art — his tales' (STH: 227).

However, if Lawrence did not like Tolstoi's moralism, he had no liking for a late comic work by Tolstoi, *The Live Corpse* (probably finished in 1908, published posthumously), which displays greater liberality than, and in certain respects rewrites, *Anna Karenina*. A man feigns suicide in order to liberate his wife to marry the man she loves, Karenin, with whom she subsequently has a child. When the fraud is revealed, the first husband shoots himself at his own trial. Lawrence saw it in its English translation by Aylmer Maude, *Reparation*, in November 1919, and described it as 'awful rubbish' (LL II: 411). Between 1919 and 1921 Lawrence slightly altered the bases of his criticisms of *Anna Karenina* and the later Tolstoi as these appear in *Study of Thomas Hardy*. He still condemned Tolstoi's Christian socialism (for example in certain authorial remarks in *Mr Noon*), but no longer celebrated Anna and Vronskii's adultery, or considered their ruin to be determined by petty social morality (*Mr Noon*: 140, 146, 190). In the first (1919) version of his essay on Nathaniel Hawthorne for *Studies in Classic American Literature*, he wrote of 'Anna Karenin', Hester Prynne, and Sue Bridehead that 'these women are never satisfied till they have shattered the man who responded to them' (SCAL: 249). Two years later, on the last page of *Fantasia of the Unconscious*, he wrote:

> If the man has no purpose for his days, then to the woman alone remains the goal of her nights: the great sex goal. [. . .] It demands at last the departure into death [. . .] Like Carmen, or like Anna Karenin.

Lawrence approved the fact that 'Tolstoi said No to the passion and death conclusion' of Anna and Vronskii, but lamented that he 'then drew into the dreary issue of a false conclusion' which was even worse:

> Better the woman's goal, sex and death, than some *false* goal of man's. Better Anna Karenin and Vronsky a thousand times than Natasha and that porpoise of a Pierre [. . .] Better Vronsky than Tolstoi himself, in my mind. Better Vronsky's final statement [. . .] than Tolstoi and Tolstoi-ism and that beastly peasant blouse the old man wore. (PUFU: 200)

Lawrence's reading of *Resurrection* in late 1924 restoked his partly Nietzschean contempt for Christian 'Tolstoi-ism', which he found to deny the Resurrection itself: 'Tolstoi writhed very hard, on the Cross. His Resurrection is the step into the tomb. And the stone was rolled upon him'. Lawrence thought that Tolstoi believed that Christ 'would go on being crucified, everlastingly', whereas Lawrence proclaimed that: 'The Lord is risen' (RDP: 233, 235).

In his essay 'The Novel', of June 1925, Lawrence criticized 'Tolstoi-ism' in the context of modern Bolshevism (although he added an optimistic remark about Bolshevism to the final typescript of the essay):

> when the lion tries to force himself down the throat of the huge and popular lamb — a nasty old sheep, really — then it's a phenomenon. Old Leo did it: wedged himself bit by bit down the throat of woolly Russia. And now out of the mouth of the bolshevist lambkin still waves an angry, mistaken, tufted leonine tail, like an agitated exclamation mark. (STH: 187)

Lawrence returned to his charge of 1914 that Tolstoi denied his own nature, with reference to *Anna Karenina*, *War and Peace*, and *Resurrection*: 'Tolstoi, being a great creative artist, was true to his characters. But being a man with a philosophy, he wasn't true to his *own character*' (STH: 186). He inflected this criticism with the charge that Tolstoi embraces 'absolutes' — a negative noun (although not always a negative adjective) in Lawrence's vocabulary from 'The Crown' (1915) onwards: 'He wanted to *be* absolute: a universal brother' (STH: 187).

In 'The Novel' Lawrence reverted to his earlier celebration of Anna and Vronskii's love, and to his accusation that Tolstoi enforces their submission to society's moral judgement:

> Nobody in the world is anything but delighted when Vronsky gets Anna Karenin [. . .] all the tragedy comes from Vronsky's and Anna's fear of society.

> The monster was social, not phallic at all. They couldn't live in the pride of their sincere passion, and spit in Mother Grundy's eye. And that, that cowardice, was the real 'sin'. The novel makes it obvious, and knocks all old Leo's teeth out [. . .] where would any of Leo's books be, without the phallic splendour? The Judas! Cringe to a mingy, bloodless Society, and try to dress up that dirty old Mother Grundy in a new bonnet and face-powder of Christian-Socialism. Brothers indeed! Sons of a castrated Father! The novel itself gives Vronsky a kick in the behind, and knocks old Leo's teeth out, and leaves us to learn. (STH: 180)

Lawrence combined these criticisms with demonstrations of the strength of the novel form, using Tolstoi more than any other author. He argued that the novel form *per se* exposes as fraudulent attempts on the part of the novelist to propound absolutes:

> in the novel there's always a tom-cat, a black tom-cat that pounces on the white dove of the Word, if the dove doesn't watch it; and there is a banana-skin to trip on; and you know there is a water-closet on the premises. All these things help to keep the balance. (STH: 181)

The novel necessarily testifies to the power of sex: 'Sex is flame, too, the novel announces' (STH: 189).

Three years later, in the year of publication of *Lady Chatterley's Lover*, the 'Introduction' to Lawrence's translation of Giovanni Verga's *Cavalleria Rusticana* again restated his 1914 charges of conventional morality (Verga 1928: 20). To these he added the new charge of worship of poverty. According to Lawrence, Verga avoids 'the Tolstoyan fallacy, of repudiating the educated world and exalting the peasant': 'What Tolstoi somewhat perversely worshipped in the peasants was poverty itself, and humility' (18–19).

To summarize, Lawrence's main criticism of *Anna Karenina* was that Anna and Vronskii suffer a tragedy of social rather than cosmic morality.[15] Around 1920 this interpretation was briefly replaced with exasperation at Anna's sex tragedy. He criticized Tolstoi in general for denying his sensuous nature, failures of artistry, worshiping humble poverty, rejecting education, and asserting ethical absolutes. Such faults are particularly visible in his novels. It should be noted that Lawrence never commented on Levin, Kiti, or Oblonskii. Jessie Chambers recorded that she, her brother and father 'felt most sympathy [. . .] with Levin and Kitty, and followed their experiments in farming with deep interest [. . .] Lawrence, however, was more interested in the problem of Anna' (Chambers 1965: 114). At the level of explicit comment, this remained the case throughout his life. The character and situation of Anna compelled his attention and (for most of his life) his sympathy. However, his silence about Levin requires careful interpretation.

I will not attempt to hoist Lawrence by his own 1907–09, 1914, 1919–21, 1925, and 1928 petards; writers' comments upon writers are frequently rhetorical for their own as well as readers' benefits. As Lawrence wrote to Edward Garnett on 1 February 1913, after describing contemporary drama as 'rather bony, bloodless drama': 'I don't want to write like Galsworthy nor Ibsen, nor Strindberg nor any of them, *not* even if I could. We have to hate our immediate predecessors, to get free from their authority'. (LL 1: 509). Instead, I will use Lawrence's emergent arguments about *Anna Karenina* as a critical perspective on both that novel and *Women in Love*. Leavis wrote of Lawrence's response to Tolstoi: 'It is astonishing that so marvelously perceptive a critic as Lawrence could simplify in that way, with so distorting an effect' (1967: 21). In fact it is not surprising; like Bakhtin, or like Tolstoi in *What is Art?*, Lawrence converted other writers into his own critical vocabulary, rather as he used locations in his travel writing. Raymond Williams claims that 'Lawrence the critic of Tolstoi was sometimes put right by Lawrence the novelist' (Zytaruk 1971: 94). However, as Chapter 4 will observe, this is not always the case, and sometimes Lawrence the critic was right in the first place.

Notes to Chapter 1

1. In this book *thing* will be used in its sense as an entity distinct from both the totality of being, and from attributes or qualities. *Entity* was rejected for this role as being ostentatiously philosophical, and *object* as being unhelpfully opposed to *subject*.

2. Charles Bernheimer opened the 1995 American Comparative Literature Association report with the statement: 'Comparative literature is anxiogenic' (Bernheimer 1995: 1). Étiemble opened his 1963 *Comparaison n'est pas raison* with the observation: 'Encore que le mot crise soit à la mode [. . .] pour raccrocher le lecteur, les auteurs d'articles ou d'ouvrages sur n'importe quoi l'accrochent n'importe où [. . .] la littérature comparée subit en effet, depuis deux décennies au moins, ce qu'il ne messied pas d'appeler une crise.' [Even though it's fashionable to use the word crisis [. . .] to grab the reader, authors of articles and works on whatever subject attach it no matter where [. . .] comparative literature has in fact, for at least two decades, been undergoing what it wouldn't be inappropriate to call a crisis.] (Étiemble 1963: 9)

3. *Ethnie* is the French term for a non-national ethnocultural group, employed in English sociology since Anthony D. Smith used it in his work *The Ethnic Origins of Nations* (1986: 13).

4. The narrator of *Daniel Deronda* uses *comparison* to mean *simile* or *analogy* when a member of the Philosophers' Club recites 'the comparison of the avalanche in his [Shelley's] "Prometheus Unbound") —

   > "As thought by thought is piled, till some great truth
   > Is loosened, and the nations echo round."' (DD: 445)

5. This and similar idioms are taken from the Wikipedia article 'Apples and Oranges': <http://en.wikipedia.org/wiki/Apples_and_oranges>.

6. For example, Blumberg (1971); Fleetwood (1980); Hardy (1997).

7. Mills (1996) also refers to *Anna Karenina*.

8. The note does not survive; the list translated in Christian's edition is taken from a copy made by Tolstoi's daughter Masha.

9. The quotation from *What is Art?* is the last sentence of the book.

10. For a full consideration of 'Why Does Daniel Deronda's Mother Live in Russia?', see the article by the present author in *George Eliot–George Henry Lewes Studies* (September 2010). I thank the editors for permission to use research from that article in this book, and for their editorial help with the article.

11. Parts of this section also appeared, in different form, in Brown (2010b). I thank the editors of *Comparative Literature* for their kind permission to use this material, and for their editorial assistance with the article.

12. For example by Bell (1992); Fernihough, (1993); Gray (1969); Pinkney (1990).

13. Cf. Murry (1916).

14. Lawrence alludes to a quotation attributed to Tolstoi: 'What difficulty is there in writing about how an officer fell in love with a married woman? There's no difficulty in it, and, above all, no good in it' (quoted in I. Tolstoi 1914: 144–45).

15. This has generated much critical debate — for example Gifford (1959) and (1960); Williams (1960); Leavis (1967: 9–32).

CHAPTER 2

Daniel Deronda

Nationalliteratur will jetzt nicht viel sagen; die Epoche der Weltliteratur ist an
der Zeit, und jeder muß jetzt dazu wirken, diese Epoche zu beschleunigen.
[National literature doesn't mean much now; the time has come for the epoch
of world literature, and everyone must work to bring it on.]
JOHANN WOLFGANG VON GOETHE, 31 January 1827; Eckermann 1948: 229

Weltliteratur

Like Daniel, Eliot wanted to avoid 'a merely English attitude in studies'; like
Mordecai, she wanted to 'drink culture at all sources' (DD: 155, 426). She educated
herself to a degree which her critics struggle to match about the history and cultures
of Germany, Spain, France, Italy, Bohemia, and Palestine, and her elective affinity
with Goethe included a shared interest in cultural breadth. Although the term
Weltliteratur appears neither in extant writings by Eliot nor in Lewes's *Life*, Eliot was
almost certainly familiar with the concept from the writings of Thomas Carlyle and
Matthew Arnold. *Daniel Deronda* both makes an attempt to constitute *Weltliteratur*,
and implicitly reflects upon the concept. According to Goethe, *Weltliteratur* fosters
geistiger Handelsverkehr [spiritual trade] between peoples by mediating the differences
between them. Authors who wish to perform such mediation often do so for the
benefit of people of their own culture, whereas, for example, modern Nigerian
writers may wish their Anglophone writing to serve as a bridge for foreigners to (a)
Nigerian culture. *Daniel Deronda* is less concerned to introduce upper-class English
society to, say, rural Russian Jews, than it is to introduce Jews to English Gentiles
— but it is also exemplary of, and concerned with, cultural mediation *per se* (Werses
1976: 36). Its characters, plots, and sensibility are influenced by European literature
including Goethe's own (Röder-Bolton 1998: 269–74). Of the forty-one (60 per
cent) of the novel's epigraphs which are not by Eliot, 45 per cent were originally
not written in English. Like Daniel Charisi's chest of family records, which contains
texts written in Spanish, Italian, Latin, Hebrew, and Arabic, the novel contains
texts from seven different countries in its covers (DD: 640). A reader from any of
these countries (England, the United States, Italy, France, Germany, Greece, and
Palestine) will find something — however small — that is familiar, and will also be
exposed to the foreign; to provide someone with both is the most rudimentary form
of mediation. Goethe stated in his journal *Kunst und Altertum* [*Art and Antiquity*]:
'daraus nur kann endlich die allgemeine Weltliteratur entspringen, daß die
Nationen die Verhältnisse aller gegen alle kennenlernen' [that is the only way for

a general world literature to finally emerge — that nations learn the relationships of everyone to everyone else] (quoted in Strich 1957: 21). *Daniel Deronda* meets this demand for comprehension of relationships which exclude the comparer's own category by noting, for example, the situation of Jews in Piedmont. But it is of course Jewish English and Gentile English readers in particular who are both made to feel at home, and exposed to what any but such aristocratically connected Jews as Deronda or Disraeli would experience as unfamiliar. Since its author was not such a person, she had to conduct a considerable amount of research in order to banish 'the spectre of amateurism' to the satisfaction of educated Jews (Damrosch 2003: 284). The novel gives the Gentile reader a touchstone in Mrs Meyrick, who found 'herself on inspection rather dim as to what the Hebrew religion might have turned into at this date', and an analogue in Daniel, whose interest of and knowledge in Judaism increase over the course of the novel (DD: 182). The same was true of Eliot's own interest and knowledge over the course of writing the novel, but hers was the most voluntary learning; Daniel finds it at first thrust upon him as a consequence of his care for Mirah, whilst the reader finds it thrust upon him as a consequence of that concern for Gwendolen which demands that he passes through the Jewish sections in order to find out what happens to her next. Like Hatem, the narrator of Goethe's *West-östlicher Diwan* [*West-Eastern Divan*], which provides the epigraph for Chapter 39, Daniel's interest in an eastern culture increases with his love for a woman; the reader, like Eliot, must be satisfied with more cerebral inducements.

Insofar as *Daniel Deronda* gives rhetorical support to Mordecai's ideas, it asserts the interdependence of language and culture. One of Mordecai's first questions to Daniel is whether he knows Hebrew, and for him it is essential that his best ideas and feelings be expressed in that language: 'If I could write now and used English, I should be as one who beats a board to summon those who have been used to no signal but a bell' (DD: 428). The novel mediates between Hebrew and English by glossing certain words ('the reader had mounted to the *almemor* or platform') and translating others, always indicating when Hebrew is being spoken (Kalonymos spoke 'in Hebrew, quoting from one of the fine hymns in the Hebrew liturgy, "As thy goodness has been great to the former generations, even so may it be to the latter"') (DD: 310, 617). However, the novel also suggests that natural language is not necessary to all thought and feeling. Daniel is moved by the liturgy in Frankfurt without knowing Hebrew:

> Deronda, having looked enough at the German translation of the Hebrew in the book before him to know that he was chiefly hearing Psalms and Old Testament passages or phrases, gave himself up to that strongest effect of chanted liturgies which is independent of detailed verbal meaning — like the effect of an Allegri's *Miserere* or a Palestrina's *Magnificat*. (DD: 310)

Similarly, when Mirah sings her mother's hymn with the senseless words which resemble what she remembers of it, Daniel comments that 'The lisped syllables are very full of meaning', and likens them to his reception of the liturgy in Frankfurt. Such *scat* singing might be thought to approach the hypothetical language of Goethe's *Weltpoesie* — literature which approximated to the *Urphänomen* [original phenomenon] of universal humanity — but a novel cannot be written in it (Strich 1957: 27).

As *Weltliteratur, Daniel Deronda* has limitations. It might have attempted to teach Gentiles considerably more about Jewish life and culture than it does; Eliot may have decided not to risk the criticisms which were levelled at *Romola* twelve years before for overburdening the reader with detail about a foreign place and time. The reader's knowledge of Hebrew is permitted on the level of that of Hans, who remarks: 'You see how far I have got in Hebrew lore — up with my Lord Bolingbroke, who knew no Hebrew, but "understood that sort of learning and what is writ about it"' (DD: 553). Nor, on the other hand, is the Gentile reader made to sense Hebrew as *other*; printing עמש would have aroused a stronger sense of the foreign than the word *Shemah*, and since the novel draws 'on the long tradition of experiments in the sublime "hebraic" style', Spivak's 'inter-diction — speaking between the two sides' is strongly biased towards the target language (Shaffer 1975: 235; Spivak 2003: 38). Mordecai is translated into language which strongly resembles his habitual English speech when he gave forth Hebrew verses with a meaning something like this:

> Away from me the garment of forgetfulness,
> Withering the heart;
> The oil and wine from presses of the Goyim,
> Poisoned with scorn.
> Solitude is on the sides of Mount Nebo,
> In its heart a tomb:
> There the buried ark and golden cherubim
> Make hidden light: (DD: 409)

Lawrence makes a similarly motivated attempt to translate a Spanish prophetic style in *The Plumed Serpent*. A member of the Mexican Aztec revivalist cult with which the novel is concerned gives the English heroine Kate 'a sort of ballad, but without rhyme, in Spanish', including the following lines:

> I heard the star singing like a dying bird;
> *My name is Jesus, I am Mary's Son.*
> *I am coming home.*
> *My mother the Moon is dark:*
> *Oh brother, Quetzalcoatl*
> *Hold back the dragon of the sun,*
> *Bind him with shadow while I pass*
> *Homewards. Let me come home.* (Lawrence 1995b: 104)[1]

Both novels concern religions to which Christianity is supplementary (Quetzalcoatl having been temporarily replaced by Mary and Jesus), but reject the claims of Christianity to have superseded them. Eliot and Lawrence both attempt to mediate these religions to modern Christians in language related to that chosen by Tyndale and King James's translators of the Hebrew Bible, but precisely because of the familiarity of that translation, they convey only a limited sense of the quiddity of a Middle Eastern and a Central American culture respectively. Whereas the cult of Quetzalcoatl is already mediated by an imperial language, *Daniel Deronda*'s attempt to give a sense of Hebrew more nearly resembles the attempt of *The Book of Mormon* to mediate the reformed Egyptian of the ancient native American Moroni, its supposed original author.[2] It is as though Eliot, if not Mordecai, heeds the objection of a Jew whom Mordecai fails to convince: 'The book of Mormon would never have answered in Hebrew' (DD: 427). But whereas Joseph Smith, Jr., succeeded in his attempt to start a new line of religion, Eliot's (and Lawrence's). attempts at proselytization are second order — their aim being primarily to make English readers receptive to others' receptiveness to a foreign religion. Daniel is largely convinced by Mordecai; Kate is partly convinced by Don Ramón and Don Cipriano; the reader is meant to be at least interested in their interest, and to judge them according to it. Such second-order mediation is fully within the spirit of Goethe's *Weltliteratur.*

However, whereas *The Plumed Serpent* for the most part teaches its readers such Spanish as it contains, *Daniel Deronda* does not translate all of its (few) Hebrew words into English. When Alcharisi says: 'I was to [. . .] think it beautiful that men should bind the *tephillin* on them, and women not', her complaint against incomprehensible exclusion will resonate in readers who do not know what *tephillin* (boxes containing verses from the *Torah* strapped onto the arm and forehead) are. The novel's failure, remedied by modern editors, to provide translations of its French, Italian, and German epigraphs and lyrics is a failure to mediate between those who share Eliot's level of education, and those who do not. Mirah's ability to complete the couplet from the *West-östlicher Diwan* quoted by Klesmer (and by Eliot in the epigraph; the response has been provided to attentive readers) exemplifies the kind of cultural breadth to which the reader should aspire (although Gwendolen and Mrs Arrowpoint's similar interchange with a quotation from Goethe warns against superficial erudition; when Gwendolen quotes Mephistopheles 'die Kraft ist schwach, allein die Lust ist gross', Mrs Arrowpoint returns: 'Ah, you are a student of Goethe. Young ladies are so advanced now. I suppose you have read everything') (DD: 416, 36; Röder-Bolton 1998: 271). On the other hand, the novel's translation into English of only Classical texts (epigraphs from Marcus Aurelius and Aristotle) makes the insular, Oxbridge, Casaubon-like erudition of which even Sir Hugo advocates having a little, and which its readers are more likely to have possessed than German, redundant. Even though Mordecai uses the example of the 'living [. . .] history and literature of Greece and Rome, which have inspired revolutions, enkindled the thought of Europe' as a model for his revival of ancient Jewish literature, the novel as a whole does not (DD: 457). The challenge which the novel presents to cultural insularity has made many English readers uneasy, particularly if, rather than recognizing the novel as *weltlich* [worldlike], they have attempted to relate it to a narrowly English tradition: 'Critics grasping in desperation and relief at the superficial resemblances of Gwendolen Harleth to Jane Austen's heroines have made it nearly impossible to comprehend *Daniel Deronda* as a whole' (Shaffer 1975: 234). Such comprehension relies on broader cultural knowledge than many readers possess, and the novel's aim is more to make readers aware of this, than to remedy it.

In one of his schemes for *Kunst und Altertum* Goethe significantly corrected 'World literature' to 'European, in other words, World Literature' (Strich 1957: 371).

Like Goethe and Mordecai, *Daniel Deronda* strives to mediate 'East and West' —
hence the repeated quotation from Goethe's *West-östlicher Diwan* (Shaffer 1975: 233).
Elsewhere in the divan appear the lines:

> Wer sich selbst und andere kennt,
> Wird auch hier erkennen:
> Orient und Okzident
> Sind nicht mehr zu trennen.
>
> [Those who know themselves and others
> Will recognize even here:
> The Orient and the Occident
> Are not to be parted again] (Goethe 1972: 437)

The Meyricks either admire the poem or share its spirit, since their cat is named
after the poet who inspired Goethe to write the poem, and the poem's narrator
to travel to Persia; Hafiz is an unobtrusive but constant presence in a household
which represents the unification of the Scottish and French, and which designates
Daniel as 'Prince Caramalzaman' and Mirah as 'Queen Budoor' (DD: 156, 178).
The aim is not merely mediation *per se*, but the instruction of the West by the
East: in Goethe's case an East which knows how to submit to fate whilst taking
physical delight, like the cat, in any situation; in Mordecai's case, an East which
inspires spiritual sublimity and struggle (although he also criticizes Europe by
the Ottoman standards: 'is there no prophet or poet among us to make the ears
of Christian Europe tingle with shame at the hideous obloquy of Christian strife
which the Turk gazes at as at the fighting of beasts to which he has lent an arena?')
(DD: 456). The narrator satirizes the arrogance of British eastern imperialism
casually but keenly: Warham Gascoigne cannot grasp the connection of 'a quotable
knowledge of Browne's Pastorals' to 'the welfare of our Indian Empire', and India is
the location of 'tiger-hunting or pig-sticking' as fondly remembered by Grandcourt
and fantasized by Gwendolen (DD: 46, 93). The narrator refers to Europe as the
extent of the civilized world, with irony: 'Klesmer was not yet a Liszt, understood
to be adored by ladies of all European countries with the exception of Lapland'
(DD: 203). Pash's characterization of Arabs as one of the 'backward nations' which
contrast to 'us in Europe' is made in the context of an argument about nationalism
which is rejected by Mordecai, Daniel, and the rhetoric of the scene (DD: 448).

Nonetheless, there are reasons why *Daniel Deronda* is called Eliot's European novel.
Of the novel's epigraphs not written by Eliot, only that from *The Book of Wisdom*
(to Chapter 3) was not written in Europe or America. Mordecai makes respectful
reference to the Persian Achaemenid Empire, but his Zionism is also strongly, and
by his own confession, based on European models of nationhood: he envisions
'a republic where the Jewish spirit manifests itself in a new order founded on the
old, purified, enriched by the experience our greatest sons have gathered from the
life of the ages'; its 'ancient community' had offered 'equality of protection' to its
people, giving it 'more than the brightness of Western freedom amid the despotisms
of the East' (DD: 459, 458, 456). His argument draws on recent theories about the
utopian republican nature of ancient Israel which did more to serve contemporary
political purposes than to describe the actual Hebrew Kingdom, and his view of the

rest of the East is by contrast Orientalist in Edward Said's sense of the term (DD: 456). Fifty years later Lawrence had a similar perception of Zionism itself: 'even in Zionists I can't really get at any gulf between me and them. They seem like one of us English just doing a Zion stunt' (LL III: 690). When Mordecai advocates the construction of 'a land set for a halting-place of enmities, a neutral ground for the East as Belgium is for the West', he likens Israel to a country which was being guaranteed independence from its neighbours by Britain, and was therefore effectively a British client state (DD: 456). Indeed, Mordecai may have sensed the power of Britain, which it exerted once it no longer supported the Ottomans, to establish an independent but client Zionist state in Palestine. Lewes's comment about Goethe, that 'while donning the Turban, and throwing the Caftan over his shoulders, he remained a true German' may to some extent be applied to Mordecai as a European, and to *Daniel Deronda* as a European novel (1911: 539).

Goethe's advocacy of *Weltliteratur* as mediation between particularity, and as rapprochement with the *Urphänomen*, did not entail the abolition of nationhood. He stated that it was not the case that 'die Nationen sollen überein denken, sondern sie sollen nur einander gewahr werden, sich begreifen, und wenn sie wechselseitig nicht lieben mögen, sich einander wenigstens dulden lernen' [nations should think alike, rather that they should simply become aware of each other, and even if they can't like each other, at least learn to tolerate each other] (quoted in Strich 1957: 25). However, he also understood the essence of art and science as transcending nationhood:

> Es gibt keine patriotische Kunst und keine patriotische Wissenschaft. Beide gehören wie alles hohe Gute der ganzen Welt an und können nur durch allgemeine freie Wechselwirkung aller zugleich Lebenden in steter Rücksicht auf das, was uns vom Vergangenen übrig und bekannt ist, gefördert werden.
>
> [There is no such thing as patriotic art and no patriotic science. Both belong to the whole world like everything great and good, and can only be supported by a general free exchange between all those who live at the same time, paying constant consideration to what has been left to us, and is known, from the past.]
> (Goethe 1972: 539)

Moreover, Goethe did not explicitly argue in favour of nationalism, whereas *Daniel Deronda* in certain respects does. Rather than arguing for what Posnett called 'the gradual expansion of social life, from clan to city, from city to nation, from both of these to cosmopolitan humanity', it stresses the need for a secure sense of a 'local habitation', and a circumscribed sphere of action (Posnett 1886: 86; DD: 16). The narrator of *Middlemarch* points out that the ego's candle makes the world's events randomly scratched on a mirror seem to orientate themselves around that flame. *Daniel Deronda* does not contradict this perception (tellingly, Gwendolen repeatedly sees herself in mirrors), but it adds the perception that a sense of geographical and cultural locality is a helpful basis from which to relate to the foreign, just as the perception of stars around one's 'homestead' is 'the best introduction to astronomy' (DD: 16). Hans feels hopelessly estranged from Mirah precisely when he feels 'cosmopolitan': ' "That is your kind way of praising me; I never was praised so before," said Mirah, with a smile, which was rather maddening to Hans and made him feel still more of a cosmopolitan' (DD: 418). At the Philosophers' Club Gideon argues for Jewish assimilation, and Pash argues that although backward nationalities such as the Arabs may revive, 'with us in Europe the sentiment of nationality is destined to die out' (DD: 451, 448). Mordecai, in denying this, uses the organicist metaphor of the body: a people 'absorbs the thought of other nations into its own forms, and gives back the thought as new wealth to the world; it is a power and an organ in the great body of the nations' (DD: 449). The metaphor moderates the apparent paradox that it is the role of nations to mediate between nations. Moreover, Mordecai argues that as well as functioning as the emotional 'heart of mankind', Israel is particularly adept at mediating between itself and other peoples, and between peoples other than itself (DD: 453). The novel's major mediatory figure, Daniel, is Jewish. Jewish analogies are used at moments of mediation, as when Mordecai describes the Philosophers' Club members as 'few — like the cedars of Lebanon', thereby giving honorary Jewish status to people who wish to exchange ideas (DD: 444)

Several reasons are suggested for Israel's talent at mediation. One is geographical: Mordecai predicts 'a new Judaea, poised between East and West — a covenant of reconciliation' (DD: 459). Diasporic Jews combine what they perceive to be a common race and religion with regional variation: the Genoese Jews have a 'way of taking awful prayers and invocations with the easy familiarity which might be called Hebrew dyed Italian', and use a 'Spanish-Hebrew liturgy which had lasted through the seasons of wandering generations like a plant with wandering seed, that gives the far-off lands a kinship to the exile's home' (DD: 586). George Steiner argued, in a way which contradicts neither the arguments nor the evidence of the novel, that Jews rose to prominence in comparative literature in the United States 'endowed, it would appear, with an unusual facility for languages, compelled to be a *frontalier* [. . .] the twentieth-century Jew would be drawn naturally to a comparative view of the secular literatures which he treasured but in none of which he was natively or "by right of national inheritance" altogether at home' (Steiner 1996: 162). Jewish theology, in contrast to pagan religions and to Christianity, insists on unity; to Mordecai the defining mark of Jewishness is the *Shemah*: 'In the multitudes of the ignorant on three continents who observe our rites and make the confession of the divine Unity, the soul of Judaism is not dead' (DD: 454). Almost at the end of *Anna Karenina* Levin comes to believe that 'одно очевидное, несомненное проявление божества — это законы добра' [the one obvious, incontestable manifestation of Godhead is the law of what is right] (AK IX: 402). But he also accepts Christian dogma, which he considers to be the particular form taken by divine truth as revealed to Russians, like the apparent motions of the stars as viewed from a fixed point (AK IX: 403). By contrast, Mordecai considers that 'the divine Unity embraced as its consequence the ultimate unity of mankind', and that the *Shemah* therefore gives 'a binding theory to the human race' (DD: 628). In addition, as *Daniel Deronda*'s narrator, Daniel, and Theophrastus Such each note, this theology has 'penetrated the thinking of half the world, and moulded the splendid forms of that world's religion' (DD: 310, 316; Eliot 1994: 148). Posnett stated in his study of comparative literature that:

Between the world-religions of Israel and Islam and the world-cultures of Alexandria and Rome there are, no doubt, very wide differences. Yet, though the former reach universality through social bonds of creed and the latter reach universality through the unsocial idea of personal culture, the outcome of both is to rise above old restrictions of place and time, and to render possible a literature which, whether based on Moses or Homer, may best be termed a 'world-literature'. (Posnett 1886: 236)

However, there are several limitations and contradictions implicit in the novel's position on nationality. One implication of Judaism's ability to mediate between nations is that its literature is particularly likely to be *Weltliteratur* — but no Jewish literature is quoted apart from Mordecai's poetry, which leads Jacob to 'stop[s] his ears with his palms' and does nothing to enlist Daniel or anyone else to his cause (DD: 551). Daniel takes the example of contemporary Italian unification as a source of hope for Zionism — a connection emphasized by Daniel's birth in Piedmont, and the fact that his and Kalonymos's faces 'may as easily be Italian as Hebrew'; Eliot may have known that Jews such as L'Olper featured prominently in the Risorgimento (DD: 310). However, the novel takes relatively little interest in other European nationalisms; its strongest division is between Jews and Gentiles, and scepticism of intra-Gentile ethnic distinction is expressed at several points. Amongst the debaters in the Hand and Banner 'pure English blood (if leech or lancet can furnish us with the precise product) did not declare itself predominantly', and the fact that Alcharisi's Князь Халм-Эберштейн [Prince Halm-Eberstein] is of an immigrant German family, is calculated (DD: 446). The ignorant, snobbish, and passive anti-Semitism of Lady Mallinger or Mrs Meyrick differs in degree more than kind from the laughter which Cohen's anti-Semitic parody raises in such Habsburg cities as Vienna, Pesth, and Prague (DD: 185). Russia is hardly described by Alcharisi, but the reader can deduce that it more resembles England than either resemble Jewish ghettos anywhere, or the Israel which Daniel hopes to create. Mordecai hopes that Israel will enter 'a new brotherhood with the nations of the Gentiles', but these 'nations' are given little reality by the novel (DD: 459).

The Jewish role of mediation might be particularly well performed by 'emancipated, liberalized, nationalized, secularized' Jews resembling 'those *esprits forts* of Feuerbach who formed the avant-garde of Christian spirituality' (Shaffer 1975: 244). Yet when liberal and conservative Judaism come into confrontation or competition in the novel, it is the former which is favoured. In the Philosopher's Club the arguments of the assimilationist Gideon are subordinated to those of Mordecai. In Frankfurt Daniel might have visited one of the most important spiritual centres of Reform Judaism in Europe, but he seeks 'not the fine new building of the Reformed but the old Rabbinical school of the orthodox', where he encounters the upholder of his family's honour (DD: 309). At the same time in Russia, Jews of the Maskilic, secularizing intelligentsia were rebelling, as Alcharisi did, against Orthodox Jewish separatism, superstition, conservatism, and sexism, and were sufficiently prominent in revolutionary movements that *нигилизм* [nihilism] was referred to as a Jewish disease — but neither she nor the novel mentions them (Irwin 1996: 84–85; Haberer 1995: 187, 110). Of course, the novel's important secular Jew is Klesmer, who preaches Mordecai's message of spiritual striving in a form which is applicable to Gentiles. Whereas the Christianity of the Reverend Tryan, Dinah, Savonarola, Pastor Lyon, and the Reverend Farebrother can be read alternatively as Christianity, or through the lens of Feuerbach, religion in *Daniel Deronda* has a split presentation — as Cabbalist Zionism, and as art. The novel has a stronger meta-aesthetic dimension than any other of Eliot's works, and at the end of the novel art stands in place of scripture when *Samson Agonistes* is quoted rather than the *Shemah*, 'which for long generations has been on the lips of the dying Israelite':

> Nothing is here for tears, nothing to wail
> Or knock the breast; no weakness, no contempt,
> Dispraise or blame; nothing but well and fair,
> And what may quiet us in a death so noble. (DD: 695)

This substitution for words from the Jewish scripture, by Christian art based upon it, is indicative of the way in which the novel mediates its Judaism to Gentiles. Nonetheless, the contradiction between Mordecai, whose religion is served by art, and Klesmer, whose religion is art, remains unresolved. Klesmer, like Levin, disapproves of Panslavism and 'looks forward to a fusion of races', whereas Mordecai advocates Jewish 'separateness unique in its intensity'; these visions are allowed to stand side by side and appeal to different readers (DD: 413; Eliot 1994: 149).[3] Shaffer considers that:

> the very closeness of poetic and religious techniques as shown by the higher criticism did not merely put religion on a new apologistical basis, but had a corrosive effect on art itself. Poetry was not a separate realm where these ideas could take refuge. (Shaffer 1975: 291)

Yet this is not quite the implication of *Daniel Deronda* precisely because Mordecai holds a conception of religion which is distinct from Klesmer's and from art, and to which the art of the novel provides respectful, if partial, support. One consequence is that both the Judaism and the art of the novel are — and are perhaps intended to be — imperfectly mediatory.

More mediatory than Klesmer is Heine, who supplies three of the novel's epigraphs, was a (converted) Jew who met Goethe, and whom Eliot considered 'as much a German as a pheasant is an English bird' (Ashton 1992: 199). Through him Judaism is connected to a nation which serves a quietly mediatory function in the novel, through its location, education, art, and hospitality. Germany is the country to which Mordecai and Daniel turn to expand their education, in which Mirah and Alcharisi have toured, which keeps Daniel's chest secure, brings people from East and West Europe together for spa cures, introduces the novel's two central characters to one another, and produced Goethe, whose literature and ideas on literature provided much inspiration for the novel. Germany prevents the novel's whole Gentile domain from appearing provincial in relation to its Jewish domain (as, in *Middlemarch*, the whole of England appears provincial in relation to Germany). At the time of the novel's action it was also the focus of nationalist aspirations, and serves many of the functions which Mordecai promises of Israel. Goethe himself used an Exodus analogy in his 1797 epic of Germany,

Hermann und Dorothea, to suggest the possibility of a mediatory, modern German cultural consciousness (whilst denying the same to the modern Jews in 'Israel in der Wüste', which appeared as a companion piece to the *West-ostlicher Diwan*) (Berghahn 2001: 4–6). Similarly Thomas Mann, in his 1923 essay on Goethe and Tolstoi, described Germany as 'an seelische Mischungen reich, zwischen Ost und West', 'das Vorbild der Völker' (rich in spiritual mixing between East and West; the model of peoples) (Mann 1923: 48). In this context, there is comparable irony in the subsequent racial arrogance and aggression of both states. *Daniel Deronda* is not responsible for these ironies; it strains to constitute an example of *Weltliteratur*, and in doing so reveals some of the difficulties of that project. It supports cultural breadth acquired in relation to a defined cultural base, and ethnic purity for such Jews as choose it, whilst questioning the possibility of English or Russian ethnic purity. It mediates Judaism to Gentiles through limited explanations, and through translation into the language of the English Bible and (relatedly) the realm of art. It has obvious appeal for comparative critics. Not only is it specifically concerned with cultural difference, but it constitutes a peculiarly complicated example of comparative literature.

Contrastive Literature

The novel's self-consciousness about mediation is related to, and an extension of, its self-consciousness about comparison and contrast. Of the latter a crude but not irrelevant quantitative indication may be found in its language: the word *comparison* appears in the novel seventeen times, *comparative* or *comparatively* fourteen times, and *contrast* sixteen times. Since such numbers acquire significance only through comparison, they will be compared to the equivalent figures for *Middlemarch* (taken as an example of another work by Eliot), and for seven other Victorian novels which, like *Daniel Deronda*, have clear morphological or conceptual binary structures: Brontë's *Wuthering Heights*, Dickens's *Nicholas Nickleby* and *A Tale of Two Cities*, Thackeray's *Vanity Fair*, Disraeli's *Sybil: or, the Two Nations*, Gaskell's *North and South*, and Wilde's *The Picture of Dorian Gray*. Allowing for the differences in their lengths, and taking all four terms related to comparison together, the closest to *Daniel Deronda* is *Middlemarch*, which reaches 83 per cent of *Daniel Deronda*'s frequency; next is *Sybil* on 56 per cent, *North and South* on 43 per cent, *A Tale of Two Cities* on 32 per cent, *Nicholas Nickleby* on 30 per cent, *Wuthering Heights* on 22 per cent, *The Picture of Dorian Gray* on 16 per cent, and *Vanity Fair* on 11 per cent.[4] All of these novels contain striking *comparisons*, in at least one of the senses outlined in the previous chapter, but none except *Middlemarch* is anywhere near as linguistically conscious of them. The small sample taken here suggests that Eliot is particularly conscious of comparison, and especially so in her last novel.

At one level, to say that *Daniel Deronda* is a novel of contrasts would be as trivial as it is true; most literature is characterized by contrasts. In *What is Art?* Tolstoi condemned 'поразительность' [striking effects] as one of four 'приёмы' [devices] which characterize the 'поддельное искусство' [counterfeit art] which he considered to make up most of European written literature:

Эффэкты эти во всех искусствах состоят преимущественно в контрастах: в сопоставлении ужасного и нежного, прекрасного и безобразного, громкого и тихого, тёмного и светлого, самого обыкновенного и самого необычайного.

[In all arts these effects consist predominantly of contrasts; in the juxtaposition of the terrible and the tender, the beautiful and the hideous, the loud and the quiet, the dark and the light, the most ordinary and the most extraordinary.] (WIA: 134)

Gwendolen makes a striking contrast to all of the females with whom she appears ('No youthful figure there was comparable to Gwendolen's'), but that is generally what heroines are called upon to do — and that she contrasts particularly sharply with the novel's other heroine is characteristic of most literary love triangles (DD: 34). Nonetheless, in comparison to most realist novels, *Daniel Deronda* makes unusual duplications and divisions: there are three broods of girls, two former-professional Jewish opera singers who have rebelled against oppressive fathers, and two sets of characters — Gentile and Jewish — most of whom never meet each other, and are only dimly if at all aware of each others' existence.

The novel is also distinctive in the narrator's relish of and interest in contrasts. At the New Year's ball at the Abbey Lady Pentreath chooses Daniel to dance with because 'Nobody is old enough to make a good pair with me. I must have a contrast'. The narrator approves her sensibility: 'Her partner's young richness of tint against the flattened hues and rougher forms of her aged head had an effect something like that of a fine flower against a lichenous branch. Perhaps the tenants hardly appreciated this pair' (DD: 379). Suspecting the tenants of lacking Lady Pentreath's sensibility, the narrator determines that the readers should share it. Moreover, the narrator's interest extends to pointing out the contrast between a contrast and its opposite; Book VIII opens by exemplifying the relativity of 'extension' with the observation that in a few months someone who leaves home may achieve great things, and return to find his neighbours much as before. This is likened to the contrast between the difference of 'the brilliant, self-confident Gwendolen Harleth of the Archery Meeting' to 'the crushed penitent' — and the relative lack of change in her family at Pennicote over the same period. Klesmer's infelicitous contrast with everyone else at the Archery meeting (at which the reader is invited to be amused: first at Klesmer, then at the English) is contrasted with the 'candle-light occasions when he appeared simply as a musician' (DD: 86). The former contrast is explained as the difference between a figure intrinsically 'well-modelled' and 'extreme', and a people which 'objects to marked ins and outs' and tends to 'nullity of face'. That is, it is the contrast of the defined and the undefined, the implication being that although 'artistic fellows' may appear as harmoniously together as well-dressed Englishmen ('Draped in a loose garment with a Florentine berretta on his head, he would have been fit to stand by the side of Leonardo de Vinci'), they would, unlike the English, appear mutually distinct (DD: 85–86). Given that definition of thought, culture, and facial profile are highly valued in the novel, it is not surprising that the members of the Philosophers' Club all have 'sharply-characterized figures' (DD: 446).

Two particularly well-defined faces contrast with each other in Cohen's bookshop; here too there is a contrast between conformity and contrast, but the conformity is internal — on the one side Daniel, financially and metaphorically 'rich in youthful health', and on the other side Mordecai, whose youth is contradicted by his premature agedness, whose intensity is contradicted by his weakness, and on whom the characteristically contradictory 'stamp of consumption' appears in a 'brilliancy of glance to which the sharply-defined structure of features reminding one of a forsaken temple, give already a far-off look' (DD: 424–45). Mordecai wishes to speak with Daniel precisely because he senses both their spiritual likeness and their outward unlikeness; he had searched for his successor 'chiefly by a method of contrast', and the sympathy between them is expressed by their common desire to reveal their contrast most forcefully:

> In ten minutes the two men, with as intense a consciousness as if they had been two undeclared lovers, felt themselves alone in the small gas-lit book-shop and turned face to face, each baring his head from an instinctive feeling that they wished to see each other fully. (DD: 405, 424)

The narrator comments: 'I wish I could perpetuate those two faces, as Titian's "Tribute Money" has perpetuated two types presenting another sort of contrast' (DD: 424). The painting's contrast is indeed of 'another sort', representing as it does the sacred and the profane in Christ and Peter (although Christ is acting as teacher to Peter, and advocating accommodation between secular and sacred tribute) (Matthew 22. 17–22). As such it more resembles the contrast between Mordecai and Cohen ('there could hardly have been a stronger contrast to the Jew at the other end of the table') or Daniel and Grandcourt (who 'might have been a subject for those old painters who liked contrasts of temperament') (DD: 339, 137). The narrator is aligned with Mordecai in responding to contrasts aesthetically; Rubens's painting stood in the National Gallery in which Mordecai searched for representations of his own contrast (DD: 405). Eliot is clearly conscious of being just such a literary painter. However, she knew that her own art form was diachronic, and that its contrasts could also be felt by the replacement of one thing by another ('The tableau of Hermione was doubly striking from its dissimilarity with what had gone before') (DD: 49). Later in this chapter Eliot's own use of transitions will be discussed.

Certain contrasts work in favour of one party, whereas others (like that of Mordecai and Daniel) are impartial and intrinsically valuable. Hans comments with characteristic self-parodic seriousness that he is destined to marry Mirah because

> 'I go to science and philosophy for my romance. Nature designed Mirah to fall in love with me. The amalgamation of races demands it — the mitigation of human ugliness demands it — the affinity of contrasts assures it. I am the utmost contrast to Mirah — a bleached Christian, who can't sing two notes in tune. Who has a chance against me?' (DD: 396)

He spoofs, and wistfully places hope in, contemporary Darwinian ideas of health through the amalgamation of diversity; his contrast to Mirah, however, is not harmonious but disjunctive. Successful marriages in Eliot are always based on greater similarity than difference (and one of the most painful marriages in her fiction juxtaposes 'she all lily-white and golden, and he with his dark glowing beauty above the purple red-bordered tunic') (*Romola*: 202). Gillian Beer describes *Daniel Deronda* as a 'dark and glittering work' — a description which fits well with the juxtaposition of misery with glittering wealth for both Gwendolen and Alcharisi (Beer 1986: 228).

The narrator is also highly conscious of the importance of comparison, and thrice recommends it to the reader: twice to avoid mistaking circumstances for causes, and once to avoid double standards (DD: 32–33, 35, 309–10). The latter argument, which concerns Jews, is reiterated by Theophrastus Such: 'There is more likeness than contrast between the way we English got our island and the way the Israelites got Canaan' (Eliot 1994: 150). One opposite of such voluntary, ethical comparison which selects its objects, is the involuntary, unconscious comparison of objects as contingently arranged and found. Comparisons of the latter kind work in Grandcourt's favour, and therefore stress the need for the former kind. Grandcourt impresses Gwendolen at their first meeting partly because she sees him 'by the light of a prepared contrast' to what she had expected (he is 'not ridiculous'); he 'had the advantage of being in complete contrast with Rex'; and his horses appear to her 'in delightful contrast with the ugliness of poverty and humiliation at which she had lately been looking close' (DD: 92, 110, 258). During the marriage which for Grandcourt follows their sexless courtship 'by the finest contrast', Gwendolen manipulates comparisons to comfort herself. She

> often pursued the comparison between what might have been, if she had not married Grandcourt, and what actually was, trying to persuade herself that [. . .] if she had chosen differently she might now have been looking back with a regret as bitter as the feeling she was trying to argue away. (DD: 277, 367)

Both characters and readers are advised to exercise judicious comparison in order to avoid poor judgements. The novel itself, however, is a peculiarly difficult patient of comparison.

Double-headed Monster

This is so principally because of its double-plotting.[5] It was mentioned above that *Daniel Deronda* contains three broods of girls and two main groups of characters: the former may be precisely counted, but the latter are more impressionistically decided. The number of plots in a novel can also be difficult to determine. In one sense, a novel has as many plots as characters who appear on more than one occasion.[6] I define a *double-plotted* novel as one which contains two plots which are of roughly equal importance to each other, but no others which are of significantly greater importance. The comparison of two *comparanda* has as long a history in comparative literature as that of three. Bassnett refers to 'the old idea of comparative literature as a binary study, i.e., as the study of two authors or texts from two different systems' — for example Greece and Rome (1993: 9). Such double-plotted novels as *Daniel Deronda* and *Anna Karenina* may be contrasted on the one hand with such mono-plotted novels as *Хаджи-Мурат* [*Hadzhi Murat*], and on the other with such multi-plotted novels as *Middlemarch*. One feature of double-plotted novels is that its two stories tend to be clearly distinguishable as such, whereas it is debatable whether *Middlemarch* has three, or more, central stories. Leontiev in 1890 compared

War and Peace to 'an Indian idol: three heads or four faces and six arms!' (quoted in Knowles 1978: 378). Since only entities may be compared, it is difficult to compare stories of which the number is unclear.

In other respects, however, multiple (more than two) stories may be easier to compare. Five stories are better able than two to create the single world of time and space which forms a consistent basis for comparison, by severally guaranteeing what Elizabeth Deeds Ermarth terms 'a single vanishing point of perspective': 'Just as in realist pictures implied perspectives are infinite, so in historical narrative a number of possible and potentially infinite perspectives support the construction of a common medium' (1997: 71, 76). Alternatively, five different vanishing points may be less apprehensible as such, and therefore less disorientating to the reader, than two. Five stories which are not connected by a single theme or argument are nonetheless likely to be connected by multiple strands of meaning in what the narrator of *Middlemarch* would call a web. Two stories, by contrast, may be isolated; Henry James

> had a mortal horror of two stories, two pictures, in one. The reason of this was the clearest — my subject was immediately, under that disadvantage, so cheated of its indispensable centre as to become of no more use for expressing a main intention than a wheel without a hub is of use for moving a cart. (1962: 83–84)

Daniel Deronda addresses a modified version of the question posed by Henry James of *The Newcomes*, *Les Trois Mousquetaires*, and *War and Peace*: what do such double-headed monsters as *Daniel Deronda* actually mean? Are their heads affronted or addorsed? And if they converse, about what? Although a double-plotted novel contains no stories or characters significantly more important than the two which justify the term, the reader must ask herself whether she is invited to understand one from the perspective of the other, or each from the other's perspective, or both from the perspective of a third point — and if the last, whether this point corresponds to any particular feature of the text, or whether it emerges from the text as a whole. It is also possible that two *comparanda* fail to be understood in relation to each other, precisely because there is no third point in terms of which they can both be understood. Which of these possibilities is the case with *Daniel Deronda* is one of the objects of investigation.

The novel's sixth chapter opens with an epigraph taken from Bernard le Bouyer de Fontenelle's popularization of Copernican astronomy, *Entretiens sur la pluralité des mondes*.[7] Written in 1686, it takes the form of five evenings of conversation between the narrator-teacher and a Countess whilst strolling in the grounds of a château. The pupil responds to her teacher: 'Croyez-vous m'avoir humiliée pour m'avoir appris que la terre tourne autour du soleil? Je vous jure que je ne m'en estime pas moins' [Do you think you have humiliated me by informing me that the earth turns around the sun? I swear to you I think none the less of myself because of it] (DD: 42). This quotation appears soon after Klesmer's mortifying criticism of Gwendolen's mediocre musical talent. Fontenelle's work as a whole, however, has an obvious application to Gwendolen's relationship with Daniel. *Entretiens* describes five evenings of conversation between the Countess and the narrator as they walk in the moonlit grounds of a château. The narrator develops the conceit that the moon may be inhabited, but that communication between earthlings and moon people is not yet possible: 'quand meme les deux planets seraint fort proches, il ne serait pas possible de passer de l'air de l'une dans l'air de l'autre' [even if the two planets were right next to each other, it still would not be possible to pass from the air of the one to the air of the other] — these being as different as air and water (Fontenelle 1955: 98). He nonetheless imagines that, one day, such contact may be possible. In *Daniel Deronda* the Gentile characters other than the Meyricks never meet its Jewish characters other than Daniel and Mirah. Mordecai and Gwendolen spend a few minutes of the narrative's two years in adjoining rooms, but she shows no interest in his existence; nor does he ever necessarily learn of hers. Daniel's partial understanding of Gwendolen's situation exceeds hers of his to the extent that she is hardly aware that he possesses a story unconnected with her own. Daniel's intervention in her life neither makes her marriage more likely nor averts its termination. His own movements are marginally determined by each of these events, but his marriage and vocation are unaffected by them. Of the novel's seventy chapters, twenty-seven concern Daniel to the exclusion of Gwendolen.

However, any approach to the novel which takes the work as a *Gestalt* must compare these stories. This is a different kind of analysis from that pursued in the first part of this chapter, since it concerns the relations of aesthetic rather than thematic objects — but both kinds of relations have implications for each other. William Empson made a number of suggestions, principally with reference to Elizabethan drama, as to the types of meaning which parallel actions can generate. Ironies may be created between stories; one story may play out the dangers inherent in another; character traits found in one person may be split between characters in a process of 'decomposition' for the purposes of analysis; an audience's scepticism at a serious action may be pre-empted by its parody; the range of human life, or of a single situation experienced by different characters, may be suggested; or a single phenomenon may be universalized, as by *King Lear*'s subplot (Empson 1950: 36, 66, 28–30, 29, 5). The implication of the last may be that there is nothing new under the sun: as Taube writes about *Vanity Fair*, 'The contrasts [. . .] create a sense of the limited possibilities of human existence' (quoted in Garrett 1980: 114). The relations of stories' meanings have their own, second order, meaning: Peter Garrett described the meanings of Victorian 'multiplot' novels including *Daniel Deronda* as *dialogical* in Bakhtin's sense, since their form is 'neither single- nor multiple-focus but incorporates both, and it is the interaction and tension between these structural principles which produces some of their most important and distinctive effects' (Garrett 1980: 8). Empson and Garrett concentrate upon synchronic and metaphoric, rather than diachronic and metonymic, relations between stories. The analysis of this and the following two chapters concentrates mainly on the former, but will also consider the latter. Neither Empson nor Garrett makes much of the distinction between two and more than two stories. Empson is chiefly concerned with double-plotting; Garrett concentrates on the binary opposition of the monologic and dialogic, the latter produced by any multiplication of stories (he gives *Wuthering Heights* as a good example of a 'multiplot' novel, because 'its formal compression permits a more concise analysis') (1980: 18).

George Eliot herself insisted that *Daniel Deronda*'s stories were connected. In October 1876 she expressed impatience with 'readers who cut the book into scraps and talk of nothing in it but Gwendolen. I meant everything in the book to be related to everything else there' (EL VI: 290). 'Related' here has adjectival and verbal validity: Eliot 'meant' the two parts of her novel to have kinship, and 'meant' the reader to perceive it. Since the mid-1970s the majority of critics have stressed the coherence of *Daniel Deronda*, although not all have considered it to be immediately apparent; Adrian Poole uncovered 'Hidden Affinities' in *Daniel Deronda* (1983). However, Barbara Hardy rightly criticized the New Critical propensity for demanding — and finding — coherence in multi-plotted novels:

> We insist that the large loose baggy monster has unity, has symbolic concentration, has patterns of imagery and a thematic construction of character, and in the result the baggy monster is processed by our New Criticism into something strikingly like the original Jamesian streamlined beast. (1971: 7)

I concur with the majority of critics since the mid-1870s who have identified a deficiency of connection between the two stories; this is not to deny that many substantial connections are present, merely to claim that certain connections are also palpably absent. Some critics, whose proportion has also increased since the mid-1970s, have found intended or unintended significance in this fact (although the line between significant disconnection, and connection, is blurred).

Double-plotted novels of which the stories are disconnected may contain a struggle for power, as one or both of the stories fails in its attempts to contextualize the other — that is, to provide the ethical or ontological terms in which the other should be understood, or a context which qualifies its importance. Eagleton writes of *Middlemarch* that 'since every destiny is significant, each is consequently relativised'; however, one or both of *two* stories may more easily contest this relativization (1978: 114). How strongly a story contextualizes or resists contextualization depends on its relative importance in the novel, which itself may depend on several criteria in addition to that of textual space. If the interpretation of one story is considered to be aided by another more than the reverse is the case, or if one story is considered to be more dominated by Jacobson's poetic function, or to be more heteroglossic, or to effect more of a shift in the reader's *Erwartungshorizont*, or to offer the reader more of Iser's interpretative *leere Stellen*, or to carry more didactic import, or more accurately to represent the world through its balanced tensions, or through its typicality, or to be more atypical, or to involve a more widespread human problem, or a more painful, urgent, or admirable emotion, or to belong to a more sympathetically involving character — then, according to the reader's comparative faculties and critical biases, this story may be judged to hold the balance of power.

There is a close connection between comparison and contests for power: one archaic meaning of *compare* is *to compete or vie*, and *comparative* could mean *in competition or rivalry* (OED 1654). Harry Levin made this connection in his observation that, when faced by equally great books juxtaposed on a shelf, 'for the sentient observer, sparks are struck by their very collocation. They are marshaled to do battle, as Swift observed in a pamphlet which was nothing if not comparative' (Levin 1972: 73). Those who have emphasized the meaningful connections between *Daniel Deronda*'s stories tend to have found Daniel's story to contextualize Gwendolen's (for example Garrett, who finds that by the end of *Daniel Deronda*, *Our Mutual Friend*, and *The Newcomes*, 'the structural dialogue appears to be resolved') (1980: 221). Many of the critics who have emphasized a deficiency of connection have considered Gwendolen's story to resist, at least partly, contextualization by Daniel's. On the other hand, for certain Jewish and Gentile readers one story has held so much more interest than the other that no power struggle has been apparent. A wide range of criteria for assessing importance accords the two stories sufficiently equal importance to render any deficiencies of connection between them problematic. Dryden had a politicized distrust of such parity: when 'two Axions' are 'equally labour'd and driven on by the Writer' then there is

> no longer one play, but two: not but that there may be many actions in a Play [. . .] but they must be all subservient to the great one, which our language happily expresses in the name of under-plots [. . .] Co-ordination in a Play is as dangerous and unnatural as in a state. (Dryden 1964: 78–79)

The Austrian-Jewish scholar David Kaufmann commented in his 1877 essay in praise of *Daniel Deronda* that:

> Two lines which cut one another at a common point of intersection make a mathematical figure, it is true; but they cannot form the subject of a work of art, the unity of which must be preserved in accordance with fundamental axioms. For a writer of fiction to couple narratives which have no essential connection does not lower his work — it sentences it to death outright [. . .] it is solely because contemporary criticism has shut its eyes to the relation of the two stories which run through *Daniel Deronda* that its value as a work of art [. . .] has not yet received full and true expression. (Kaufmann 1877: 47–48)

However, *Daniel Deronda* takes more risks, in this respect, than Kaufmann identifies.

Stories exist diachronically as *фабулы* [*fabulae*] and *сюжеты* [*siuzhets*], but certain stories may also be conceived spatially, as occupying different worlds. The word *world* is used in *Daniel Deronda* in a variety of senses, including 'the earth and all created things upon it', 'a group or system of things or beings associated by common characteristics', and 'the sphere within which one's interests are bound up or one's activities find scope' (OED 888, 1673, 1586). The 'spheres' in which most of Gwendolen's and Daniel's 'activities find scope' are also intersubjective 'group(s) or system(s) of things or beings associated by common characteristics'. These spheres will be referred to as domains. Their common characteristics may be geographical, aesthetic, social, or connected to the domain's most important character. The numbers of a novel's dominant stories and domains do not necessarily coincide; the stories of Moll Flanders, Tom Jones, Latimer (in 'The Lifted Veil'), Nekhliudov (in *Воскрессение* [*Resurrection*]), and Mr Noon traverse several domains, whereas stories co-habit a domain in *Sense and Sensibility*, *Vanity Fair*, *Romola*, *Братья Карамазовы* [*The Brothers Karamazov*], Tolstoi's '*Фальшивый Купон*' ['The Forged Coupon'], and *Women in Love*. Two stories occupy two separate domains in *Daniel Deronda*, *Anna Karenina* (Saint Petersburg and the country), Arnold Bennett's *The Old Wives' Tale* (Bursley and Paris), Hermann Hesse's *Narziss und Goldmund* (the monastery and the world), Mikhail Bulgakov's *Мастер и Маргарита* [*The Master and Margarita*] (Moscow and ancient Palestine), and Patrick White's *Voss* (Sydney and the Bush). *Daniel Deronda*'s Gentile domain covers most of the novel's geographical territory, whereas the Jewish domain consists perforce of actual and metaphorical ghettos within it (in Holborn, Frankfurt, and Genoa). The fact that the novels contain a plurality of worlds has ethical implications for the relations of the heroine and hero, the divergence of their fates, and the interaction of the domains' genres.

Scapegoats

In melodramas, and Miss Prism's three-volume novel 'of more than usually revolting sentimentality', 'the good [end] happily and the bad unhappily' (Wilde 2006: 26). The juxtaposition of stories of justified failure and success permits the exhibition by the latter's protagonist of those virtues which the former's protagonist suffers for lacking, and makes both the downfall and success appear of greater magnitude by contrast. Tolstoi's tales 'Два старика' ['The Two Old Men'] and 'Хозяин и работник' ['Master and Man'] are of this kind. Alternatively, since two stories carry the risk of mutual independence, some didactic tales (such as the Parable of the Talents) contain three protagonists who experience varying levels of success. Eliot had denounced narrative eschatology in her 1855 defence of the 'Morality of *Wilhelm Meister*':

> Just as far from being really moral is the so-called moral denouement, in which rewards and punishments are distributed according to those notions of justice on which the novel-writer would have recommended that the world should be governed if he had been consulted at the creation. The emotion of satisfaction which a reader feels when the villain of the book dies of some hideous disease, or is crushed by a railway train, is no more essentially moral than the satisfaction which used to be felt in whipping culprits at the cart-tail. (Ashton 1992: 130)

Two decades later, *Daniel Deronda* both invites and frustrates interpretation in terms of a moral denouement. For example, the suffering which results from Gwendolen's egotism accords imperfectly with notions of justice which the novel itself suggests. Downfall or suffering which exceeds the demands of retributive justice is either not interpretable in ethical terms, or else indicates persecution of the victim. Since it is in the nature of fiction to attribute a representative quality to those whom it depicts, fictional victims of persecution may sometimes be interpreted as *scapegoats* in the broadest sense of that term — that is to say, those who are punished as representatives of a category. This use of the term of course contradicts several elements of the original, Mosaic Jewish, conception: that the scapegoat was *not* sacrificed on an altar, that violence against it was prohibited, and that it was recognized as innocent of the crimes for which it was expelled. Nonetheless, since the seventeenth century (in which Hobbes observed that Jesus Christ served the role both of sacrificial goat and scapegoat), the word *scapegoat* has been applied to actual victims of violence, and of persecution more broadly conceived.

René Girard analysed the phenomenon of scapegoating in and outside of fiction in his 1982 *Le Bouc émissaire* — a book which has proved of particular interest and use to literary critics. In it he made a helpful distinction between those who are presented as victims *in* a text, and those who are victims *of* the text itself:

> Nous avons donc deux types de texte qui ont un rapport avec le 'bouc émissaire'. Ils parlent tous des victimes mais les uns ne dissent pas que la victime est un bouc émissaire et ils nous obligent à le dire pour eux: Guillaume de Machaut, par exemple, et les textes mythologiques. Les autres nous dissent eux-mêmes que la victime est un bouc émissaire: les Evangiles.

> [We therefore have two types of text which have a relationship to the 'scapegoat'. They both talk about victims but one type doesn't tell us that the victim is a scapegoat and obliges us to say it for them: Guillaume de Machaut, for example, and mythological texts. The others tell us themselves that the victim is a scapegoat: the Evangelists.] (Girard 1982: 170)

Le Bouc émissaire contains scapegoats *within* its text, since it explicitly describes them as such. It also quotes texts which enforce 'le mécanisme du bouc émissaire' [scapegoat mechanism] against their victims — for example, the transcript of a seventeenth-century witch trial. These cases are clear-cut. In most cases, however, determining the existence, nature, and extent of a character's scapegoating relies on two judgements, both of which may be difficult to reach. First, it relies on determining the causes of a character's downfall or sufferings, which is as philosophically fraught a process in a fictional as in the non-fictional world. The critic assumes the role of an investigator determining the causes of injuries or death on the basis of evidence which may be ambiguous, and vulnerable to interpretation according to the critic's ethical perspective. For this reason accusations of scapegoating inside and outside of fiction have varied according to ethical fashion; Girard locates his 1982 study in a historical process of the progressive discovery of scapegoating. Secondly, if persecution is detected, the critic must assess to what extent this judgement is supported by the narrative's rhetoric. A scapegoat cannot be *of* the text if the narrative's evidence overwhelmingly denies, or supports, a punitive discourse, or if this state of conflict is significantly acknowledged by one of the narrative's discourses. Certain circumstances, however, are iridescent with regard to scapegoating, since when they are considered in different lights they either increase, or mitigate, a character's status as a scapegoat of the text.[8] A feature which undermines sympathy for a suffering character may validate, or undermine, the justice of her suffering. A feature may exemplify, or acknowledge, the narrative's ethical disjunctions. Lesser suffering on the part of equal or greater offenders may indicate scapegoating either in or of the text, depending on the attitude of the narrative towards the discrepancy. A character may therefore indeterminately be a scapegoat in and of a text. This is true of Falstaff at the end of *Henry IV Part II* and of Shylock in *The Merchant of Venice*; directors of the latter, in which the ambiguity is sustained, must perforce narrow the range of possible interpretation in their production. It is also possible (although Girard does not mention such a type) that a character be a scapegoat if the reader's opprobrium is unfairly directed at her or him, even if she or he does not suffer; indeed, the absence of suffering may make these characters objects of particular opprobrium, whereas their conspicuous suffering might have aroused the reader's sympathy. Since all of the three novels under discussion in this book contain examples of characters who do suffer unjustly, however, my comparisons will focus on this type.

Fictional scapegoating intersects in complex ways with the genres of tragedy and comedy. Of course *tragedy* in particular has long been the subject of fierce critical contestation. In this book the adjective *tragic* will be applied to a character of some spiritual stature whose sufferings are imperfectly just; these characteristics accord with Vladimir Dal´'s 1882 definition of *трагедия* [tragedy] as a *'высокая трогательная и печальная драма'* [*a lofty, moving, and sorrowful drama*] (although *comedy* will not be used to imply a corresponding lack of stature) (Dal´ 1955 IV: 425). Not every scapegoat is a tragic figure, nor is every tragic hero a victim of persecution. However, the denial of a character's tragic status by other characters may itself form part of that character's scapegoating in the text; by the same token, the denial of tragic status by a text may contribute towards that character's scapegoating by the text. That is, as with scapegoating, a text may contain discourses which deny its own evidence that a character possesses tragic status. Alternatively, there may be a contradiction between the two: Girard considers the scapegoat status of 'Œdipe' to be occluded by the ostensible nature of his tragedy (Girard 1982: 39). The common enemy of both tragedy and persecution is justice.

The scapegoat (William Tyndale's mistranslation via the Septuagint and Vulgate of the Hebrew לעזאזל [*Azazel*]) is a Jewish concept. In Leviticus 16.21–34 God orders that a goat representatively bearing the sins of the people be driven into the wilderness on the Day of Atonement, and this was a Jewish practice from the time of the Exodus to that of the temples in Jerusalem. The term *scapegoat* was not used in English to refer to any victim of representative persecution until the nineteenth century, and then it was not particularly applied to Jews, although they had repeatedly served as such in Christendom. Girard made the connection; the first chapter of *Le Bouc émissaire* is titled 'Guillaume de Machaut et les Juifs', and concerns Guillaume de Machaut's reference, at the beginning of his *Jugement du Roy de Navarre*, to a massacre of Jews in Northern France in response to what Girard considers to have been an outbreak of the plague (1982: 1–11). The Jews were accused of poisoning the Christians, but it is clear to Girard that they were being scapegoated. Eliot knew about the Jewish ritual of scapegoating; in her *Daniel Deronda* notebook she notes the 'Story of a Scape-Camel, à propos of scape-goat' and refers to Milman's note on the story of a camel which was killed outside a town, having been blamed for many iniquities — 'After which the men retired, fully satisfied as to the wrong they had received from the camel' (Irwin 1996: 245). In 'Silly Novels by Lady Novelists' Eliot satirizes 'the Evangelical lady novelist, [who] while she explains to you the type of the scapegoat on one page, is ambitious on another to represent the manners and conversations of aristocratic people' (Ashton 1992: 314). *Daniel Deronda* gives no explanation of scapegoating, but it does include several *types* of scapegoat, and represents the manners and conversations of aristocratic people. Mordecai and Mirah are intensely conscious of the history of Jewish persecution referred to in the quotation from Zunz's *Die Synagogale Poesie des Mittelalters* which opens Chapter 42; and when Mirah is contemplating whether to commit suicide, one factor in favour is her recollection of the mass suicides of oppressed Jews.

However, the Jews in *Daniel Deronda* are not in any way scapegoated *by* their text; nor are they scapegoated *in* their text, other than by virtue of being the objects of mild anti-Semitic prejudice on the part of such Gentiles as Lady Mallinger. Mordecai dies because his father absconded with his sister, he caught a cold on his resultant return home, and then went into physical decline. He is treated with sympathetic respect by the members of the Philosophers' Club, and dies a death in which there is

> nothing to wail
> Or knock the breast; no weakness, no contempt,
> Dispraise, or blame (DD: 695).

Nor, one might add, tragedy. Admittedly, the Jewish people itself is presented as tragic. Zunz describes Jewish history as a 'National Tragedy lasting for fifteen hundred years, in which the poets and the actors were also the heroes'; Eliot inserts the word 'National', which does not appear before the German 'Tragödie', and this epigraph is emphasized by being followed by Daniel's reading of the same quotation (DD: 441). Mordecai counts his sufferings as part of this tragedy. However, his Zionism is projected to redeem it sooner or later as a comedy. Modern Italy's example to Zionism is unconsciously adduced by Mirah in her rendition of Leopardi's 'Ode to Italy', which begins with recitative, followed by 'a mournful melody, a rhythmic plaint. After this came a climax of devout triumph' (DD: 414). This resembles tragicomedy as defined by Guarini in his *Compendio della Poesia Tragicomica* (1602) in which the tragedy is arrested by means of 'a credible miracle' in the fifth act (as in *The Winter's Tale*, in which Gwendolen acts) (Hirst 1984: 20). The Jewish National tragicomedy also has a synchronic aspect, however; Mordecai comments that:

> our lot is the lot of Israel. The grief and the glory are mingled as the smoke and the flame. It is because we children have inherited the good that we feel the evil. These things are wedded for us, as our father was wedded to our mother. (DD: 636)

The tragedy which is ultimately to be redeemed is 'social tragedy' ('a civilisation destroyed or destroying itself', in Raymond Williams's definition) rather than 'personal tragedy' ('men and women suffering and destroyed in their closest relationships'), but it is reduplicated at the level of 'closest relationships': Mirah is saved physically, and Mordecai spiritually, by the tragicomic miracles of their meetings with Daniel (R. Williams 1966: 121).

Although Mordecai considers the Jewish tragedy to be ongoing, for Gideon there is in contemporary society very little tragedy in their situation: he points out, with comedic equanimity, that 'Many of our people are on a footing with the best, and there's been a good filtering of our blood into high families' (DD: 451). The Cohen family is similarly insusceptible to the concept or experience of tragedy. One reason why the Jews of the novel are not presented as the victims of active Gentile persecution is quite simply that over the three decades before the novel is set (and the further decade until it was written, the events of which may have affected Eliot's decisions in representing the mid-1860s), legal anti-Jewish discrimination in all of the countries concerned by the novel had been largely or entirely abolished. In England this abolition occurred in the stages of successive Acts of Parliament in 1833, 1837, 1845, and 1858; when Alcharisi speaks to her son, a converted Jew had just become Chancellor of the Exchequer, and when Eliot was writing the novel, the same man was Prime Minister (and inadvertently stoking anti-Jewish hostility in Russia by his pro-Ottoman foreign policy). In Frankfurt Daniel visits Germany's largest, and one of its oldest, Jewish ghettoes. Yet since 1796 Jews had been free to live where they chose in the city, and in the year before Daniel's visit they had been granted civic equality. Eliot and Lewes visited the *Juden-gasse* in 1873 as part of their research for the novel, but in the following year half of it was demolished as part of the city's redevelopment (the remainder was demolished a decade later). In Daniel's birthplace, Piedmont, Jews were emancipated by stages in 1848 and 1859, and by the time the novel was written Italian Unification had brought equality for Jews across the Kingdom of Italy. Alcharisi moved to Russia under Nikolai I, who on coming to power in 1825 had introduced harsh measures to persuade Jews to convert to Christianity. However, by the time of her arrival he had switched to a policy of assimilation through accommodation: Jewish schools based on Хаскала [*Haskalah*] (Jewish Enlightenment) principles, and state rabbinical seminaries, were permitted within the Pale. By the time that Alcharisi visited Daniel in the mid-1860s, Aleksandr II had abolished juvenile conscription for Jews, and made Jews graduating from tertiary education eligible for state, professional, and commercial employment across the Empire (Haberer 1995: 10–13).

The only factor which may have made Eliot, at the time of writing *Daniel Deronda*, fear for European Jews would have been reports from Russia about growing anti-Semitism (the word is only just anachronistic, being a German coinage of 1879 adopted by English two years later). Lewes's acquaintance Laurence Oliphant travelled in the Pale to verify reports of the pogroms which started in 1880 and intensified following the assassination of Aleksandr II in the following year; Jews in England were prominent in organizing relief (Polowetzky 1995: 138). Eliot knew Anton Rubinstein, and may have heard from him that his music was criticized for being insufficiently Russian by the *Могучая Кучка* [*Mighty Handful*] of five romantic nationalist composers (Balakirev, Kyi, Musorgskii, Rimskii-Korsakov, and Borodin) — an accusation almost certainly coloured by anti-Semitism. Eliot wrote in her notebook that in Russia and Poland the Jews 'are still dreadfully oppressed. Their worst endurance is the conscription — twenty-five years of service without hope of advancement'. She considered many such Jews to be culturally 'in deep darkness' (as mentioned before, she showed little interest in the Russian Jewish intelligentsia) (Irwin 1996: 84–85). She also noted in her notebook: 'Jews now everywhere emancipated except in Russia & Roumania' (Irwin 1996: 300). Shortly before she wrote the scene in which Alcharisi meets her son, she and Lewes had read to one another a collection of Ivan Turgenev's short stories including the 1846 'Жид' ('Le Juif' in Mérimée's translation) of which the eponymous Jew is venal, treacherous, preposterous, and physically disgusting.[9] However, the anti-Semitic stereotype of her Russian friend's protagonist is not much stronger than that of her English friend's (Dickens's) Fagin, and she died before the threat to Russia's

Jews was clearly apparent. Theophrastus Such, in 'The Modern Hep! Hep! Hep!', refers to the European treatment of Jews largely without specification. In *Daniel Deronda* she had no intention to present Jews living in 1860s London, Frankfurt, or Genoa — or a converted Jew married to a Russian Prince — as scapegoats of Gentile society. On the contrary, the novel attaches to Jews various kinds of *gentility* (identity as an ethnic *genus*, and gentleness and high breeding), whilst deflecting the mechanism of scapegoating onto Gentiles. This reversal of associations does much to connect the two parts of the novel, and is also involved in their disjunction. It may be investigated through a consideration of two equivocally Jewish characters.

Lapidoth falls from the relatively high estate of being young, handsome, talented, and with a beautiful, loving wife, to being a penniless widower, gambling addict, and thief. But he is presented as neither a scapegoat (since he is responsible for his own troubles), nor as tragic (since he remains physically and mentally sprightly, and finally escapes with a precious ring to gamble another picaresque day). Leonora Alcharisi in several respects resembles him. Both of them change their names, lie about the death of a relative, prioritize professional singing over duty to their dependents (Alcharisi would have wished precisely such a father for herself as Lapidoth), reject and ridicule Judaism, try to bring up their children in ignorance of the Jewish faith, pass the peak of their talent, and go into decline. However, their differences are significant. Whereas Alcharisi only makes Daniel's early life difficult (and it would perhaps have been more difficult, and more resembled Mirah's, had she not done what she did), Lapidoth brings misery if not death to the three members of his family. Despite this, Alcharisi suffers far more. Her country of residence is metonymically connected by several references in the novel to Siberia: Lush says 'I am not to be exiled to Siberia', and Sir Hugo (with reference to Halm-Eberstein) quotes Leroux as remarking that: 'A man might as well take down a fine peal of church bells and carry them off to the steppes' (DD: 270, 375). Alcharisi seems, as some convicts were, physically broken by the experience (Kalonymos 'took a journey into Russia to see me; he found me weak and shattered'), or even killed ('she looked like a dreamed visitant from some region of departed mortals') (DD: 547, 571). She is forty-five, but, like Eliot who was fifty-seven at the time that she created her, fears that she does not have long to live: she is sometimes 'in an agony of pain' (DD: 545). She is what Armgart terms 'A pensioner in marriage', and repeatedly fulfils the reproductive role of a wife (Eliot 2005: 150). In this respect her location is poignant, since the position of women in Russian aristocratic society was in several respects better than that of women in British bourgeois society. She is not scapegoated *in* the text: she has extremely handsome offers of marriage, including from Sir Hugo and then her Prince (it would have been scandalous for a Russian aristocrat to have married a Jewess). Rather, the fact that she suffers far more than Lapidoth, and for apparently smaller crimes, is a sign of her possible scapegoating *by* the text.

This hypothesis is favoured by a comparison of Alcharisi with her probable model. There are several reasons why Eliot may have chosen Russia as the location of Alcharisi's retirement: Alcharisi may have wished to live as far away as possible from those who knew of her first marriage, and may have been attracted by the possibility of access to the world's richest court.[10] To Eliot Russia connoted both barbarism and decadent luxury — but also Slav cultural strength, from which the retired Alcharisi is painfully excluded. A further possible reason for Eliot making Alcharisi marry a Russian is that the only Russian whom Eliot knew well, Turgenev, was devoted to the French-Italian mezzo-soprano Pauline Viardot (née García) (Pope 1994: 143). Viardot, like Alcharisi, was born in 1821, and acquired European-wide fame as an opera singer. Both singers were trained by an older female relative: in Alcharisi's case, by her Aunt; in Viardot's, by her mother (soprano Joaquína Sitchez) and elder sister (Maria Malibran). Both were married young, at someone else's persuasion (Alcharisi's father's and George Sand's), to men who loved them dearly and supported them in their careers. Like Alcharisi, and despite her marriage, Viardot had many admirers. Turgenev left Russia for her and spent most of his life after the age of twenty-five following the Viardots around Europe, supporting them financially, and eventually moving in with them and their children; he died in their house (Pope 1994: 165). As Alcharisi says: 'Men followed me from one country to another' (DD: 537). According to Viardot's biographer Fitzlyon, Viardot 'always put her work first, and all personal considerations second', whereas for Turgenev his love for Viardot predominated (1964: 207). It was because of the Viardots' enforced residency in London during the Franco-Prussian War that Eliot became acquainted with both them and Turgenev. Pope considers that 'Eliot and Viardot were friends, moving in many of the same artistic and intellectual circles. Indeed, Viardot occupied in the world of music a place parallel to Eliot's in the realm of letters' (1994: 143).[11] Of the singers Viardot, Alcharisi, and Armgart, the real one had by far the happiest life — a fact which lends support to the thesis that Eliot denied her heroines her own level of success and happiness, even when (as in the cases of Armgart and Alcharisi) they are exceptionally gifted and have a real-life model of success. Viardot combined her career with a supportive marriage and the rearing of four children, all of whom became musicians. Unlike Armgart and Alcharisi, Viardot did not have a scare about her voice. She continued operatic singing until 1863, and then — like Armgart but unlike Alcharisi — settled down to concert singing and teaching (Grove and Blom 1954: 762). Alcharisi has one man who supports her career for just a few years, whereas Eliot had one such man for most of her adult life, and Viardot had two such men for most of her adult life.

If Alcharisi's sufferings are taken as punishments imposed by the text upon her, there are several possible motives for them. She flatly rejects the religion of which the novel does much to approve, and puts herself beyond the pale of the Jewish national tragicomedy. There is a poignancy, of which Eliot would have been aware, with which Kalonymos may have berated her, and which Alcharisi herself may have embraced, in her decision to convert to the Christianity of the most assertively Christian great power of the world. She evinces no interest in the condition of its Jews. Kaufmann commented appositely: 'Her life as we see it is a broken existence — a picture of apostasy punished' (1877: 80). In addition, she moves to Russia in a year (probably 1851) in which Russia broke off relations with her mother's (and Eliot's) native country in the build-up to the Crimean War. Two years later Eliot, who was suffering from a cough, had hoped that 'the cough will soon take its flight from me and wing its way across the Baltic to the Emperor Nicolas' (EL II: 143). She furnishes a sharp contrast to the conspicuously chaste Mirah. Her sexual activity between her marriages is not recorded, but she may well have had lovers, as her more famous model, Rachel Félix, certainly did; the latter was also born, a Jewess, in 1821, toured Russia in the 1840s as a tragic actress, had her health broken by living in Russia, and, according to Lewes, could not act feminine tenderness (Stokes 1984: 774–75). Alcharisi comments: 'I was never willingly subject to any man. Men have been subject to me' (DD: 571). Viardot was widely accused of keeping Turgenev an emotional captive, and was significantly described by some as 'a crafty Jewess, who was bleeding him to death' (Fitzlyon and Viardot-Garcia 1964: 419).[12] Finally, she is a gifted actress in a novel which, through the character of Mirah in particular, expresses distrust of acting.

Nonetheless, many of Alcharisi's criticisms of Orthodox Judaism for misogyny and superstition are posed forcefully and remain unanswered. Shortly before writing *Daniel Deronda*, Eliot was rereading Greek tragedy; Alcharisi is not only a tragic actress, but is presented as belonging to a tragic sphere: 'It seemed as if he were in the presence of a mysterious Fate' (DD: 536). She hubristically aspires beyond the conditions of her society via mastery in marriage and a career. She shuns her son, then falls from the high estate of being 'the greatest lyric actress of Europe'; 'some vengeance' sends Kalonymos to cause the *anagnorisis* which leads her to reveal herself to Daniel: 'My father's threats eat into me with my pain' (DD: 548; 545; 547). Belonging to neither Jewish nor Gentile society, she suffers alone. She asserts:

> If my acts were wrong — if it is God who is exacting from me that I should deliver up what I withheld — who is punishing me because I deceived my father and did not warn him that I should contradict his trust — well, I have told everything. I have done what I could. (DD: 567–68)

This both demonstrates her tragic nobility, and acknowledges the possibility of divine, and by extension, authorly, punishment. By her criticisms of Judaism, her integrity, and her capacity to suffer, the reader is inclined partially in her favour, and her scapegoating by the text itself is mitigated.

Gwendolen too bears marks of Greek tragedy; she too has a regal aspect and hubristically aspires to mastery in marriage; her reduction from middling estate by the turn of the international roulette wheel which bankrupts Grapnell & Co. provokes her *hamartia*. On the night of accepting Grandcourt, she experiences a semi-conscious premonition of *anagnorisis* in 'the first onslaught of dread after her irrevocable decision', informed by her horrified memory of Lydia Glasher (DD: 262). On her wedding night, her *peripeteia* begins with the arrival of a letter from Mrs Glasher, which is likened to the 'Furies' (DD: 303). Thereafter her *anagnorisis* develops slowly into ethical consciousness. She bears her situation with an affected 'proud cold quietude' (DD: 348). Her catastrophe confirms omens, such as the sudden revelation of a picture of a drowned face, and Gwendolen's comment to her mother that 'all the great poetic criminals' were 'women!' (DD: 44). Following Greek convention, the death of the protagonist, Grandcourt, is kept off the narrative stage — first to be seen by anonymous witnesses at the Genoese quayside, and later to be described by Gwendolen. Like Alcharisi, she has an unhappy marriage of bejewelled idleness, entered to avoid a perceived worse fate. These marks, however, do not in themselves mean that the text endorses her as tragic; until their operations in the texts are understood, 'We recognise the alphabet; we are not sure of the language' (DD: 91).

Sousa Correa comments that:

> Like the Princess, Gwendolen has an affinity with the tragic women she once played at being. In Gwendolen's story, the satirical musical references at the beginning of the novel are simultaneously prophetic of later tragedy. At the time of her greatest theatrical aspirations, Gwendolen provides a superficial, yet prophetic, defence for her high voice as more becoming to a tragic heroine [. . .] Whatever the derogatory associations with Jenny Lind, Bellini, and immoral operatic heroines committing desperate acts, hers promises to become the authentic voice of tragedy and despair. (2002: 165–66)

In part, however, Gwendolen suffers by comparison with Alcharisi. She has less nobility, intelligence, integrity, and talent; Gwendolen's ideas of becoming a discoverer of 'the North-West Passage or the source of the Nile' — or, indeed, a singer and actress, are girlish parodies of Alcharisi's achievable ambition, at a younger age, to become 'the greatest lyric actress of Europe' (DD: 113). One consequence of the comparison is that Gwendolen's is not *the* 'authentic voice of tragedy and despair' in the novel. However, the circumstances of the two women's presentations are imperfectly comparable. In the two scenes in which Alcharisi appears, the times, the place (her Genoa apartment), the lighting (light, then dark), her costume (black, then 'dusky orange') are chosen by herself, and she dominates the dialogue. Her audience is receptive to her tragedy (Daniel feels that he 'had gone through a tragic experience which must forever solemnize his life'), and the scene's secondary audience is induced to feel similarly (DD: 571). On the other hand, this secondary audience is also told that 'experience immediately passed into drama, and she acted her own emotions' — that is, is made conscious that Alcharisi acts, furnish it with no chorus, in a theatre of her own devising — whereas Gwendolen acts in scenes which are emphatically not of her devising, and which give her tragedy no resonance, furnish it with no chorus. Her domain cannot conceive of the potential tragedy of her situation because it is comic in the banal sense denounced by Mirah when she describes hearing Christians' irreverent laughter:

> the world seemed like a hell to me. Is this world and all the life upon it only like a farce or a vaudeville, where you find no great meanings? Why then are there tragedies and grand operas, where men do difficult things? (DD: 184)[13]

The terms *comedy* and *comic* are used throughout *Daniel Deronda* synonymously with Mirah's 'farce or a vaudeville', even by those characters whom the novel considers trivial — as in Mrs Arrowpoint's reaction to Catherine's announcement of her engagement to Klesmer, 'It is a comedy you have got up, Catherine. Else you are mad' (DD: 209). Those members of Gwendolen's domain who criticize their society for its lack of seriousness are trivial by the standards of Mordecai or Daniel: Mrs Vulcany, preferring a supernatural to a materialist explanation for the opening of the panel door in the theatricals, professes to find Gascoigne 'a little too worldly for her taste' (DD: 50). This banal comedy is directly implicated in Gwendolen's sufferings, for example through Gascoigne's refusal to take seriously the rumours he hears concerning Grandcourt's illegitimate family.

Gwendolen, then, is denied tragic status by a society which itself is represented as trivial and culpable. However, the novel also undermines her tragic status in a manner which sometimes sits uneasily with its criticism of that society. Eliot wrote to Blackwood in November 1875 that: 'It will perhaps be a little comfort to you to know that poor Gwen is spiritually saved, but "so as by fire"' (EL VI: 188). Paul tells the Corinthians:

> if any man build upon this foundation [of Christ] gold, silver, precious stones, wood, hay, stubble; Every man's work shall be made manifest: for the day shall declare it, because it shall be revealed by fire; and the fire shall try every man's work of what sort it is. If any man's work abide which he hath built thereupon, he shall receive a reward. If any man's work shall be burned, he shall suffer loss: but he himself shall be saved; yet *so as by fire*. (I Corinthians 3. 11–15)

By the end of the novel Gwendolen resembles *Romola*'s burnt Savonarola almost as much as she resembles the 'spiritually saved' Romola. Heyns notes that Eliot's Puritanism is directed particularly at female charm and vanity, and that 'Whereas Bess [in *Adam Bede*] is brought to her terrified repentance through Dinah's exemplum, Eliot's other women are subjugated by the novelist's own plot' (Heyns 1994: 30–34, 151). Paul's theology makes no accommodation for tragedy. One implication of the Pauline passage is that Grandcourt serves as Gwendolen's 'fire', in effect punishing her for accepting him, and acting in concert with Daniel to effect her partial ethical redemption. The personal stature on which her potential tragic status relies is limited. Certainly, she exceeds the standards of her society in her consciousness of guilt, but since this society is banally comic, her superiority reaches merely a realistic rather than a high mimetic standard (in Frye's senses of these terms) (Frye 2006: 142). She does not have, as Dorothea Brooke has, 'the impressiveness of a fine quotation from the Bible, — or from one of our elder poets, — in a paragraph of to-day's newspaper' (M: 29).

Moreover, she is contrasted not only with Alcharisi but with Mrs Glasher, who also belongs to the Gentile domain, but shares more of Alcharisi's tragic stature and resonance. Like Alcharisi, Mrs Glasher presents herself largely in scenes of her own devising; perforce living away from society, she makes contact with others rarely, and, apart from with Grandcourt, in times and places of her own choosing. Relative to Mrs Glasher, Gwendolen suffers conspicuously for her transgressions; the former lives quietly without encountering the disapproval of the curate and his wife, has children whom she loves, and eventually achieves a fortune for her son. Gwendolen's sin of ruining the prospects of a woman to whom she had given a promise to the contrary is made by the novel to appear of far greater magnitude than Mrs Glasher's sin of leaving a husband and child for an attractive younger man (the sin which furnishes half the concern of *Anna Karenina*). Grandcourt, the villainous oppressor of both women, is killed swiftly and at the peak of such pleasure as life by then afforded him. Such uneven treatment of transgressors is one potential indication of scapegoating by a text. Another such indication pertains to agency; as Heyns comments: 'Creating Gwendolen as a representative of her society and then according her the duty to aspire beyond that society, Eliot in effect asks of her to reach beyond the limits of her own definition' (1994: 171). She has, in Bernard Williams's (1993: 41) sense, bad 'moral luck', for which she is held to account.

Nonetheless, the marks of tragedy upon her remain. When Daniel finds Mirah on the brink of the Thames, 'His mind glanced over the girl-tragedies that are going on in the world, hidden, unheeded, as if they were but tragedies of the copse or hedgerow, where the helpless drag wounded wings forsakenly' (DD: 160). This description applies far less to Gwendolen than to Hetty Sorrel in *Adam Bede*; she has too much in common with Mrs Glasher and Alcharisi for such a classification. The marks of tragedy, denied by her domain, both accord to Gwendolen a hypothetical tragic status, and stress the extent of her failure to attain it. In so doing they both augment and measure the extent to which she is the victim of her text.

Daniel's Contribution

The effect on Gwendolen's treatment of the existence of Daniel and the novel's Jewish domain is ambivalent. Daniel does not condemn Gwendolen as much as he condemns her society, which tends both to produce and overlook Grandcourt's kind of guilt ('"What right had he to marry this girl?" said Deronda, with disgust') (DD: 371). He affords her some support, and makes her more likely to find happiness in the future than if she had become as coldly calculating as Rosamund Lydgate in *Middlemarch*, and sought a second splendid marriage with a more pliant husband. On the other hand, many readers of the novel have had the same reaction as Edith Simcox who (as she wrote to Eliot in October 1879) was 'more struck by the pathos of Gwendolen's rejection than by the healing power of Daniel's virtuous conduct and counsel' (EL ix: 275). Gwendolen opens and enters the novel as the object of Daniel's benevolence, but departs from and almost closes it in a letter which equivocates as to whether he has rendered her any help whatsoever: 'It is better — it shall be better with me because I have known you'. This is only a small advance on her claim of almost a year before: 'It may be — it shall be better with me because I have known you' (DD: 695, 389). Daniel's attempts to alleviate the effects of her actual and metaphorical gambling losses humiliate her, give Grandcourt occasion to punish her, sharpen her already poignant sense of guilt, and awaken and disappoint her love. When they part, Gwendolen is left in chastity and misery, and Daniel in the opposite state — as they are both well aware. After the end of her letter to Daniel on his wedding day, the novel's next paragraph begins: 'The preparations for the departure of all three to the East began at once'. Although this is immediately followed by the ostensible reason for their departure ('for Deronda could not deny Ezra's wish'), the effect of the sentences' order is that after Gwendolen's letter has been read, the preparations for departure *therefore* begin immediately (DD: 695). Daniel is aware of the contrast of his own fate with Gwendolen's, even without the benefit of Hans's reproach 'do you want her to wear weeds for you all her life — burn herself in perpetual suttee while you are alive and merry?' (DD: 685–86). James's fictional critic Constantius suggests that the effect is intentional:

> Her finding Deronda pre-engaged to go to the East and stir up the race-feeling of the Jews strikes me as a wonderfully happy invention. The irony of the situation, for poor Gwendolen, is almost grotesque, and it makes one wonder whether the whole heavy structure of the Jewish question was not built up by the author for the express purpose of giving its proper force to this particular stroke. (1964: 46)

Certainly the narrative is *aware* of the irony. It can be interpreted either as contributing towards Gwendolen's scapegoating by her text — or else as sufficiently pointed as to induce sympathy for her.

However, the unobtrusive ironies of the novel's titles tend more decisively to work against Gwendolen. Kaufmann commented that: 'It has been frivolously asked why the book is called "Daniel Deronda" and not "Gwendolen Harleth," or "Ezra Mordecai Cohen"? We might reply in the old Biblical words, "Thou dost not inquire wisely concerning this"' (1877: 56–57). He might have considered querying why the title did not encompass both main protagonists less frivolous. *Daniel Deronda* is named only for its successful protagonist. The gap between its title and its epigraph coincides with the novel's fault-line, since the latter (beginning 'Let thy chief terror be of thine own soul') is of no direct relevance to the Jewish plot — apart from to the apostate Alcharisi. Those of the book's titles which do acknowledge Gwendolen are either directly critical of her ('The Spoiled Child'), or else elevate into the novel's formal structure the ironies which work against her at the level of plot. In 'Meeting Streams' Gwendolen meets Grandcourt, and Daniel meets Mirah, ensuring that Gwendolen and Daniel's streams will not merge. The demure diction of 'Maidens Choosing' misrepresents Gwendolen's passive acceptance of Grandcourt, and has no application to Mirah's contrasting history of vigorous, maidenhood-preserving choice. 'Gwendolen Gets Her Choice' again overstates the free will involved in her acceptance of Grandcourt, and points to her resultant loss of choice. 'Fruit and Seed' contrasts Grandcourt's seed which dies fruitlessly in Gwendolen with the new beneficiaries of his illegitimate fecundity, and the devoutly anticipated fecundity of Daniel and Mirah.

Under-acknowledged irony exists also in the fact that the resemblances, inversions, and parallels which connect Daniel's and Gwendolen's stories are not interpretable in ethical terms. Both characters are ignorant about a parent, but only Daniel is eventually enlightened; they are simultaneously in a Leubronn gambling hall after simultaneously meeting their future spouses in England, but only Gwendolen is fleeing from hers; they lack a focus for their energy, but only Daniel finds one; Gwendolen unsuccessfully aspires to the masculine role of dominance within marriage, whereas Daniel successfully plays a feminine, nurturing role to Mirah; in Genoa Gwendolen loses her husband whilst Daniel finds his mother, with the result that she loses her potential husband whilst he gains his wife. The overarching irony is that, in Leavis's phrase, 'Gwendolen *has* no Zionism' (1948: 84). The implications of this fact are stressed by Mordecai's repetition of *because* in his assertion: 'ideas, beloved ideas, came to me, because I was a Jew. They were a trust to fulfil, because I was a Jew. They were an inspiration, because I was a Jew' (DD: 425–26). Several factors disrupt the Jewish–Gentile dichotomy in *Daniel Deronda*, but none of them decisively. The Meyricks are virtuous, happy, idealized, and Gentile. However, theirs is an exceptional, part-foreign, Gentile household, which forms as it were an anti-chamber to the novel's Jewish domain. It is not fully part of the latter because of the limited physical and spiritual scale of its parlour and inhabitants (Mrs Meyrick has some of Lady Mallinger's narrowness). Rather, it is an enclave of peace and virtue reminiscent of such Dickensian parlours as that of *Oliver Twist*'s Maylies, in which a starving, hunted child is also given refuge. The strikingly virtuous Gentile who belongs to Gwendolen's own society is Rex, who is incapable of understanding and moving Gwendolen as Daniel can since he lacks the wise and vocal seriousness for which she apparently yearns. Only if her redemption 'so as by fire' has cured her of this need is a future match between herself and Rex possible.

The irrelevance of Judaism to Gwendolen is suggested not so much by her own lack of interest in it — 'the phrase "reading Hebrew" had fleeted unimpressively across her sense of hearing' (if anything, it suggests the reverse) — but by the Jewish lack of interest in her (DD: 507). Mordecai is so absorbed in his explanation to Mirah of the *Shemah* as the mark of Jewish distinctness (in fact he is preaching to the reader, not her, since she would have known all he says already) that he fails to notice her misery. Had he done so, and enquired after the reason for it (jealousy of Gwendolen), he might for the first time have been made aware of Gwendolen's existence; as it is, an exposition of the *Shemah* keeps him in ignorance. He, apparently, shows no more interest in Gwendolen's presence in the room next to him than Gwendolen does in the presence of Mirah's brother 'reading Hebrew' in the next room to her (DD: 505). As mentioned above, a secular equivalent to Judaism is preached to the novel's and its readers' Gentiles by Klesmer. However, Carroll rightly says that the distance between Gwendolen's life and Daniel's is 'not more extreme, in truth, than the contrast between life's limits and conditions as dimly guessed by Gwendolen and its unconditioned boundlessness through Art as felt by Klesmer' (1971: 392–93). The Gentile Hans is an alternative, talented artistic figure whose facetiousness, however, contrasts with Klesmer's seriousness, and whose negligible understanding of Gwendolen prevents him from constituting a source of alternative value for her. She can no more acquire artistic talent than Judaism. Like Judaism, the gospel of art must be taken by her as a metaphor — as a vision of striving to spiritual or aesthetic excellence which may be replaced by specific alternative ideals by individuals according to their gifts. It is easier, however, for the novel's readers to respond to its ideals in this way; Gwendolen lives in the fictional world in which they are presented as having value, and appears to have no alternative with which to replace them. Romola's lot of looking after her late husband's mistress and illegitimate child is austere, but not a poor substitute for any form of excellence attainable by women which the novel promulgates; Gwendolen's aspiration to become 'one of the best of women' is indeed a poor substitute for being a pious Jewess or a great artist, in part because it is a widely available goal rather than being centred in a delimited human essence, or a 'local habitation' (DD: 694).

Of course, Daniel and his domain are established as an ethical and spiritual example not only to Gwendolen but to her whole domain — like Tacitus' Germania to Rome (Kaufmann also makes this comparison to the novel), or like a Jewish 'lune' from which the 'éclipse de terre' of Gentile society can be viewed (Kaufmann 1877: 49; Fontenelle 1955: 83–84).[14] Indeed, the moon is prominently associated with Daniel. Mirah enters Daniel's life under the light of the rising moon. At the New Year's Eve party Daniel invites Gwendolen and Grandcourt to see 'the finest possible moonlight on the stone pillars and carving, and shadows waving across it in the wind'; Grandcourt tells Gwendolen that 'Deronda will take you' (DD: 381). As he waits to see his mother, Daniel watches the moon sinking every night over Genoa, whilst Gwendolen 'watched through the evening lights to the sinking of the moon with less of awed loneliness than was habitual to her — nay, with a vague impression that in this mighty frame of things there might be some preparation of rescue for her'. An hour before Daniel actually appears to her, she wakes from 'a strangely-mixed dream in which she felt herself escaping over the Mont Cenis, and wondering to find it warmer even in the moonlight on the snow, till suddenly she met Deronda, who told her to go back' (DD: 579). However, Gentiles can neither reach a Jewish moon, nor can most of them reach the moon of artistic excellence.

The differences between the domains may also be expressed in terms of the Hellenism and Hebraism adumbrated by Matthew Arnold in *Culture and Anarchy* five years before the novel was written. Terry Eagleton's argument that the 'fruitlessly Hellenistic' Daniel receives 'the essential corrective' of Hebraism from the Jewish world is correct (1978: 122). Daniel is impelled into constructive action by Mordecai, whose vision is not one of 'sweetness and light', and by Kalonymos and the memory of his grandfather, who represent the most strictly Hebraic side of Judaism (M. Arnold 1965: 90). However, Arnold associates Hebraism no more with modern Judaism than with Christianity, and advocates the improvement of contemporary, unreflecting, Hebraic, English society by Hellenic reflectiveness. Gascoigne, Sir Hugo, and Bult are *Daniel Deronda*'s laxly Hebraic Philistines, whereas the widely cultured Mordecai, Daniel, and Mirah represent the best not only of Hebraism but also of Hellenism. This Hellenism is not only, like them, associated with modern Germany — but is 'more Orientalising than Arnold's and Winckelmann's Hellenism, being concerned with the meeting of ideas in the Hellenistic period and early Christianity' (Shaffer 1975: 288, 14).

The stories may also be compared in generic terms. A comedy may ontologically contextualize a tragedy contained within the same work by guaranteeing that the narrative universe itself is not tragic — or it may denature the tragedy as such. Auerbach, in a comment which neither asserts nor denies Shylock's status as a scapegoat of his text, says that the power of the Venetian comedy denies his tragic status:

> überhaupt fehlt es ihm nicht an Tiefe der Problematik, Eindringlichkeit der Erscheinung, Kraft der Leidenschaft und Gewalt des Ausdrucks. Dennoch läßt Shakespeare die Motive des Tragischen am Ende in achtloser, olympischer Heiterkeit fallen [. . .] am Schluß läßt Shakespeare ihn ohne Größe, als geprellten Teufel, so wie er es in seinen Vorlagen fand, und nach seinem Abgang gibt er noch einen ganzen Akt poetischen Märchen- und Liebesspiels, in welchem Shylock vergessen und versunken ist. Ohne Zweifel haben also die Schauspieler, die aus Shylock einen tragischen Helden machen wollen, unrecht

[. . .] Für ihn [Shakespeare] ist Shylock, ständisch und ästhetisch, eine niedere Figur, des Tragischen unwürdig, dessen Tragik einen Augenblick beschworen wird, aber doch nur eine Würze ist in dem Triumph einer höheren, edleren, freieren, und auch aristokratischeren Menschlichkeit.

[overall he doesn't lack depth of problems, vividness of character, power of suffering, and violence of expression. Nonetheless, at the end Shakespeare drops these tragic motifs with heedless Olympian serenity. [. . .] In the end Shakespeare leaves him without greatness, as an outwitted devil, as he found him in his sources, and after his departure he gives another whole act of poetical fairy-tale and love-sport, in which Shylock is forgotten and sunk. So there is no doubt that the actors who have wanted to make Shylock a tragic hero have been wrong [. . .] For him [Shakespeare] Shylock is, in terms of class and aesthetics, a low character, unworthy of tragedy, whose tragedy is guaranteed for a moment, but is after all only a spice added to the triumph of a higher, nobler, freer, and also more aristocratic humanity.] (1946: 300–01)

However, *Daniel Deronda* does *not* invert *The Merchant of Venice* and give to the Jews 'poetical fairy-tale and love-sport', and suffering to the novel's leading Gentile. Since Daniel and Mirah can conceive of tragedy, they are capable of giving the recognition and resonance to Gwendolen's tragedy which her own domain denies: Daniel finds her to have undergone 'a tragic transformation', whilst Mirah feels that 'genuine grand ladies' such as Gwendolen 'impressed her vaguely as coming out of some unknown drama, in which their parts perhaps got more tragic as they went on' (DD: 656, 478). Indeed, Mirah — and Ortega y Gasset — define the tragic and the comic in terms very similar to those in which the novel's Jewish domain is the former, and its Gentile domain the latter. According to Ortega y Gasset, in tragedy 'The noble heroic fiction rises above the inertia of reality through the greatest exertions; it lives by aspiration. The future is its witness'; the comic world, however, is 'drawn back and frozen in the present', 'undermining the aspiration of someone to be different in the future, by contrasting that vision with what they currently *are*' (McKeon 2000: 290). Gillian Beer notes that '*Daniel Deronda* is a novel haunted by the future'; Daniel's story reaches towards the future and vindicates precisely such aspiration (1983: 181). Ortega y Gasset argues that 'the novel' itself is 'a tragicomedy' in which 'The upper level [. . .] is a tragedy, from which the muse descends, following the tragic as it falls into comedy', but he concedes that 'The tragic element, of course, may expand a great deal and even vie in scope and importance with the comic matter of the novel. All degrees and oscillations are possible here' (McKeon 2000: 291). In *Daniel Deronda* the tragic not only vies with, but is given a rhetorical victory over, the comic. As Kaufmann says, 'the morality of Deronda's surroundings is greater than that of Gwendolen's, and their vital purport *deeper* and more hearty' (1877: 50).

However, the Jewish domain contains a complex mixture of genres: the Jewish National tragicomedy, which is also its Epic, the personal tragicomedies of Mordecai and Mirah, the romance of Mordecai and Daniel's meeting, the romantic comedy of Daniel and Mirah's marriage, and the Cohens' low-mimetic comedy (DD: 156). The effect of the last might be that of tragicomedy as conceived by Plautus and Sidney, in which tragic and low comic action are interspersed, were not the Cohens themselves evidence of the tragedy, and embraced by the comedy, of the national tragicomedy. Gwendolen's tragedy, albeit recognized by Daniel and Mirah, has little resonance with any of these genres. Daniel's story, in contrast to Gwendolen's, contains 'elements of mythopoeic story, of universal type, of spiritual intention, and high art'; Garrett notes that it 'unfolds not as a sequence of choices and consequences but as a process of discovery, of prophecy and fulfilment, where meaning is determined by a remote, mysterious origin and a remote, beckoning goal' (Shaffer 1975: 239; Garrett 1980: 168). Gwendolen's story also fulfils omens, but, unlike the successful prophecies in Daniel's story, these are not recognized by the characters themselves. Gwendolen is the victim of a moribund Gentile society of which the decline is neither mourned nor presented as tragic. This is due partly to its own faults (for example its Philistine prejudices against Jews and Caribs), and partly to its lack of gravity.[15] This difference of the two domains itself tangentially contributes to Gwendolen's scapegoating by the text, since her tragedy, unlike Mirah's, has no national context which gives it resonance.

The generic distinction of the novel's domains is reinforced by other disjunctions. Whereas Gwendolen's society is established at the beginning of the novel, Daniel's Jewish society appears to be created as he discovers it over the course of the novel, giving it a further aspect of inaccessibility to Gwendolen. Each story has a characteristic narrative voice: that of a dryly witty Gentile who is knowledgeable about Judaism and sharply critical of Gentiles, and that of an earnest person identified by Doyle in the comment 'Daniel and the narrator have the same styles' (1981: 161). The former observes: 'We English are a miscellaneous people'; and the latter: 'the velvet canopy never covered a more goodly bride and bridegroom, to whom their people might more wisely wish offspring' (DD: 85, 693). The Gentiles tend to be more thickly described: Gwendolen's history before her trip to Leubronn is presented as a series of episodes, whereas Daniel's before his trip is given in a more continuous line of character description. The Gentiles are more physically substantial. Admittedly, Mordecai's body is present in its pain, and Mirah's in its small-scale, pictorial descriptions. However, the Jews have less physical volition than the Gentiles: Gwendolen and Grandcourt have 'physical antipathies', and match each other respectively in revulsion from sex, and sexual sadism, whereas Daniel's attraction to Gwendolen is weaker than his observers suppose, and his marriage to Mirah has hardly more a sexual aspect than that of Edmund and Fanny in *Mansfield Park* (DD: 101). Only in the Gentile story are animals (horses, dogs, and prawns) present in reality, rather than being used exclusively as similes, as they are in the Jewish story.

Some of those features which connect the worlds have less the aspect of *de facto* commonality than of signifying connectedness. Gambling, with studied parallelism, ruins Grapnell & Co., Gwendolen, and Lapidoth; jewels lie scattered across both stories. Beer notes that 'parallel narratives are fleetingly condensed through allusion to opera, myth, legend, politics'; however, the fact of condensation is palpable (1986: 215). As Soussa Correa notes, 'Connections are indeed constantly proposed through musical allusions which increase our sense of the novel's formal coherence. Nevertheless, they frequently dissolve and are rarely permitted narrative fulfillment. Music is involved in both the creation and disruption of narrative unity' (Sousa Correa 2002: 174–75). Newton argues that the novel is 'something akin to the *Gesamtkunstwerk*' in which, as in *Waverley*, a romance narrative is grafted on to historical material and absorbed within it (1981: 245). The epigraph to Book VI, taken from Aristotle's *Poetics*, rationalizes this absorption: 'This, too, is probable, according to that saying of Agathon: "It is a part of probability that many improbable things will happen"'' (DD: 434). However, such absorption as occurs, and such meta-aesthetic bridges as exist, fail entirely to eliminate the reader's sense of the generic distinction of the domains. Gwendolen and the novel do not have the optimism of Fontenelle's narrator that in the future communication may be possible between the earth and moon ('je ne veux plus jurer qu'il ne puisse y avoir commerce quelque jour entre la lune et la terre' [I don't want to insist any more that there can never be contact one day between the moon and the earth]) (Fontenelle 1955: 92). Gwendolen, then, is rendered partially a victim in relation to Daniel's world in that her own is discontinuous with his, and she is excluded from the ethnic and aesthetic categories correspondent to the novel's ideals. In addition, her downfall throws his success into relief. Nonetheless, Eliot is not one of Girard's wholly 'persécuteurs naïfs' [naïve persecutors] who '*ne savent pas ce qu'ils font*' and '*ne se doutent pas qu'en rédigeant leurs comptes rendus ils donnent des armes contre eux-mêmes à la posterité*' ['*do not know what they are doing*' and '*do not suspect that by writing their accounts they are arming posterity against them*'] (Girard 1982: 17).

The narrative's awareness of its contradictions is apparent in the ambivalent personal relations of Gwendolen and Daniel. Her modest degree but problematic type of attraction for him analogizes the partial resistance of her story to ethical contextualization. In the Leubronn gambling hall their power relations are ambiguous: Daniel, the narrator, and the reader, attempt to judge Gwendolen for three pages before she first sees him, during which time her mind is closed to the reader, whereas Daniel's is open. Gwendolen enquires, Juliet-like, about the identity of Daniel near the door, but has neither spoken to nor kissed him. Daniel, and the novel named for him, are partly conscious of his limited ability to help Gwendolen, and of his implication in her pain. Moreover, although Mordecai's absorption in reading Hebrew and expounding the Shemah cause him to remain in ignorance of Gwendolen's existence and suffering, Daniel is twice distracted from his thoughts of Jewish matters by thoughts of Gwendolen:

> Deronda found himself after one o'clock in the morning in the rather ludicrous position of sitting up severely holding a Hebrew grammar in his hands (for somehow, in deference to Mordecai, he had begun to study Hebrew), with the consciousness that he had been in that attitude nearly an hour, and had thought of nothing but Gwendolen and her husband. [. . .] 'What is the use of it all?' thought Deronda, as he threw down his grammar, and began to undress. 'I can't do anything to help her — nobody can, if she has found out her mistake already.' (DD: 354)

In Genoa, the information from a porter that Mr and Mrs Grandcourt have 'gone out boating' 'had somehow power enough over Deronda to divide his thoughts with the memories wakened among the sparse *taliths*' (DD: 586). These two

incidents are indicative: in the earlier, he is completely distracted, and in the later
— when he is closer to his own happiness — only partly so. Yet he also recognizes
that Gwendolen's sufferings stemmed from 'her mistake'. For the fact that she made
that mistake, and suffered so much as a result of it, the responsibility is divided
between her and the novel.

Tragi-comedy

The relationships between the stories are also affected by the transitions between the
two. Since they must succeed each other, the reader is repeatedly put in the position
of performing asymmetric comparison of them — reading each new segment (a
section of narrative concerning one story rather than the other) in comparison to
the segment which she has just left. A contrastive structure is established by half way
through the novel. Gwendolen's story dominates the first half of *Daniel Deronda*: of
the first thirty-one chapters, up to her marriage, twenty-four concern Gwendolen,
after which only five chapters concern her story exclusively (Doyle 1981: 161).
One result is that the unhappy story appears to be followed by the happy one.
Gwendolen's history up to the point of meeting Daniel is given before Daniel's, and
five out of the novel's eight books (which coincide with the instalments in which it
was published) begin with Gwendolen. Daniel's story in fact overtakes Gwendolen's
during the segment in which he discovers Mordecai, and remains largely ahead
of hers for the rest of the novel — but since six of the novel's segment transitions
are from mixed segments to Daniel's segments, Daniel often appears in his role as
Gwendolen's adviser *before* he appears in his own domain (recapitulating his first
appearances in the novel). For example, the revelation of Mordecai and Mirah to
one another is suspended around the musical evening at Park Lane, permitting
Daniel to appear to minister to Gwendolen before attending to his own business,
and attenuating the reader's sense of her victimization. In fact, Daniel discovers
Mordecai during the first seven weeks of Gwendolen's marriage, which period
is never narrated for Gwendolen, who is left screaming among her diamonds.
Gwendolen's chronology reaches only one month ahead of Daniel's at the time of
her wedding — in relation to what is in both stories two years of narrative time
(Schultze 1982: 24–25). There is a sense, then, that the hero's story catches up with
and avoids the mistakes of the heroine's.

   Of course, a *fabula* is an extrapolation rather than a reality. Eliot did not write
two stories and splice them together *a posteriori* in the manner of a film editor; she
wrote, as it were, to the *breakdown* (a shooting script) of cuts between segments.
Two alternative modes of reading the novels are in relation to the assumed totality
of two *fabulae* extrapolated from the *siuzhets*, and as a continuous 'Tale' of different
'phases' (Blackwood referred to Mordecai's 'phase of the Tale') (EL VI: 222). Certain
features of *Daniel Deronda* encourage the former reading, and certain the latter. Both
modes of reading may have each of two contrary effects on a sense of the plurality
or otherwise of the stories' worlds. Independently existent *fabulae* may appear to
constitute different realities, or may, like discrete objects coexisting in space-time,
appear to share a common reality. Two *phases* of a single *siuzhet* are united by that

siuzhet, but they cannot share homogeneous time. A common reality may constitute a ground for equal opportunity on the part of characters, and for fair ethical comparison on the part of readers — thus limiting the possibility of scapegoating by a text. The pluralist ethics which may correspond to a pluralist ontology may create the double standards on which scapegoating relies. Alternatively, however, it may permit a plurality of judgements, which qualifies a narrative's condemnation of a transgressor.

These effects may be considered in relation to the coincidence or otherwise of the novel's segment boundaries with its formal boundaries. In *Daniel Deronda* a few segment boundaries occur within chapters, and only one occurs at a book boundary (from Daniel's segment to a mixed segment at the beginning of Book VII), meaning that the novel's first readers always started a new instalment, and sometimes a new chapter, in the story which they had last read. This construction suggests the close relationship and common reality of the two stories. Segment transitions tend to be semantically rather than structurally reinforced. Many of the transitions between Daniel's and Gwendolen's segments end or begin with what may be called hypotactic sentences which indicate their temporal, geographical, or thematic relation to the action to come or just passed. For example, 'This was the history of Deronda [. . .] up to the time of that visit to Leubronn in which he saw Gwendolen Harleth at the gaming-table' is followed by 'It was half-past ten in the morning when Gwendolen Harleth, after her gloomy journey from Leubronn' (DD: 193–94). The books themselves, by contrast, make no concessions to the reader's memory. However, just as a dissolve on screen is the softest and one of the most alienating modes of transition between shots, authorial mediation draws attention to the fact of transition. The chapter epigraphs with which most of the segments begin also indicate the author's intervention (even if the reader doesn't read them; Beer considers readers 'tacitly licensed to skip' them) (1983: 191).

Bakhtin's 1953 article 'Проблема речевых жанров' [The Problem of Speech Genres] offers a model for interpreting the *siuzhets* as two speakers holding a conversation (1979: 237–80). Since the speakers have independent reality, but are taking part in a single conversation, this model may be interpreted either in terms of distinct realities, or in terms of a single *siuzhet* with two aspects. Although Bakhtin considers 'диалога' [dialogue] to be 'наиболее простая и классическая форма речевого общения' [the simplest and most classical form of speech communication], he allows that the same structure may pertain to more complex forms: 'Сложные по своему построению и специализированные произведения различных научных и художественных жанров при всем их отличии от реплик диалога по своей природе являются такими же единицами речевого общения' [Complexly structured and specialized works of different scientific and artistic genres, despite all their differences from replies in dialogue, manifest by their nature the same units of speech communication] (1979: 253–54, 254). He states that the 'завершенная целостность высказывания' 'определяется тремя моментами (или факторами)': '1) предметно-смысловой исчерпанностью; 2) речевым замыслом или речевой волей говорящего; 3) типическими композиционно-жанровыми формами завершения' ['finalized completedness of utterances' 'is determined by three aspects (or factors)': '1) the semantic exhaustiveness of the subject; 2) the speaker's contemplation or will in speaking; 3) typical compositional-generic forms of finalization'] (1979: 255). In the first case, of 'semantic exhaustiveness', a certain result has been achieved before the other *siuzhet* is allowed to 'speak'. Many transitions in *Daniel Deronda* are of this kind. A mixed segment at the Abbey over New Year ends within half a page of Gwendolen's exit from Daniel's presence with the words: 'It may be — it shall be better with me because I have known you' (DD: 389). These words mark the furthest extent to which their relationship can proceed (she repeats them twice in the novel). Although she and he may have further meetings during the month of *fabula* which ensues before Daniel's departure for London at the beginning of the next segment, nothing is narrated of this period. Other segments end with Gwendolen's acceptance of Grandcourt, the reunion of Mordecai with Mirah, and the reunion of Daniel with his mother. Such endings conform to the contours of the individual *fabulae*. However, by giving to the 'utterance' the aspect of a self-contained contribution to a conversation, they also gesture towards Bakhtin's second type of finalization, by the speaker's will.

Some segments are ended by the will of the character dominating its action. Gwendolen is several times the victim of the termination of her segments by another person's will. Grandcourt reduces the narrator to the novel's only one-word sentence, and ends Gwendolen's *siuzhet*, by telling Gwendolen that Lush will be dining with them: ' "He is useful to me; and he must be treated civilly." Silence' (DD: 483). Later, when Grandcourt tells Gwendolen 'No; you will go [yachting] with me', he silences Gwendolen until such time as she is found on the yacht in 'the domain of the husband' (DD: 522, 573).

Certain segments end precisely despite the participating characters' will, at the determination of what Bakhtin calls 'типическими композиционно-жанровыми формами завершения' [typical compositional and generic forms of finalization] — as, for example, at moments of high tension (1979: 255). *Daniel Deronda* might make more use of such endings than it does. It does not indulge in 'The sudden transitions from tragic to comic and vice versa, which outraged classicists and emboldened romanticists, [and which] were deliberate effects [. . .] based upon a new esthetic of contrasts, appropriate to a climate which favored hybrid growths' (Levin 1966: 111). However, it does make some use of them. Gwendolen ends a segment 'pallid, shrieking as it seemed with terror, the jewels scattered around her on the floor' (DD: 303). Bakhtin notes that 'такие реальные паузы — психогогические или вызванные теми или иными внешними обстоятельствами — могут разрывать и одно высказывание' [such real pauses — psychological, or prompted by one or another external circumstance — can also interrupt a single utterance] (Bakhtin 1979: 253). One of Daniel's segments is internally ruptured on a point of high emotion: the sentence 'It seemed one impulse that made the two men clasp each other's hand for a moment' is separated by a book break (and, in the four-volume edition of 1876, by a volume-break) from 'This was the letter which Sir Hugo put into Deronda's hands' (DD: 524, 529). Such moments are, however, rare.

Bakhtin argues that an utterance, as opposed to a sentence, is distinguished by 'адресованность' [*addressivity*], meaning that 'Говорящий кончает свое высказывание, чтобы передать слово другому или дать место его активно ответное понимание другого' [The speaker ends his utterance in order to allow the other to speak or to make room for his active responsive understanding of the other] (1979: 275, 250). At certain of the novel's segment transitions the speaker of one *siuzhet* responds to what the other has said by providing corresponding information — for example, Gwendolen's history up to the point of meeting Daniel at Leubronn is followed by the equivalent for Daniel. At certain other transitions, the second speaker is prompted to describe an emotion related to the one with which the other speaker has just concluded. Transitions based upon parallels between *fabulae* and characters are an obvious location for ethical comparison. A submerged contrast between Gwendolen and Mirah exists at the segment boundary which juxtaposes Mirah's near-ruin and travel to England to find her mother, with Gwendolen's reluctant return to England and her own ruined mother. However, the novel tends to avoid such contrasts.

In his article 'Проблема текста в лингвистике, филологии и других гуманитарных науках: опыт филосовского анализа' [The Problem of the Text in Linguistics, Philology, and Human Sciences: the Experience of Philosophical Analysis] Bakhtin writes that:

> Два сопоставленных чужих высказывания, не знающих ничего друг о друге, если только они хоть краешком касаются одной и той же темы (мысли), неизбежно вступают друг с другом в диалогические отношения. Они соприкасаются друг с другом на территории общей темы, общей мысли.
>
> [Different people who know nothing about one another if they only slightly converge on one and the same subject (idea), inevitably enter into dialogic relations with one another. They come into contact with one another on the territory of a common theme, a common idea.] (1979: 281–307; 293)

He also considers that:

> Любые два высказывания, если мы сопоставим их в смысловой плоскости (не как вещи и не как лингвистические премеры), окажутся в диалогическом отношении. Но это особая форма ненамеренной диалогичности.
>
> [Any two utterances, if we juxtapose them on a semantic plane (not as things and not as linguistic examples), present themselves in a dialogic relationship. But this is a special form of unintentional dialogicity.] (1979: 296)

This 'special form' is not that 'dialogicity' of mutual comprehension which Bakhtin described as being peculiar to the novel in 'Слово в романе' ['Discourse in the Novel'] (1934). It more resembles the interaction of two autonomous, non-coinciding consciousnesses which do not complete one another, and do not invite comparison on a single ethical scale. In *Daniel Deronda* Daniel himself crosses many of the segment transitions: these transitions are often mediated by the narrator, and the very contrast of domains and genres forms a kind of dialogue. Fontenelle's narrator refers to 'le choc que se fait à l'endroit où deux tourbillons se poussent et se repoussent l'un l'autre; je crois que dans ce pas-là une pauvre planète est agitée assez rudement, et que ses habitants ne s'en portent pas mieux' [the turbulence which is produced when two vortices repel one another; I think that in such a case a poor planet is rudely shaken, and its inhabitants fare no better] (Fontenelle 1955: 138). When, in *Daniel Deronda*, genres and modes affront each other directly at segment boundaries, it is often the heroine's domain which is the more strongly shaken. After Mordecai 'has recovered a perfect sister, whose affection is waiting for him', the narrator asks:

> And Gwendolen? She was thinking of Deronda much more than he was thinking of her [. . .] it was as far from Gwendolen's conception that Deronda's life could be determined by this historical destiny of the Jews, as that he could rise into the air on a brazen horse. (DD: 466–67)

The irony of the sharper-toned 'Gentile' narrator is here inverted against scepticism of the kind of idealism with which the preceding segment ends. The intervening epigraph (beginning 'Faerie folk a-listening') works in the opposite direction to the same end: it is apparently fantastical, pastoral, and escapist in its tripping trochaic tetrameter, but in its last three lines it delivers the point that: 'Thus all beauty that appears | Has birth as sound to finer sense | And lighter-clad intelligence' (DD: 467). It is precisely such intelligence which Gwendolen lacks. At such segment boundaries it is apparent that 'the triumph of idealism over irony is written into the very structure of the novel's double plot' (Newton 1986: 210). Moreover, idealism is here associated with *lightness*, and irony with dull heaviness, in a reversal of common English and Philistine assumptions.

However, on certain occasions in both novels the hero's *siuzhet* appears facile in its proximity to the heroine's. After Gwendolen's last spoken words in the novel (her bleak assertion to her mother that 'I shall live. I shall be better') the narrator effuses that 'Among the blessings of love there is hardly one more exquisite than the sense that in uniting the beloved life to ours we can watch over its happiness' (DD: 692–93). The latter sentence, which aims to inflect Daniel's romantic comedy with ethical responsibility, perforce emphasizes also the fact that Daniel will no longer be watching over Gwendolen. The epigraph ('In the chequered area of human experience the seasons are all mingled [. . .] in the same moment the sickle is reaping and the seed is sprinkled') attempts to mediate between Gwendolen's disaster and Daniel's happiness by claiming their co-temporality to be typical, and implying in its second sentence — 'Nay, in each of our lives harvest and spring-time are continually one, until Death himself gathers us and sows us anew in his invisible fields' — that Gwendolen's bitter emotional harvest may also be her spiritual spring (DD: 693). The latter suggestion is faint, and the former is of no comfort to Gwendolen. This is tangentially acknowledged in the narrator's confession that Mirah 'knew nothing of Hans's struggle or of Gwendolen's pang' (DD: 693). At this transition the hero's domain offers no solutions to the problems of the heroine's, as is acknowledged by the failure of Daniel's attempts to offer such solutions.

On a few occasions Daniel's *siuzhet* is even ironized by its juxtaposition with Gwendolen's. For example, Daniel's reflections to Sir Hugo on Gwendolen's increased womanliness and attractiveness since her engagement are undermined by the narrative's preceding image of Gwendolen screaming amongst her diamonds

(DD: 303–04). Daniel's subsequent involvement in Sir Hugo's financial calculations about Grandcourt's estate has the aspect of low comic relief. Such moments are revealing, but temporally restricted. Daniel's *siuzhet* quickly loses its air of comparative levity; Blackwood told Eliot in November 1875 that:

> It seemed hard to be torn away from Gwendolen after she read that 'horrible' letter and Grandcourt came down 'dressed for dinner,' but so exquisitely do you work the other chain of your story that one is speedily as engrossed as ever.
> (EL VI: 195)

Such speedy engrossment necessarily limits the resonance of Gwendolen's tragedy with the reader.

The relations of the novel's genres are most palpable towards its end. Gwendolen fades rapidly within *Daniel Deronda*'s Book VIII. Of the book's thirteen chapters, Daniel appears in eight and Gwendolen in only three, mainly in conversation with him. She falls silent (she is frequently present at the conversation of others, but, for the first time in the novel, does not speak), asleep (she takes sleeping draughts), prone (her last appearance in the novel is lying in bed), and is finally rendered two-dimensional (her last presence in the novel is in a letter). At the end of Book VII Gwendolen is left on the floor 'in hysterical crying [. . .] She was found in this way, crushed on the floor. Such grief seemed natural in a poor lady whose husband had been drowned in her presence' (DD: 601). Eliot was determined that the instalment should end here, and defended the short seventh book in April 1876 to Blackwood (whilst demonstrating her concern for narrative sequence): 'It is inadmissible to add anything after the scene with Gwendolen, and to stick anything in, not necessary to development, between the foregoing chapters, is a form of "matter in the wrong place" particularly repulsive to my authorship's sensibility' (EL VI: 240). The segment's last line, with its hint of comedy, prepares the transition to the following scene, which resembles the transition to the fourth act of *The Winter's Tale*. Rather than the scene changing to a sheep-shearing festival in Bohemia, with the Shepherd, his son, and the flourishing Florizel, Perdita, Dorcas, and Mopsa, it moves to 'the faint murmurs of the garden' on 'a July afternoon', with Gascoigne, his flourishing son Rex, and the Davilow girls (DD: 605). Gascoigne is engaged in 'Peaceful authorship!, living in the air of the fields and downs' of 'two ecclesiastical articles' which no one who knows their authorship troubles to read, and no one who reads troubles to comment upon (DD: 604). This authorship brings 'a more suffusive sense of achievement than the production of a whole *Divina Commedia*' — the comparison accentuating the relative superficiality of the domain's comedy (DD: 604). The Meyricks accept the drowning of Grandcourt more easily still than the Clown and Shepherd accept the drowning of the Sicilian ship's crew and the eating of Antigonus, immediately turning their attention to 'things new-born' in speculation on Gwendolen's possible children by her first or a second marriage (*The Winter's Tale*, III. 3. 112). In fact the novel's Hermione is hardly revived, but is left partly paralysed by horror. Mirah, on the other hand, is a Perdita who, after surviving persecution by, and forgiving, her father, marries a prince in disguise. The narrator, in a similarly alienating intervention as that made by Time in *The Winter's Tale*, reflects on 'the year's experience which had turned the brilliant, self-confident

Gwendolen Harleth of the Archery Meeting into the crushed penitent impelled to confess her unworthiness where it would have been her happiness to be held worthy'. This segment transition therefore both denies resonance to Gwendolen's tragedy, and stresses the failure of its conversion into a tragicomedy (at least in the short term; the tranquil family life to which Gwendolen will return offers a chance of rehabilitation in the longer term). Daniel's comedy at times successfully contextualizes Gwendolen's story; at other transitions 'Satire and melodrama, visionary romance and domestic realism [are] brought into uneasy confrontations', and the comedy is temporarily troubled (Garrett 1980: 8–9).

Eliot used an organic metaphor, amongst others, for connection in art. Six years before starting *Daniel Deronda*, in 'Notes on Form in Art', she wrote that: 'The highest Form, then, is the highest organism, that is to say, the most varied group of relations bound together in a wholeness which again has the most varied relations with all other phenomena'; 'forms of art can be called higher or lower only on the same principle as that on which we apply these words to organisms; viz. in proportion to the complexity of the parts bound up into an indissoluble whole' (Ashton 1992: 356, 358). This metaphor is helpful: *Daniel Deronda* is an organism in which the vital organs work imperfectly together, and which must die when their relationship breaks down completely. The Cabbalistic title story could be called an *overplot*, which (in Berlin's sense) makes a hedgehog-like attempt at control (Berlin 1994: 22–81). This attempt has only partial success, as the novel's rhetoric partially acknowledges. Carroll goes too far, however, in saying that 'an essential feature of any comprehensive world-view in Eliot's fiction is the inevitability of its self-deconstruction' (1992: 313). Mordecai's theories are not deconstructed, merely shown to be of non-infinite relevance in the novel's universe. The novel's ending is not, in Henry James's words: 'a distribution at the last of prizes, pensions, husbands, wives, babies, millions, appended paragraphs, and cheerful remarks' (quoted in Kermode 1967: 22). Rather, the ending of *Daniel Deronda* both tends towards this condition, and is sharply aware of the respects in which it fails to reach it. Tragicomedy has been variously theorized and defined since Plautus coined the term to apply to *Amphitryon*, and since Sidney introduced it to the English language in 1581. The kind of tragicomedy discovered in *Daniel Deronda* is neither Plautine nor Guarinian, but an imperfect version of Miss Prism's definition of fiction, in which 'the good [end] happily and the bad unhappily' (Wilde 2006: 26). What I call *tragi-comedy* makes an imperfectly satisfactory suggestion that its protagonists' respective disasters and successes are justified. This imperfection is partly acknowledged. It is one of the problems of such *problem comedies* as *The Merchant of Venice*, where an ethical disjunction separates the vanquished Shylock from the Venetian Christians. Unlike the Venetian Christians, however, the hero of *Daniel Deronda* is only slightly involved in the novel's injustice. He is not personally responsible for the extra-narrative logic in which 'events are justified by their appropriateness to a thematic structure', making events the 'products of meaning'; he plays only a secondary role in Gwendolen's suffering, and, therefore, in her scapegoating by the text (Culler 1981: 173).

In this novel Eliot reverses the stereotype of Jewish victimhood and scapegoating by giving the Jewish story ethical dominance, and the generic character of epic tragicomedy, as contrasted to the muted tragedy of the Gentile story. The dominance is achieved at the partial expense of coherence: knowledge of Judaism is imperfectly mediated to the Gentile reader, rather as the ethical relevance of Judaism is imperfectly mediated to Gwendolen. Mordecai's claims about the Jewish talent at mediation are not justified either by his own or by Daniel's efforts in the novel. The novel strives strongly to mediate, but, like nineteenth-century comparative literature which reinforced national distinctions precisely in the attempt to read literature supranationally, its success is moderated by its very insistence on its claims. Leavis, twelve years after arguing that the 'good part' of *Daniel Deronda* could and should be prised from the 'strongly, and very questionably, emotional' part and called 'Gwendolen Harleth', admitted that 'the surgery of disjunction would be a less simple and satisfactory affair than I had thought' (Leavis 1986: 63). On the other hand, Eliot's surgery of *con*junction, for all the sensitivity demonstrated at its segment boundaries, may have been a less simple affair than she had initially anticipated.

In the Meyricks' parlour hangs a collection of engravings which, like *Daniel Deronda* itself, are 'there through the medium of a little black and white'. 'The Tragic Muse' hangs with other Classical, Christian, and secular icons, which are named in apparently random order:

> the Virgin soaring amid her cherubic escort; grand Melancholia with her solemn universe; the Prophets and Sibyls; the School of Athens; the Last Supper; mystic groups where far-off ages made one moment; grave Holbein and Rembrandt heads; the Tragic Muse; last-century children at their musings or their play; Italian poets. (DD: 179)

These are described as 'a glorious silent cloud of witnesses', and are apparently harmonious. Their silence, however, might be considered to resemble that of Leubronn's gambling table, with its 'striking admission of human equality' in what Carroll describes as 'a parody of [the] divine unity' (DD: 4; Carroll 1992: 279). If the 'silent witnesses' were to be conjured into animation on the stage of the Meyricks' parlour wall, then the apparent harmony with which they coexist would disintegrate. The Virgin would glide off the stage with her cherubic escort and return wearing *tephillin*. She would join hands with one of the grave Holbein figures and with the Prophet, whose other hand would be held by grand Melancholia, now much happier. The Tragic Muse would grasp the hand of one of the playing girls, but would be invisible to all of the characters including herself. The two groups would face each other, whilst the girl's former companions would continue to play. The Holbein figure would reach out his free hand to the girl, who would stretch out her own in answer, but they would not be able to take hold.

Notes to Chapter 2

1. Pilar Giralt, in his 1980 translation of the novel into Spanish (*La serpiente emplumada*), tries to give a sense of the possible hypothetical original by imposing a more regular rhyme and metre than belong to the supposed English translation: 'La oí cantar como un ave moribunda: | *Mi nombre es Jesús, soy Hijo de María*' (Lawrence 1980: 135).

2. Whereas Eliot was able to carry her wish for the title *Daniel Deronda*, which Blackwood thought too foreign-sounding, Lawrence was persuaded by his publisher Knopf to translate *Quetzalcoatl* into *The Plumed Serpent*.

3. Extracts from the half of the novel concerning Jews were published in Hebrew and Russian translations in the country to which Alcharisi exiles herself, where it was used 'to preach up-to-date Zionism' 'by various Zionist societies in Russia' (Werses 1976: 36). Schapira noted, with reference to the pogroms which started within a few years of its publication, that the novel appeared in Russia 'like forked lightning to illuminate our night' (McKay 2003: 8–9). Between 1876 and 1915 three full and two abridged translations of the novel into Russian were made; two full and one abridged Hebrew translations appeared in 1893, 1935, and 1953–54, and one Yiddish translation (possibly two) appeared in 1914 and 1920 (Baker 2002: 351).

4. *Contrast* stands at 85 per cent of *Daniel Deronda*'s usage in *Middlemarch*, 50 per cent in *A Picture of Dorian Gray*, and 13 per cent in *A Tale of Two Cities* and *Vanity Fair*. *Nicholas Nickleby*, *Wuthering Heights*, and *North and South* do not use the term, and only *Sybil* is slightly (6 per cent) higher than *Daniel Deronda*.

5. Parts of the rest of this chapter also appeared, in different form, in Brown (2009). I thank the editors of *Essays in Criticism* for their kind permission to use this material, and for their editorial assistance with the article.

6. In a term such as *double-plotted* the morpheme *plot* is used to denote a *фабула* in Vladimir Shklovskii's sense of the term: a series of events in which a character or group of characters is involved, otherwise denoted by *fabula*, *histoire*, or *story*. When the distinction between *фабула* and *сюжет* (*conte*, *récit*, or *plot*) is required, the Russian terms will be used in transliteration (*fabula* and *siuzhet*).

7. Eliot owned an 1866 French edition which she marginally marked in pencil; quotations in this book are from the 1955 Oxford Clarendon Press edition.

8. *Iridescence* is an important concept for Eliot; the narrator of *Daniel Deronda* refers to 'the iridescence of [Gwendolen's] character — the play of various, nay, contrary tendencies' (DD: 33). However, the iridescence referred to here entails that different perspectives afford views of different aspects of the same subject ('a moment is wide enough for the loyal and mean desire'). In my own usage, the same aspect of a single subject must be judged differently when viewed from different interpretative perspectives. It is a function of the complexity of *Daniel Deronda* that no single perspective presents itself as adequate.

9. As such he resembles other Jews portrayed in Russian literature. *Anna Karenina* is by these standards not anti-Semitic. Oblonskii's mild, aristocratic anti-Semitism is narrated with detachment, whereas Mikhailov's painting of Jesus as an *еврей* [Jew] — not a Christian or a *жид* [Yid] — is taken seriously.

10. For a full consideration of 'Why Does Daniel Deronda's Mother Live in Russia?', see Brown (2010c). I thank the editors for permission to use research from that article in this book, and for their editorial help with the article.

11. Viardot knew many languages, designed her own costumes and researched their historical accuracy, composed music, and was George Sand's closest female friend. She and Eliot had many acquaintances in common including Sand, Clara Schumann, and Liszt, who had taught Viardot how to play the piano. On 26 April 1871 Eliot and Lewes had Turgenev and others to lunch, and Viardot 'sang divinely and entranced every one' (EL 5: 143–44).

12. Henry James, who attended the Viardots' salon in Paris, tells a version of this story: 'I meant to add about poor Turngenieff that there [are] insuperable limits to seeing much of him, for the poor man is a slave — the slave of Mme. Viardot. She has made him her property, is excessively jealous, keeps him to herself etc. [. . .] Such is the tale I am told.' (1978: 16)

13. Mirah's perspective resembles Samuel Smiles's 1859 quotation of Douglas Jerrold: 'I am convinced the world will get tired (at least I hope so) of this eternal guffaw about all things. After all, life has something serious in it. It cannot be all a comic history of humanity. Some men, would, I believe, write a Comic Sermon on the Mount. Think of a Comic History of England, the drollery of Alfred, the fun of Sir Thomas More, the farce of his daughter begging the dead head and clasping it in her coffin on her bosom. Surely the world will be sick of this blasphemy.' (Smiles 1996: 203–04)

14. *The Plumed Serpent* similarly uses Neo-Aztec Mexico as a standpoint from which to criticize decadent Europe, holding up the example of a non-European religion which was at its height several centuries before the novel's present. Its adherents were colonized by European invaders and now hope to re-establish a great nation.
15. The narrator notes tartly that the reputation of Christians among Caribs for thieving is not without justification (DD: 176).

CHAPTER 3

Anna Karenina

Juxtaposition difficile enfin, presque acrobatique, des morceaux du 'paysage au lever de soleil' alternativement aperçus par les deux carreaux opposés du wagon de chemin de fer entre Paris et Balbec, et qui oblige le héros à 'courir d'une fenêtre à l'autre pour rapprocher, pour [. . .] avoir une vue totale et un tableau continu.

[A difficult, almost acrobatic, juxtaposition of the fragments of the 'landscape at sunrise' alternatively viewed out of the two opposing windows of the train carriage between Paris and Balbec [. . .] obliges the hero to 'run from one window to the other to bring together, to [. . .] have a total view and a continuous picture.]

GENETTE 2007: 102

The story oscillates from side to side 'like an express train' on a winding route.

Anonymous review of *Anna Karenina*, Boston *Literary World* 1886;
quoted in Knowles 1978: 341

Мир [Peace/The World/Society/The People]

Like Mordecai's anticipated 'new Judaea', Goethe's house in Weimar became a meeting ground 'between East and West' (DD: 459). Seven years after Eliot and Lewes visited the house, so did the 33-year-old Lev Tolstoi (Koelb 1984: 224). He had admired Goethe, as had Eliot, from an early age, and listed *Hermann und Dorothea* among those books which had a 'very great' influence on him between the ages of twenty and thirty-five, which was the period in which he began *War and Peace* (Orwin 1993: 33; Tolstoi 1978: II, 486).[1] However, unlike Eliot but like Lawrence, Tolstoi turned against most of the writers whom he initially admired. In *What is Art?* he denied Goethe's status as a true artist, and in *On Shakespeare and Drama* criticized him for immorality, referring to 'бессодержательные драмы, каковы драмы Гете, Шиллера, Гюго, у нас Пушкина, хроники Островского, Алексея Толстого', 'без всякого не только религиозного, но и нравственного содержания' [contentless plays, like those of Goethe, Schiller, Hugo, and our Pushkin, or the chronicles of our Ostrovskii, of Aleksei Tolstoi, which are not only without any religious, but also moral, content] (Tolstoi 1950: 270). This criticism fits closely with Eliot's characterization of those who consider *Wilhelm Meister's Apprenticeship* immoral: 'Goethe, it is sometimes said, seems in this book to be almost destitute of moral bias: he shows no hatred of bad actions, no warm sympathy with good ones' (Ashton 1992: 129). Moreover, Goethe, who was 'в то время диктатором общественного мнения в вопросах эстетических', 'провозгласил Шекспира великим поэтом' [at that time the dictator of public opinion on aesthetic questions declared Shakespeare a great poet] — in Tolstoi's opinion a harmful error (Tolstoi 1950: 265).

Yet in both writers Tolstoi was rejecting qualities which he was aware of himself possessing. Thomas Mann noted some of the affinities of 'Goethe und Tolstoi' in his 1923 lecture of that name. He pointed to their shared, Rousseauian, creative non-intellectualism, and contrasted them to their 'großen Gegenspieler' and 'Kinder der Idee' [great opposites, children of ideas], 'Schiller und Dostojewskij' (Mann 1923: 19). His comments apply particularly to the early Tolstoi, but he might also have pointed out the irony that the kind of art advocated by *What is Art?* bears strong resemblances to Goethe's idea of *Weltliteratur*:

> Христианское искусство, то есть искусство нашего времени, должно быть кафолично в прямом значении этого слова, то есть всемирно, и потому должно соединять всех людей. Соединяют же всех людей только два рода чувства: чувства, вытекающие из сознания сыновности богу и братства людей, и чувства самые простые — житейские, но такие, которые доступны всем без исключения людям, как чувства веселья, умиления, бодрости, спокойствия и т. п.

> [Christian art, that is art of our time, should be catholic in the literal sense of the word — that is, belonging to all the world, and for that reason it should unite all people. All people can only be united by two types of feeling: the feelings arising from the consciousness of filiality to God and brotherhood to man, and the very simplest feelings — everyday, but such as are accessible to all people without exception, such as the feelings of joy, tenderness, cheerfulness, tranquillity and so on.] (WIA: 197–98)

Mann further notes that Tolstoi protested against the confusion of Europe or Western Europe with humanity in general, and that he demonstrated 'Asiatismus' (1923: 35). Certainly, he demonstrated an early interest in non-European Eastern cultures by studying Arabic and Turko-Tatar at the University of Kazanʹ, and like Goethe became increasingly interested in Eastern religions when he was older.

However, Mann rightly notes that Tolstoi's 'Asiatismus' is anti-Petrine. To this extent it is, certainly in the case of *Anna Karenina*, anti-European and nationalist; and here a point of divergence with Goethe appears. Levin is frustrated by reading European political economists such as Mill, because 'он никак не видел, почему эти законы, неприложимые к России, должны быть общие' [he didn't at all see why these laws, inapplicable to Russia, should be general]; rather, Russian peasants have a 'призвание заселять и обрабатывать огромные незанятые пространства сознательно' [vocation to settle and develop the vast unoccupied expanses consciously] (AK VIII: 364; 365). Whereas Eliot's and Tolstoi's nations, located at opposite sides of Europe, both considered that continent to be a foreign place, to Eliot openness to European culture was consistent with openness to Eastern culture, whereas for Tolstoi these cultures generated competing interpretations of Russia itself. *Anna Karenina* and *Daniel Deronda* envisage a life lived east of Europe which improves upon Europe's secularism and materialism, but for *Anna Karenina* this vision is consistent with patriotism, whereas for *Daniel Deronda* the reverse is true. According to Strich, 'Goethes Ahnenschaft [. . .] ist bei den sogenannten Westlern zu erkennen' [Goethe's influence [. . .] can be seen amongst the so-called Westernizers]; accordingly, by the time of *Anna Karenina*'s composition, Goethe had passed the peak of his influence on Tolstoi (1957: 312). Insofar as Levin and Kiti represent the good life, it is a Russian way of life.[2] It is endorsed by Kiti when she chooses to honeymoon on the land, and by her father who exaggerates his Russianness when abroad (his Westernizing wife does the reverse). Levin develops his idea of the particular characteristics of the Russian peasant, to which European measures are inappropriate:

> Он доказывал, что бедность России происходит не только от неправильного распределения поземельной собственности и ложного направления, но что этому содействовали в последнее время ненормально привитая России внешняя цивилизация, в особенности пути сообщения, железные дороги, повлекшие за собою централизацию в городах, развитие роскоши и вследствие того, в ущерб земледелию, развитие фабричной промышленности, кредита и его спутника — биржевой игры.

> [He maintained that the poverty of Russia arises not only from the unjust distribution of landed property and wrong-headed reforms, but that in recent times what had contributed to it was the unnatural cultivation in Russia of foreign civilization, especially means of communication such as railways, leading to centralization in towns, the development of luxury, and consequently the development of manufactures, credit and its companion speculation — to the detriment of agriculture. (AK IX: 55)

Levin reads in as many languages as Daniel, but without profit. Whereas *Middlemarch* implies that Casaubon's mythological project is doomed unless informed by European higher criticism, Levin on investigation decides that European philosophy and science are irrelevant to the future of Russian agriculture. Turgenev described the novel as a 'Muscovite swamp', 'all sour, with an odour of Moscow, incense, spinsterhood, the Slavophile thing and the gentry thing' (quoted in Turner 1993: 187). Correspondingly, Dostoevskii praised it as 'perfection as a work of art', demonstrating laudable religiosity and anti-Westernism (Dostoevskii II: 1069). The novel held its somewhat problematic place in the Soviet canon largely on the basis of Lenin's argument that Tolstoi's realism reflected late Tsarist social reality *невольно* [involuntarily] (Thorlby 1987: 107).

Yet 'the Slavophile thing' to which Turgenev refers is not pan-Slavism, from which Levin and Shcherbatskii distance themselves as clearly as does Klesmer Mann rightly pointed out that Goethe and Tolstoi were nationalists despite Goethe's opposition to Teutonic brotherhoods, and Tolstoi's to Slavic ones (1923: 44). Altogether, the nationalism of *Anna Karenina* is of a strictly limited kind. When Levin in his epiphany accepts Christianity as revealed to the Russian people, he considers this merely the particular form of truth accessible to *him*. The novel's presentation of debates about the Russification of the Poles is agnostic. Levin dislikes the Russians' use of French, but the novel projects no sense that nationality inheres in language, and, like *Daniel Deronda*, suggests that natural language can be circumvented by feeling (as by the acronymic language with which Levin and Kiti become engaged; the reverse is presented in Koznyshev and Varenka's apparent failure to understand each other's double-entendres when hunting for mushrooms). National distinctiveness itself is satirized in the appetite of the 'иностранный принц' [Foreign Prince] for the particular pleasures of the countries he visits (AK VIII: 375). Levin considers 'Это слово "народ" так неопределенно' [That word *people* is so undefined] (AK IX: 394), and in contrast to Mordecai he does not believe in a people's will. The novel's presentation of Europe itself is neutral; it affords emotional healing for Kiti, and (eventually) boredom for Vronskii and Anna (Pinney 1968: 83). Moreover, as mentioned in Chapter 1, *Anna Karenina* itself is orientated towards West European models of the novel. The use of ostentatiously Anglicized familiar names, although rejected by Shcherbatskii, is nonetheless maintained by the narrator throughout the novel — demonstrating the novel's ambivalence about the Westernizing of which its most prominent positive characters disapprove.

Nonetheless, it is not a major purpose of the novel to mediate either European or Eastern culture to its Russian readers.[3] Its main mediatory role is to recommend Russian country life to town dwellers. Levin's decision to spend most of his time on his estate, like Daniel's decision to spend his time amongst Jews, is seen by his social equals as eccentric. The inhabitants of the two novels' Gentile, and urban, domains view the proletarian and peasant inhabitants of the Jewish and rural domains with social and intellectual contempt, and seek their society only for pleasure, or when they have fallen on hard times. Conversely, working Jews and peasants enter high society only on business, and few of them make the return of ethical contempt. Levin's domain constitutes a more conventional pastoral than Daniel's urban slums — but the novel's contrasting Saint Petersburg atmosphere is not as corrupt as it had been represented by Pushkin, Gogol´, and Dostoevskii, and the contrasting pastoral is itself strongly qualified.

For most of the novel Levin struggles to manage peasants who are composed of Platons, Kirillovs, and Fedors (the good, the bad, and the indifferent) in roughly equal measure. The model of saintliness, Platon, is merely described to Levin by another peasant as a 'правдивый старик' [righteous elder] who does not extort rent, in contrast to the Platon of *War and Peace*, who is dramatically represented as 'олицетворением всего русского, доброго и круглого' [the personification of everything Russian, kindly, and round] ([AK IX: 380; WP VII: 51]. The earlier novel's conflation of the concepts of Christianity and the Russian peasantry (*христианство* and *крестианство* respectively) occurs as an unconscious verbal slip on the part of Platon, whereas in *Anna Karenina* the same conflation takes place in Levin's conscious observation and hope (WP 3: 190). Moreover, Levin accuses Koznyshev of what Lawrence called the 'Tolstoyan fallacy' of 'repudiating the educated world and exalting the peasant' (Verga 1928: 18–19).

> Точно как же, как он любил и хвалил деревенскую жизнь в противоположность той, которой он не любил, точно так же и народ любил он в противоположность тому классу людей, которого он не любил, и точно так же он знал народ как что-то противоположное вообще людям. В его методическом уме ясно сложились определенные формы народной жизни, выведенные отчасти из самой народной жизни, но преимущественно из противоположения. Он никогда не изменял своего мнения о народе и сочувственного к нему отношения.

[Just as he loved and praised country life in contrast with the life he did not love, so he loved the peasantry in contrast to that class of people he did not love, and so thus he knew the peasantry as a class opposed to people in general. In his methodical mind peasant life was clearly divided into distinct forms, deduced partly from that life itself, but chiefly by means of contrast. He never changed his opinion of the peasantry and his sympathetic attitude towards them.] (AK VIII: 254)

Levin and the novel are critical of categorization, and of deduction from presumed contrasts. Like *Daniel Deronda*, the novel indicates how emotional responses can be affected by found contrasts: Vronskii is durably, and Levin temporarily, attracted to the intelligent, womanly Anna as contrasted to the artless, girlish Kiti. Anna is attracted to Vronskii as contrasted with her husband, and is then the less attracted to her husband as contrasted with Vronskii. The terms *контрасть* [contrast], *сопоставление* [contrast], *противоположность* [opposition], and *противоположение* [opposition] are used with half the frequency of *contrast* in *Daniel Deronda* — which is still a relatively high rate; by contrast, *сравнение*, *сравнительный*, and *сравнительно* are used with only 3 per cent of the frequency of terms related to *comparison* in *Daniel Deronda*. Whereas Daniel is keenly aware of the differences between himself and Gwendolen (one of them being precisely her own relative inability to compare), neither Levin nor Anna are apparently aware of the obvious parallels and contrasts between their lives — nor does their narrator exhort the reader to observe them. Whereas *Daniel Deronda* is consciously occupied with the importance of comparison, *Anna Karenina* represents a very different kind of comparative literature.

Divided Art

Its two main stories are more disconnected than in *Daniel Deronda*, since there is no regular contact between their central characters.[4] After Vronskii's pursuit of Anna frees Kiti to marry Levin, the couples have no significant effect on each other. Vronskii and Anna's adultery, and their perceived mistreatment of Kiti, give both couples reason not to see one another. Thereafter Levin and Vronskii meet thrice, Anna and Levin meet for a few hours, and Anna and Kiti meet for a few minutes. The couples make no effort to learn more of each other's stories; Dolli and Oblonskii follow the two couples' stories with near-equal interest, but they also fail to compare them. Tolstoi himself asserted that 'The structural link is not the plot or the relationships (friendships) between the characters, but an inner link [. . .] the very thing that made the work important for me' (TL I: 311). Such a *link* might justify his comment that, in contrast to what he called the 'orgy' of *War and Peace*, *Anna Karenina* was a well-finished novel:

задумал лица и события, стал продолжать, потом, разумеется, изменил, и вдруг завязалось так красиво и круто, что вышел роман, который я нынче кончил начерно, роман очень живой, горячий и законченный, которым я очень доволен.

[I thought up characters and events, started on it, and then, of course, changed it — then suddenly everything became so tightly and beautifully bound-up that

> a novel emerged, which I finished today in draft form, a very lively, passionate, well-finished novel, with which I am very pleased.] (Donskov 2003: 1, 101)[5]

There are strong similarities between critical treatments of the double-plotting of *Daniel Deronda* and of *Anna Karenina*, which reflect both critical fashions and the novels' similarities. Critics have divided into those who have stressed the connection of *Anna Karenina*'s stories (particularly in the last four decades), and those who have stressed their disconnection, some of whom (also more recent) have found significance in this condition. Those who have stressed disconnection have often remarked on the failure of the hero's story wholly to contextualize the heroine's. As has been the case for many Gentile readers of *Daniel Deronda*, the heroine's story has held the balance of interest. The Russian critic Avseenko wrote in the journal *Русский мир* [*The Russian World*] in 1875 that the Levin scenes 'lack the dramatic element and slow down the development of the story' (quoted in Knowles 1978: 265). Leavis found that:

> there is no sign that Tolstoi, the highly and subtly conscious artist, could have recognized the novel's significance as being anything but what the tragedy of Anna, implicitly commented on by the context in general and the Levin–Kitty theme in particular, conveys. (1967: 14)

Most criticism of *Anna Karenina*, in most countries, has concerned Anna's story. The French translation of the novel to which Nathan Haskell Dole referred retained only part of Levin and Kiti's story, as have several of the film adaptations of *Anna Karenina*; Clarence Brown's, Julien Duvivier's, and Alexander Zarkhi's versions of 1935, 1947, and 1967 respectively, all end with Anna's suicide (Birdwood-Hedger 2006: 72). Of these the first gives more time to Oblonskii and Dolli than to Levin and Kiti, returning the novel towards the state of its first draft, before Levin had been introduced (Schultze 1982: 13). In the standard final version of the novel, by contrast, slightly over half of the 239 chapters (126) concern Levin and his associates to the exclusion of Anna and hers. As Alexandrov flatly notes: the author 'did not make it clear what the relations between the two halves are' (2004: 95).

The other perennial question of *Anna Karenina* criticism is to what extent and how justifiably Anna is suggested by the novel to be deserving of her fate. This chapter is based on the perception that the relations of this question to that of the novel's double-plotting have not yet been sufficiently considered. Some critics have found Anna to deserve her fate, others have found her not to, and some in each category have found the novel to concur with them. Early European critics such as Matthew Arnold and Melchior de Vogüé endorsed what they judged to be the novel's condemnation of Anna, whereas Russian critics including Lev Shestov, Nikolai Strakhov, and Dmitrii Sviatopolk-Mirskii, interpreted the novel in a similar way, but criticized it for this. Some critics, including Amy Mandelker, have found the novel not to condemn Anna. However, many have found the novel to be internally conflicted. Viktor Shklovskii, Mark Aldanov, Henri Troyat, Judith Armstrong, George Steiner, Mary Evans, and Harold Bloom all proposed variants of the idea that Tolstoi's condemnation of Anna was contradicted by his love and admiration for her; D. H. Lawrence and Peter Jones found his condemnation of Anna to be subverted by the novel's artistry (and, in Lawrence's case, by Tolstoi's deeply sensual nature). Mann found the novel's attitudes towards the society which condemns Anna to be self-contradictory. Isaiah Berlin, A. N. Wilson, and Sidney Schultze found a contradiction in the novel between what Mikhail Bakhtin would term *разноречие* [*the monologic*] and *многоязычие* [*the heteroglossic*]: between condemnation of Anna, and agnosticism as to her guilt. Vladimir Alexandrov found the whole novel to be polyphonic, with every issue capable of several different interpretations. A majority of the novel's critics have found in the novel at least some impulse to condemn Anna, and of these, many have found other aspects of the novel to contradict it; overall, however, critics have complained louder and longer about Anna's treatment than about Gwendolen's. Certainly, the later Tolstoi had no qualms about the imposition of narrative justice. Although his own didactic tales rarely juxtapose simple reward and punishment, he approved of tales which did, giving as examples of 'настоящее искусство' [real art] Christ's parables, which include stories of men who build their houses on rock and on sand, and of wise and foolish virgins; the fact that Tolstoi also classified *Adam Bede* as 'религиозное искусство' [religious art] suggests that, like Eliot herself, he did not entirely shun what she denounced as the 'moral denouement' (WIA: 200; Ashton 1992: 130).

Anna, Leviticus, and Deuteronomy

In Anna's as in Gwendolen's case, the concept of the scapegoat is of some relevance in exploring this condition. Tolstoi was aware of the concept: 'Войдя в гостиную, Степан Аркадьич извинился, объяснил, что был задержан тем князем, который был всегдашним козлом-искупителем всех его опаздываний и отлучек' [On entering the drawing room Stepan Arkadich apologized, explaining that he had been detained by that prince who was the constant scapegoat for all his latenesses and absences] (AK VIII: 405). *Anna Karenina* implicitly suggests that Anna is a scapegoat of her urban, aristocratic domain, and therefore *in* her text. Men and women in *свет* [high society] practice adultery and fornication with impunity, but Anna is singled out for persecution because she commits adultery in a manner which befits her erstwhile membership of the 'совесть[ю] петербургского общества' (conscience of Petersburg society) — with deep consciousness of guilt, and (eventual) transparency towards Karenin and society (AK VIII: 136). As Shklovskii put it, 'это не адюльтер, а большая любовь' [this is not adultery, but a great love]; as such, discreet adulteresses such as Vronskii's mother and Betsi Tverskaia refuse to countenance it (1967: 348). Of course, they do not shun Vronskii; as a woman Anna belongs to a group which, as Girard argues is often the case with scapegoats, is 'particulièrement exposée[s] a la persecution' [particularly susceptible to persecution] (1982: 30)

Anna's downfall, like Gwendolen's, has a tragic aspect. Tolstoi had taught himself Ancient Greek just before starting *Anna Karenina*, and although there is no firm evidence that he read Greek tragedies, this was a period in which he intensively read plays, and it is highly likely that he did so (Troyat 1968: 453–54). Anna's story bears some of the characteristic marks of a Greek tragedy. She falls from high estate (the aristocracy of the world's most powerful land empire) to suicide as a result of yielding to her passion after 'почти целый год' [almost a whole year] of resistance (AK VIII: 159). After capitulating to Vronskii, her *anagnorisis* is immediate and fully conscious. Her *peripeteia* occurs in stages, and is sometimes itself reversed, as during her initial happiness with Vronskii in Italy, and on his estate — but it nonetheless results in her destruction. She bears her situation with frankness and dignity, as Golenishchev and Levin perceive. Her catastrophe fulfils omens: the killing of a worker by the train which brings Anna to Vronskii, and the comment of 'приятельница Анны' [Anna's friend] that 'женщины с тенью обыкновенно дурно кончают' [women with a shadow usually end badly] (AK VIII: 145). The dead protagonist is kept off the narrative stage, first to be seen by an anonymous witness (at Obiralovka station), and only later to be described in Vronskii's memory. Like Gwendolen's, Anna's domain offers her no chorus, because it is unable to conceive of tragedy. Betsi Tverskaia speaks with equanimity in explaining to Anna that the same thing (for example Liza Merkalova's chronic adultery) 'можно смотреть трагически и сделать из нее мученье, и смотреть просто и даже весело. Можеть быть, вы склоны смотреть на вещи слишком трагически' [can be looked at tragically and turned into a misery, or can be looked at simply and even cheerfully. It could be that you're inclined to look at things too tragically] (AK VIII: 317). Even those inhabitants of St Petersburg society who condemn its triviality (Lidiia Ivanovna and her circle) are Christian, and inimical to the idea of tragedy. Betsi Tverskaia and her circle, in their inability to imagine tragic adultery, shun those who do imagine it. When Anna asks 'Хуже ли я других, или лучше? Я думаю, хуже' [Am I worse than others, or better? I think, worse], Betsi's response, 'Ужасный ребенок, ужасный ребенок' [*Enfant terrible, enfant terrible*] both exemplifies the light-hearted tone which Betsi considers more appropriate to the discussion of adultery, and implicitly endorses Anna's self-criticism as being worse than other adulteresses' complacency (AK VIII: 317). One of the causes and effects of Anna's scapegoating by her society is its refusal to recognize her as tragic.

Yet certain features of the narrative itself undermine Anna's possible tragic status. They include those which imply that her suffering is justified, and those which lower her stature. The deterioration of Anna's character, her abandonment of her son, and her lack of interest in her daughter, make her suffering seem more inevitable and appropriate. Her insistence on attending the theatre in Saint Petersburg after her return from Italy is less defiant than febrile, as her response to Madame Kartasova's insult reveals. She becomes obsessed with attracting Vronskii — a phenomenon interpreted by Lawrence as her 'great sex goal', demanding 'at last the departure into death [. . .] Like Carmen, or like Anna Karenin', and which he praises Tolstoi for rejecting (PUFU: 200). During her final journey she is presented as psychologically disturbed — but there is no suggestion, as in Greek tragedy, that such disturbance has been externally imposed. Although she suffers by virtue of relative superiority within her own domain, compared to Levin's domain she appears an exemplar as well as a victim of its faults. As in Gwendolen's case, there is a problem of agency. Anna's religious and ethical education is shallow, and even by the end of the novel she is insufficiently percipient to criticize society for its responsibility for her faults. The ignoble aspect of her character and her spiritual decline, like that of Macbeth, may be seen to undermine both her tragic status, and any possibility that she is scapegoated *by* her text.

However, since her characterization is inconsistent, some of her flaws can be attributed to authorial imposition. Whereas Gwendolen's suffering is a credible outcome of her encounter with Grandcourt given the initial presentation of her character, Anna's ethical and emotional decline after finding happiness with Vronskii in Italy is not predictable from her character as initially presented. Peter Jones finds Anna's failure and Levin's relative success to be 'equally false conclusions in the light of everything else we have been shown in the novel; they are conclusions apparently imposed by the author upon the implicit argument, and against its principal burden' (1975: 110). It is as though the progression which Anna's character had made through successive drafts of the novel from the plump, crude, seductive coquette Tatiana who 'берет жемчуг в губы, разговариваем слишком громко' [takes her pearls in her mouth whilst talking too loudly], to the woman whom Vronskii encounters at the station in Moscow, is partially reversed over the course of the novel — Tolstoi's earlier impulse to punish female adultery having come again to the fore (Shklovskii 1967: 348). (An alternative thesis to the idea that Tolstoi's punishment of Anna is contradicted by his love for her is that Tolstoi was testing how good and apparently noble he might make an adulteress.) However, as Shklovskii notes, 'первые наброски и первые свойства героев не изчезнут, они не будут сняты совсем, а войдут как елементы противоречия в роман' [the first outlines and the first characteristics of the leading characters will not disappear, will not be completely taken away, but they will go as elements of contradiction into the novel] (1967: 348). Vladimir Solov´ev, reviewing that part of the novel which had been published by 1875, had already found her characterization to bifurcate: 'one [Anna] comes directly out of the novel while the other from the author's own attitude to her. Therefore when he writes about her directly it seems that he is not speaking about the woman he is describing' (quoted in Knowles 1978: 249). Anna's presentation can be inconsistent even within the space of a few pages. When Anna appeals to Dolli to forgive her brother 'Участие и любовь непритворные видны были на лице Анны' [Sympathy and unfeigned love were visible on Anna's face] (AK VIII: 76). Yet when Dolli has left the room, 'Стива, — сказала она ему, весело подмигивая, крестя его и указывая на дверь глазами. — Иди, и помогай тебе бог' ['Stiva,' she said to him, winking merrily, making the sign of the cross on him, and indicating the door with her eyes, 'Go, and God help you'] (AK VIII: 80). Bernard Williams argues that 'however inevitable Tolstoy ultimately makes [Anna's downfall] seem, it could, relative to her earlier thoughts, have been otherwise', yet rather than attributing this to the author's will, he attributes it to 'a matter of intrinsic luck, and a failure in the heart of her project' (1993: 41). In fact, Anna's downfall is partly the result of her scapegoating by her text. Lawrence blamed Tolstoi for implying that her and Vronskii's 'tragedy' stems from 'phallic' sin, since 'all the tragedy comes from Vronsky's and Anna's fear of *society* [. . .] They couldn't live in the pride of their sincere passion, and spit in Mother Grundy's eye' (STH: 180). Written in the year after his elopement, this indirect exhortation to himself and Frieda ignores the fact that Tolstoi, as part of his own punishment of phallic sin, makes Anna incapable of living in the pride of her sincere passion.

There exists a contradiction between Anna's scapegoating in the text and her scapegoating by the text, since the narrative not only criticizes those who censure Anna for and only for the openness of her adultery, but also implicitly supports them in condemning open adultery more than discreet adultery. Newton comments that 'it is difficult to think of any other novel that convincingly suggests that a bad marriage is preferable to an extra-marital affair in which there is genuine love on both sides; *Anna Karenina* is such a novel' (1986: 170). It also suggests that had Anna remained with Karenin whilst conducting her affair, she would have wronged Karenin and Sergei less, and not have destroyed Vronskii and herself. (The only detail which suggests the contrary is the fact that Sergei seems hardly traumatized by his mother's disappearance, and appears to grow up healthily in Karenin's care.) The implication that Anna's *hubris* lies in her attempt to 'spit in Mother Grundy's eye' is supported by Tolstoi's comment to Kramskoi in the summer of 1875 that: 'One thing's certain. Anna's going to die — vengeance will be wreaked on her. She wanted to rethink life in her own way'. His answer to Kramskoi's question 'How should one think?' is: 'One must try to live by the faith which one has sucked in with one's mother's milk and without arrogance of the mind' (quoted in Wilson 1988: 278). Betsi Tverskaia's circle has absorbed neither mother's milk nor faith, but nonetheless collaborates with the narrative in punishing Anna's double transgression. Thomas Mann was right to find 'a certain contradiction inherent in the author's originally moral theme, in the charge he raises against society; for one wonders what weapon of punishment God might use if society behaved other than it does' (AK G: xix–xx).

The tension between Anna's scapegoating in, and by, her text can be explored in relation to the divergent interpretations which have been offered of the novel's epigraph. 'Мне отмщение, и аз воздам' is the standard Slavonic translation of one of God's prophecies quoted by Paul to the Romans. The passage from the King James Authorized translation of the Bible (italicized below) is:

> Dearly beloved, avenge not yourselves, but rather give place unto wrath: for it is written, *Vengeance is mine; I will repay*, saith the Lord. Therefore if thine enemy hunger, feed him [. . .] Be not overcome of evil, but overcome evil with good. (Romans 12. 19–21)

The second and third sentences quoted above make clear that Paul cites in the spirit of the passage from Leviticus in which God tells Moses:

> Thou shalt not avenge, nor bear any grudge against the children of thy people, but thou shalt love thy neighbour as thyself: I am the Lord. (Leviticus 19. 18)

However, Paul is not quoting this passage, but is slightly misquoting from Moses' song in Deuteronomy (the degree of misquotation is similar in Hebrew, Russian, and English):

> To me belongeth vengeance, and recompence; their foot shall slide in due time: for the day of their calamity is at hand, and the things that shall come upon them make haste. For the Lord shall judge his people. (Deuteronomy 32. 35–36)

An emphasis on the Levitican and Pauline senses points to the novel's censure of scapegoating in the text (three chapters before the passage quoted above from Leviticus, God institutes the practice of using scapegoats, which *protected* men from the consequences of their sins) (Leviticus 16. 21–34). It therefore also points to the injustice of Anna's suffering. Kropotkin found that 'it was the opinion of the Betsies — surely not Superhuman Justice — which brought Karénina to suicide', and Shklovskii concurred that 'не бог, а люди, те люди, которые ненавидели самого Толстого, бросает Анну под колеса поезда' [not God, but people, those people who hated Tolstoi himself, pushed Anna under the wheels of the train] (Kropotkin 1916: 135, and Shklovskii 1967: 349). These interpretations are supported by Tolstoi's admiration for four books by other authors, at around the time of writing *Anna Karenina*. In March 1872 Tolstoi wrote to Pisemskii in praise of his novel of the previous year, *Во Водоворотъ* [*In the Whirlpool*], which refrains from judgement of an adulteress who commits suicide (Tolstoi 1910: 97). In 1891 he stated that between the ages of thirty-five and fifty (1863–78) Mrs Wood, Trollope, and George Eliot had had a great influence on him (Tolstoi 1978 II: 486). I shall take these authors in the order in which Tolstoi listed them. In *East Lynne* (1861) the character Carlyle quotes Romans 12. 20 in order to explain why he will not take action against a man who has wronged him (Wood 2000: 563). In *Phineas Redux* (1876) Kennedy unsuccessfully defends himself from a charge of vengefulness by quoting the same passage to Phineas (Trollope 1964 I: 250). In 1885 Tolstoi specifically expressed his admiration for *Felix Holt* (1866), in which Mrs Transome's adultery is treated sympathetically and even tragically. Eikhenbaum thought that Tolstoi chose his epigraph after finding it quoted by Schopenhauer in *Die Welt als Wille und Vorstellung* [*The World as Will and Representation*] (first read by Tolstoi in 1869), where Schopenhauer uses it in support of his condemnation of *jus talionis*. This condemnation is congruent with the 'Christliche Ethik, welche alle Vergeltung des Bösen mit Bösem schlechthin untersagt [. . .] "die Rache is mein, Ich will vergelten, spricht der Herr". Röm. 12, 19' [Christian ethic, which absolutely prohibits every repayment of evil by evil [. . .] 'Vengeance is mine, I will repay, says the Lord'. Romans 12. 19] (Schopenhauer 1987: 515). Eikhenbaum himself comments: 'no person has the authority of power to set himself up as a purely moral judge and avenger', for which reason 'the Bible says *Vengeance is mine*' (1974: 170–71). Dostoevskii, in relation to *Anna Karenina*, thought that:

> Ясно и понятно до очевидности, что зло таится в человечестве глубже, чем предполагают лекаря-социалисты, что ни в каком устройстве общества не избегнете зла, что душа человечкствая останется та же, что ненормальность и грех изходят из нее самой и что, наконец, законы духа человеческого столь еще неизвестны, столь неведомы науке, столь неопределены и столь таинственны, что нет и не может быть еще ни лекарей, ни даже судей *окончательных*, а есть Тот, Который говорит: 'Мне отмщение и Аз воздам'.

> [It is clear and understood to the point of obviousness that evil lies deeper in humanity than the doctor-socialists suppose, that no ordering of society will be able to expel evil, that the human soul will remain as it is, that abnormality and sin come from the soul itself, and, finally, that the laws of the human soul

are so still unknown, so unknown to science, so undefined and so mysterious, that there is not and cannot yet be any healers, nor even a judgment that is *final*, but there is He Who says: 'Vengeance is mine, I will repay'.] (Dostoevskii n.d.: 280)

Tolstoi went further in a letter of May 1873 to Strakhov:

> Объективой сущности жизни человек понять и выразить не может — это первые. Сущность же жизни — то, что заставляет жить, есть потребность того, что мы называем неправильно добро. Добро есть только противоположность зла, как свет — тьмы, и как и света и тьмы абсолютных нет, так и нет добро и зла. А добро и зло суть только матерьялы, на которых образуется красота — т.е. то, что мы любим без причины, без пользы, без нужды.

> [The objective essence of life can't be understood or expressed by humans — that's the first thing. The essence of life — that which makes us live, is the demand for what we wrongly call good. Good is only the opposite of evil, as light is of darkness, and just as there is no absolute light and dark, so there is no good and evil. Rather, the essence of good and evil are only materials out of which beauty is formed — that is, that which we love without cause, without profit, without need.] (Donskov 2003 1: 110)

In the same letter he wrote that he had finished a draft of *Anna Karenina*.

His position here exemplifies what Orwin calls Tolstoi's 'metaphysics of opposites'. In *Толстой в Современнике* [*Tolstoi in 'The Contemporary'*] Eikhenbaum identified an appetite for contraries in Tolstoi's unwillingness to choose between the rival ideological positions of the journal and Russian society at large in the mid-1850s, and noted that Chernyshevskii found in Tolstoi a love which reconciled seeming contradictions. He also quoted from Tolstoi's notebook of April and May 1857:

> There are two minds. According to one, the logical, small mind, for civilization to advance is a good thing; the good according to the other, which looks down from above, is an equal compensation in the absence of civilization. According to a third, even higher, into whose realm I can glance only for a moment at a time, both together are just. (quoted in Orwin 1993: 76)

In the same year Tolstoi wrote *Luzern*, which includes the comment:

> кто видел такое состояние, в котором бы не было добра и зла вместе? И почему я знаю, что вижу больше одного, чем другого, не оттого, что стою не на настоящем месте? И кто в состоянии так совершенно оторваться умом хоть на мгновение от жизни, чтобы независимо сверху взглянуть на нее?

> [Who has seen a situation in which there was not good and evil together? And how do I know that I see more of one than the other because I am not standing in the right place? And who is able to tear his mind even for a moment away from life so as to view it independently from above?] (Tolstoi 1921: 25)

At the same time, his diaries reveal that he had been reading Goethe intensively; the God in *Faust* defends the necessity even of Mephistopheles. Orwin concludes from this: 'Both indirectly, then, and directly through Goethe's work Tolstoy knew of the theory of polarity as a primal phenomenon of life. *War and Peace*', even in its title, 'is saturated with the idea' (Orwin 1993: 80). Levin changes his mind repeatedly over the course of *Anna Karenina*, his likeable friend Sviazhskii acts in a way sharply contrary to his firmly expressed convictions, and many of the debates between characters are recounted with narrative agnosticism.

The Pauline quotation of the novel's epigraph can itself be thought of as self-contradictory: 'Здесь все противоречиво, как противоречат себе обычно религиозные нормы. "Побеждай зло добром", но бог покарает, то, что ты простил, значит самое прощение есть возмездие' [Everything is contradictory here, just as the religious maxims usually contradict themselves. 'Overcome evil with good': but God will punish what you have forgiven, which means that forgiveness itself is vengeance] (Shklovskii 1967: 349). The embrace of opposites cannot, except at a second order level, be reconciled with its contrary, and *Anna Karenina* (written when Tolstoi was beginning to turn against Goethe) also contains strong suggestions of condemnation. A number of critics have argued that Tolstoi takes on the role of Deuteronomy's God. In 1900 Shestov wrote: 'Ей ждет отмщение. Ей воздаст гр. Толстой' [Vengeance is waiting for her, and Tolstoi will give it to her]:

> Она согрешила и должна принять наказание. Во всей русской, а, может быть, и в иностранной литературе ни один художник так безжалостно и спокойно не подводил своего героя к одижающей его страшной участи, как ето сделал гр. Толстой в своем роман с Анной. Мало сказать безжалостно и спокойно — с радостью и торжеством. Позорный и мучительный конец Анны для графа Толстого — отрадное знамение.
>
> [She has sinned and she must be punished. In all of Russian and possibly even foreign literature no artist has so pitilessly and calmly led his hero to the awful fate which awaits him as has Tolstoy Anna. And not only pitilessly and calmly but joyously and triumphantly. For Tolstoy the shameful and tormented end of Anna is a pleasing sight.] (1907: 3)

Eikhenbaum, notwithstanding his observation concerning Schopenhauer, argued that 'Дело не в том, что Толстой передает решение вопроса о виновности и преступности на волю бога, а в том, что этот самый бог (уже, несомненно, по воле Толстого как автор романа) считает, по-видимому, нужным "воздать" Анне ее преступления' [The issue is not that Tolstoi makes the deciding of the question of guilt and criminality subject to the will of God, but that this God (already, doubtlessly, subject to the will of Tolstoi as the author of the novel) apparently decides that it is necessary to 'repay' Anna for her crime] (Eikhenbaum 1974: 161). Eikhenbaum also argued that Tolstoi increased Anna's guilt after reading Dumas's treatise *L'Homme-Femme* (1872), which countenances the murder of faithless wives (1974: 170). Tolstoi praised that novel for its 'lofty understanding of marriage' three weeks before starting *Anna Karenina*; the epigraph itself was first attached to an early draft (quoted in Turner 1993: 111; Schultze 1982: 12). Shklovskii noted that 'Дюма-сын написал книгу, которая внезапно очень понравилось Толстому; там решается дело просто: "убей ее, убей неверную жену" — она преступница' [Tolstoy took a sudden liking to the book by Dumas the younger, in which a simple solution is proposed: 'Kill her, kill the unfaithful wife' — she is a criminal] (Shklovskii 1967: 348). Before completing *Anna Karenina*, Tolstoi had started work on *Крейцерова соната* [*The Kreutzer Sonata*] (1889), in which Pozdnyshev blames his wife for devoting herself to her sexual attractiveness; Anna's chief concern by the end of her life is to maintain her attractiveness to Vronskii.

Tolstoi's own interventions in the critical disputes concerning the meaning of the epigraph favour the interpretation of the epigraph as vengeful. Thirty years after completing *Anna Karenina* he wrote that 'I chose the epigraph simply in order to explain the idea that the bad things people do have as their consequence all the bitter things, which come not from people, but from God, and that is what Anna Karenina herself experienced' (quoted in Orwin 1993: 81). On balance the effect of the novel is such that the epigraph's Pauline context of love and *its* Levitican source are somewhat weaker than the vengeful spirit of the quotation's direct Deuteronomic source. Anna is 'repaid' more thoroughly than is the society which arrogates to itself God's responsibility, and the representation of Anna's scapegoating in the text is partly undermined by her scapegoating *by* the text. Those features of Anna's presentation which accord her a hypothetical tragic status measure the degree of her failure fully to attain it. Yet since the failure is not absolute, they function less at Anna's expense than at that of the society which denies her tragic status because it cannot conceive of tragedy. They also ensure that Anna is always nobler than two of the adulteresses with whom Tolstoi and his contemporary readers would most have been inclined to compare her: Hélène Kuragina and Emma Bovary.

Anna, Vronskii, Levin, and Oblonskii

In relation to the high society which condemns Anna, Vronskii's function is complex. On the one hand he epitomizes its venality and banality to a greater degree than Anna ever does, and when he is chosen to show Russia's pleasures to the epicurean visiting Prince, sees himself unflatteringly reflected. On the other hand, he rises as far as Anna above the level of casual adultery despite the greater social sanction for men to act on this level. The dual aspect to his character is less strikingly contradictory than is the case with Anna, but it is also the residual effect of his initial characterization (in his case, as a rake). As a result of this contradiction, his position in the novel has aspects of three distinct types: a Mephistophelian representative of a corrupt society who successfully tempts Anna to her downfall; a man who sins but who, not being married, a mother, or a woman, does so less than Anna and is accordingly less completely destroyed; and a man who devotes himself to his love as completely as Anna but who, in contrast to her, does not degenerate into jealousy and hatred. The first correlates with the novel's implied condemnation of both Anna and her society, but not with Vronskii's love for Anna. The second fits with the hypothesis of Anna's scapegoating either in or by her text. The third allows Vronskii to be seen as a touchstone of decency and sanity, who is also willing to set society at defiance. The last aspect aroused Lawrence's respect: he noted that Frieda found 'Anna very much like herself, only inferior — Vronsky is not much like me — too much my superior' (although at the end of the letter he added 'Forgive this rubbish') (LL, 1, 463). Vronskii loves Anna even in her damaged condition; unlike Medea, who rightly accuses her abductor Jason of abandoning her to marry a young Princess, Anna wrongly suspects Vronskii of the same, and ruins his life in retaliation for it. Vronskii therefore both counters the text's implied condemnation of Anna, and contrasts with her in a manner which undermines her claim to tragic status, and indicates a rival tragic status of his own. He falls from the high estate of the Saint Petersburg officer class to virtual suicide in battle because of a love to which he claims himself to be passive ('Я не могу иначе' [I cannot do otherwise]) (AK VIII: 112). Like Oedipus, he suffers a disastrous reversal of happiness in his relationship with a woman, in the wake of which she commits suicide and he effectively destroys himself; like Theseus, he abandons life after the death of the woman he abducted. Like both, he gains in stature through his suffering, announcing at his departure for Serbia: 'как орудие, я могу годиться на что-нибудь. Но, как человек, я — развалина' [as a weapon, I may be useful for something. But, as a person, I — am a ruin] — a claim particularly admired by Lawrence, who commented: 'Better Vronsky's final statement [. . .] than Tolstoi and Tolstoi-ism and that beastly peasant blouse the old man wore' (AK IX: 366; PUFU: 200). In almost his last appearance in the novel he is ignoring what the inveterately comic Oblonskii has to say to him (AK IX: 360).

Nonetheless, despite its limitations, Anna's tragedy is dominant over Vronskii's. The fact that the latter arouses more pity from people of their own society (a Princess at the railway station says 'Как ни говорите, меня трогает судьба этого человека' [Say what you like, I am moved by this man's fate]) does not work in its favour (AK IX: 360). Vronskii's mother's perspective that Anna is responsible for his downfall is consistent with Lawrence's view that Anna is 'never satisfied' until she has 'shattered the man who responded to' her — but not with Vronskii's initial, protracted, pursuit of her (SCAL: 249). Anna is not an Emma Bovary or a Rosamund Vincy, who ruins a serious, career-minded husband. Vronskii's tragedy is most apparent in the shadow of those moments in which Anna's is most apparent. He tries to commit suicide after a visit to Anna when she seems to be dying; when he in effect tries again, it is in the wake of her having successfully done so. Her volubly excited mind before her suicide is quoted at length, whereas of Vronskii it is merely stated by his mother that for six weeks he did not speak: 'Prostration complète, говорил доктор. Потом началось почти бешенство' ['Prostration complète' the doctor said. And that was followed almost by madness] (AK IX: 364). On the journey from Moscow to Tsaritsino the narration is focused not on Vronskii but on the doubtful worth of his fellow volunteers. The omens concerning the peasant working on the railway track are witnessed and dreamed by Vronskii as well as Anna, and apply also to him, who is also last seen at a railway station — but only secondarily. When his toothache is forgotten in his mental anguish, the content of that anguish is Anna:

> Щемящая боль крепкого зуба, наполнявшая слюною его рот, мешала емуговорить. Он замолк, вглядываясь в колеса медленно и гладко подкатывавшегося по рельсам тендера.
> И вдруг совершенно другая, не боль, а общая мучительная внутренняя неловкость заставила его забыть на мгновение боль зуба.

[He could hardly speak for the throbbing ache in his strong teeth, which were like rows of ivory in his mouth. He was silent, and his eyes rested on the wheels of the tender, slowly and smoothly rolling along the rails.

And all at once a different pain, not an ache, but an inner trouble, that set his whole being in anguish, made him for an instant forget his toothache.] (AK IX: 366)

Levin's comedy is not so easily overshadowed by Anna's tragedy, but its effect upon her representation is equally complex. Levin condemns Anna neither as much as does the novel as a whole, nor as much as he condemns the society which shuns her. Although he does not invite Anna to visit Pokrovskoe, or visit her himself at Vozdvizhenskoe, he counteracts society's isolation of her to the extent of providing the horse which Dolli uses to visit her. His most strident condemnation of promiscuous women is undermined by the scene in which it occurs, as he himself becomes aware. When he asserts to Oblonskii in the Англия [England] restaurant, of illicit love, that 'При такой любви не может быть никакой драмы [. . .] А для платонический любви не может быть драмы, потому что в такой любви все ясно и чисто, потому что' [In such love there can't be any kind of tragedy [. . .] And in Platonic love there can't be tragedy, because in that kind of love everything is clear and pure, because] and then suddenly recollects 'своих грехах и о внутренней борьбе, которую он пережил' [his own sins, and the inner struggle he had lived through], Oblonskii's sceptically twinkling eyes, and Levin's absurd situation eating a gargantuan gourmet meal which he does not enjoy and will pay for, undermine his idealism (AK VIII: 49). His denial of the tragedy of adultery is negatively implicated by its repetition in Betsi Tverskaia's subsequent assertion to Anna. In two later conversations about adultery during hunting expeditions with Oblonskii, Levin is non-committal.

His domain, which consists of the Russian countryside in general and his estate at Pokrovskoe in particular, is more serious than Anna's. Like Tolstoi, Levin strives continuously to perfect himself. However, his and Daniel's domains differ more than do Anna's and Gwendolen's banally comic domains, which have much in common. Neither his nor his peasants' view of life is epic, tragic, or tragicomic; his own views veer from despairing atheism to ecstatic theism. Some of the differences between the conceptions of good offered by the heroes' domains can be expressed in terms of Arnold's Hellenism and Hebraism, adumbrated in *Culture and Anarchy* three years before *Anna Karenina* was started. *Anna Karenina* makes no positive representations of German academia, and implicitly criticizes the novel's intellectuals and Levin for what in Arnold's terms may be described as excessive Hellenism (revealing a strain of anti-intellectualism which connects Tolstoi to Lawrence but not to Eliot). That part of Anna's domain which centres on Betsi Tverskaia lacks Hebraism even of Gascoigne's kind, whereas Hebraism is represented in Levin's domain by Platon, Kiti, and Shcherbatskii. Daniel's Helleno-Hebraic domain, then, contrasts with Levin's Hebraic domain. It differs from it also in the grandeur of its idealism. To compare their impoverished, prophetic, dying consumptives: Nikolai has a 'период(е) набожности, постов, монахов, служб церковных, когда [. . .] никто не только не поддержал его, но все, и он сам, смеялись над ним [. . .] звали его Ноем, монахом' [pious stage, of fasts, monks, church services, when [. . .] not only had no-one encouraged him, but everyone, and he (Levin) himself had jeered at him [. . .] called him Noah and Monk] (AK VIII: 94). Mordecai lives similarly, but with the sustained rhetorical support of the narrative, his death is more hopeful, and his contribution towards the creation of a state of Israel is taken far more seriously than is Nikolai's projected 'артель слесарную' [locksmith's workshop] as a step towards communism (AK VIII: 97). In contrast to *Daniel Deronda* neither domain of *Anna Karenina* demonstrates much faith in art. On the other hand, Plautine comedy, such as that with which Eliot depicts the Cohen family, is absent from Levin's peasantry. As Auerbach observes in *Mimesis*, in Russia the Classical association of the lower social orders with the comic had never pertained to the same extent as in Europe. Russians had:

> die Möglichkeit, das Alltägliche auf ernste Weise zu begreifen [. . .] eine klassizistische Ästhetik, die eine literarische Kategorie des Niedrigen grund-sätzlich von ernster Behandlung ausschließt, in Rußland niemals sicheren Boden zu gewinnen vermochte. Zugleich drängt sich bei Betrachtung der russischen [. . .] Realistik die Beobachtung auf, daß sie auf einer christlich-altpatriarchalischen Vorstellung von der kreatürlichen Würde eines jeden Menschen beruht, gleichviel welchen Standes und welcher Lage; daß sie also in ihren Grundlagen eher dem altchristlichen Realismus verwandt ist als dem modern-westeuropäischen.

> [the possibility of taking everyday things seriously [. . .] a Classicizing aesthetics which excludes from serious treatment a literary category of the low could never gain a firm hold in Russia. Then as soon as we think of Russian realism [. . .] we cannot avoid observing that it is based on a Christian old-patriarchal concept of the natural dignity of every person regardless of social rank and position, and therefore that it is fundamentally more closely related to old-Christian than to modern occidental realism.] (Auerbach 1946: 463)

Nonetheless, the effect of the hero's domain on the heroine is similar to that in *Daniel Deronda*: Levin's changing visions of goodness, culminating in an epiphanic vision of divine comedy, give limited resonance to Anna's tragedy.[6] In addition, the two protagonists' stories contrast ostentatiously in ways which suggest ethical comparison at Anna's expense. The patterning which reveals their differences extends even to triviality: Anna returns to Saint Petersburg to find her dress unmade because her instructions have been ignored; Levin returns to Pokrovskoe to find his buckwheat burned because his instructions have been ignored. Oblonskii, Anna, Vronskii, Kiti, and Levin begin their stories in Moscow, where Anna and Levin meet Vronskii, and both see Kiti. From this middle ground Anna and Vronskii, and Levin, travel in opposite directions geographically and ethically to Saint Petersburg and Pokrovskoe. Anna and Vronskii elope whilst Kiti and Levin marry, but Anna gives birth before this time, whereas Kiti does so afterwards. Anna and Vronskii travel in Italy, whilst Kiti and Levin honeymoon in the country. Later both couples live on the land, where they are visited by friends and relatives. Anna and Levin study agricultural treatises, and draw opposite conclusions from them. Anna is shunned by, and Levin is shunning, *свет* [society]. The couples return to Moscow, where Levin and Anna meet, Levin becomes a father, and Anna (at Obiralovka) commits suicide. Thereafter Vronskii and Levin aspire towards suicide, but only

Levin finds reason to live. Insofar as Levin's story successfully makes Anna's sufferings seem relatively deserved, his presence reduces her scapegoating by the text — the more convincingly, since he is not involved in her scapegoating *in* the text. On the other hand, insofar as Anna's downfall is perceived to be on its own terms underjustified, and a foil to Levin's relative success, Levin can be considered to be an involuntary agent of Anna's scapegoating *by* her text; as Empson remarked, 'This power of suggestions is the strength of the double plot; once you take the two parts to correspond, any character [. . .] seems to cause what he corresponds to' (1950: 34). As Anna became increasingly sympathetic in successive drafts, Levin's role expanded, as though in counterbalance. Shestov found that:

> Если бы Анна могла пережить свой позор, если бы у ней осталось сознание своих человеческих прав и она умерла не раздавленной и уничтоженной, а правой и гордой, у гр. Толстого была бы отнята та точка опоры, благодаря которой он мог сохранить свое душевное равновесие. Пред ним явилась альтернатива — Анна или он сам, ея гибель или его спасение. И он пожертвовал Анной, которая при живом муж пошла за Вронским

> [If Anna could have survived her shame, retained a consciousness of her rights as a person, and died not overwhelmed and annihilated but righteous and proud then Tolstoi would have lost that fulcrum which allowed him to retain his spiritual equilibrium. The alternative presented itself to him — Anna or himself, her destruction or his salvation. And he sacrificed Anna, who had gone to Vronskii whilst her husband was alive] (1907: 3–4)

Two under-acknowledged factors mean that unmediated comparison of their behaviour is unfair. First, they are at very different stages in their marriages. Several of Tolstoi's protagonists before and after *Anna Karenina* pursue other women after they have married (as Tolstoi himself did). It would appear that Levin is fortunate to have outgrown the promiscuous lust which his diaries record; Anna, on the other hand, has only ever known Karenin. Since she is nine years into her marriage, the fairest comparison is not of Anna with Levin or Kiti as they are, but as the reader projects they might be nine years on. Secondly, Anna is effectively restricted to her own domain, and has no access to the kind of countryside in which Levin's idea of goodness resides; Peterhof, which is a rural Court, and Vozdvizhenskoe, a mechanized estate, are denatured countryside. Karenin is a parody of Daniel, in his capacity as an ethical guide. There is also, as in *Daniel Deronda*, a difference of mode between the actions narrated in the two domains. Whereas Anna's story aspires towards the condition of a European novel, Levin's has more of the aspect of autobiography. Tolstoi only very infrequently wrote in his diary whilst writing the novel, as though writing Levin's story served in part to replace its function (Tolstoi 1985 I: vii). Wilson describes reading Anna's and Levin's stories respectively as:

> rather like wandering into what appears to be a new house. On our left the dining room, finished and complete, with its furniture, pictures, characters and conversation. On our right, however, we fling open the door of the ballroom and find ourselves in an open field, with the architect and builders still looking at the plans. (Wilson 1988: 280)

He exaggerates. Nonetheless, the characterization of counterfeit art in *What Is*

Art? (made with reference to West European literature — particularly French — from Boccaccio to Prévost) applies more obviously to Anna's than to Levin's story: 'Прелюбодеяние есть не только любимая, но и единственная тема всех романов [. . .] Так что вследствие безверия и исключительности жизни богатых классов искусство этих классов обеднело содержанием' [Adultery is not only the favourite, but the only theme of all novels [. . .] Thus because of the lack of belief and exceptional lifestyle of the wealthy classes, the art of those classes became impoverished in its subject matter] (WIA: 97, 98).

Yet the differences of the domains should not be overstated: as noted, the novel is on guard against the very phenomenon of categorization. Tolstoi added that a sense of the melancholy of life (such as Levin suffers from) had also become very fashionable, and was also a common subject of aristocratic art. With the exception of Anna's decline, which is exceptional, Anna's domain operates with the same level of realism as Levin's. Both are established near the beginning of the novel, employ the same narrative tones and modes, and their protagonists have equivalent physical presence: Levin's and Anna's sexualities are both implied rather than depicted. The domains' differing characteristic images (trains and metalwork, mushrooms and bears) are credibly connected to city and country life. There is sufficient moral variation between the characters belonging to both domains that social location is not presented as wholly determinative of them; the town-dweller and European-educated Lvov is a positive character. Moreover, Anna and Levin have far more striking similarities as individuals than do Gwendolen and Daniel. These affinities permit and are signalled by the parallelism between them. Their intellects are comparable: Gwendolen and Anna both read widely, but Gwendolen skims 'a miscellaneous selection — Descartes, Bacon, Locke, Butler, Burke, Guizot [. . .] hoping that by dipping into them all in succession, with her rapid understanding she might get a point of view nearer to his level', whereas 'все предметы, которыми занимался Вронский, она изучила по книгам и специальном журналом, пак что он [. . .] удивлялся ее знанию, памяти' [all subjects that occupied Vronskii, she [Anna] studied in books and specialist journals, so that he [. . .] was amazed at her knowledge, her memory] (DD: 467–68; AK IX: 224). Anna's is the real learning of a Mary Garth, who also writes for children, or of an amateur Marian Evans, although Anna is more hidden away than Marian Evans from the opprobrium of society for her adultery. Her reading is more productive than Levin's, who reads nothing that helps him with his farming; Anna's mind requires no 'mountainous travel [. . .] before it could reach' his (DD: 688). When they meet they agree on public philanthropy. They are both capable of extreme mental states: Anna during her last journey, and Levin on the night of his engagement, experience opposite extremes of misanthropy and philanthropy; Anna immediately before her suicide, and Levin immediately before his conversation with Fedor, fail to understand why anyone should live. As Hardy points out: 'Anna and Vronsky and Levin are all tempted to suicide — the difference between them and Oblonsky is most easily, if crudely, summed up in this fact' (1971: 196). Shestov asks:

> Отчего добро пришло благословить Левина, а не других действующих лиц романа? Отчего Анна погибает и заслуженно, Вронский — обращается

в развалину, Кознышев — влачить призрачное существование, а Левин мало того, что ползуется всеми благами жизни, еще приобретает право на глубокий душевный мир — прерогативу немногих и исключительных людей? Почему судьба так несправедливо оделила Левина и так жестоко обидила Анну?'

[Why has good arrived to bless Levin but not the other characters in the novel? Why does Anna die and deserve to, why is Vronskii ruined, why does Koznyshev drag out an illusionary existence, while Levin, who enjoys all the blessings of life, still acquires the right to a profound spiritual world — the prerogative of a very small and exclusive group of people? Why has fate favoured Levin so unjustly and dealt so cruelly with Anna?] (1907: 8)

This question takes some of its force from their similarities as individuals.

Not only do they have similarities, but the novel in several ways undermines the apparent contrast of their stories. 'Все счастливые семьи похожи друг на друга, каждая несчастливая семья несчастлива по-своему' [All happy families are similar to each other; every unhappy family is unhappy in its own way] asserts a difference far stronger than the novel justifies: the Levins, Shcherbatskiis, Lvovs, Sviiazhskiis, and Parmenovs have little more in common than do the Karenins with Nikolai and Masha (AK VIII: 5). Anna and Vronskii are in certain respects more successful than Levin and Kiti. When Vronskii lives on his estate, 'дело его, все больше и больше занимая и втягивая его, шло прекрасно' [his business, which occupied and absorbed him more and more, went excellently]; unlike Levin, he makes a return on modern machinery, and 'умел выдерживать цену' [knew how to keep up the prices] (AK IX: 224). Dolli 'даже завидовала ее здоровому виду [. . .] Ни один из ее детей так не ползал' [even envied her [Annie's] healthy appearance [. . .] Not one of her own children had crawled like that] (AK IX: 198). Whereas she struggles to discipline her own children, Sergei causes Anna no problems.

Even the difference of Anna's and Levin's endings is not absolute. Although Levin's romantic comedy with Kiti — like Daniel's with Mirah — retains an ideal, only semi-sexualized, aspect until the end of the novel, it is more verisimilitudinous and troubled than the other. Levin's acceptance of Christian dogma is psychologically and intellectually insecure. Levin himself, at one stage of his epiphany, is aware of the danger that he will again fall victim to his intellect. As Shestov notes of Tolstoi, 'Убивший ее, он приводит Левина к веру в Бога и заканчивает свой роман' [Having killed her, he leads Levin to a belief in God and ends his novel]; there is a sense that the novel must end where it does, before Levin loses his arduously attained faith (Shestov 1907: 3). Leavis rightly finds that 'With the advantage of hindsight' one 'can see that the breakdown of Tolstoy into the old Leo is here portended' (Tolstoi decisively rejected Orthodoxy soon after finishing *Anna Karenina*, although Shklovskii exaggerates in arguing that Levin's self-deception was intentionally ironic) (Leavis 1967: 31; Fleetwood 1980: 40). Soviet critics who wished to downplay the ending of a novel which, unlike Dostoevskii's novels, was included in the Soviet canon, found it relatively easy to dismiss as unsuccessful. Kermode points out that there is a distinction between the meaning of the ending of *Anna Karenina*, and the meaning of the end of Levin's *siuzhet*; the latter affects, but does not constitute, the former (1967: 176). However, the connection is close, in part because of the importance of Levin to the novel, and in part because the reader believes in Levin's future life. The very existence of the novel's Part VIII — an instalment published fifteen months late, and continuing the novel after Anna's death — gestures towards open-endedness. The insecurity of Daniel's ending is relatively superficial by comparison. No complacent happiness contrasts disturbingly with Anna's misery. The novel is sensitive to such juxtapositions, just as Shcherbatskii — otherwise a bluff character — is at the spa resort:

> Утро было прекрасное [. . .] но чем ближе они подходили к водам, тем чаще встречались больные, и вид их казался еще плачевнее среди обычных условий благоустроенной немецкой жизни. Кити уже не поражала эта противоположность [. . .] но для князя свет и блеск июньского утра и звуки оркестра, игравшего модный веселый вальс, и особенно вид здоровенных служанок казались чем-то неприличными и уродливыми в соединении с этими собравшимися со всех концов Европы, уныло двигавшимися мертвецами [. . .] Он испытывал почти чувство человека неодетого в обществе.

> [The morning was lovely [. . .] but the nearer they got to the waters the more often they met sick people, and their appearance seemed even more lamentable amongst the ordinary conditions of comfortable German life. Kiti was no longer struck by this contrast [. . .] but to the Prince the light and brilliance of the June morning and the sounds of the orchestra playing a fashionable merry waltz, and especially the appearance of the healthy attendants, seemed somehow unseemly and monstrous in conjunction with these despondently moving corpses gathered from all parts of Europe. [. . .] He almost felt like a man not dressed out in society.] (AK VIII: 242–43)

Insofar as Anna is not excluded from an exclusive or secure type of happiness, her scapegoating in relation to Levin's domain is reduced. Moreover, she is not excluded from a type of happiness belonging to ethnic or aesthetic attributes (as is Gwendolen), nor one reliant on the acceptance of dogma: Levin's final vision of good is existential rather than dogmatic. Stenbock-Fermor observes, 'The novel certainly has a message, yet it is not the peremptory teaching of Tolstoy's later period; there is no absolute certitude as to what man should do. Rather it tells the reader where the evil and the danger lie in wait for him, what to avoid, what not to do' (1967: 111). Anna has not had the advantages of good moral examples, but nor is she presented as ethically helpless. This fact too can be considered to undermine her scapegoating by her text.

The relationship of Anna's tragedy to Levin's comedy can be explored in terms of Lukács's perception that: 'Da nun der Roman auf die Gestaltung der extensiven Totalität des gesellschaftlichen Lebens ausgeht, ist in seiner Darstellung die bis zu Ende ausgetragene Kollision nur rein Grenzfall, ein Fall unter vielen anderen' [Since the subject of the novel is the total span of social life, a fully carried-through collision can only be a marginal case existing alongside many others] (Lukács 1955: 171).

> Wenn also im Drama eine Parallelhandlung als Tragödie angelegt wird, so dient sie dazu, die Hauptlinie der Kollision ergänzen und unterstreichen [. . .] Ganz anders im Roman. Tolstoi legt z.B. zum tragischen Schicksal seiner Anna

Karenina verschiedene Parallelhandlungen an. Die dem Paare Anna–Wronski entsprechenden Kontraste Kitty–Lewin, Darjo–Oblonski sind nur die großen Zentralergänzungen, daneben gibt es noch eine Fülle von anderen, starker episodischen Parallelhandlungen [. . .] In *Anna Karenina* unterstreichen die Parallelhandlungen gerade die Tatsache, daß das Schicksal der Heldin wohl ein typisches und notwendiges, aber dennoch gerade ein extrem individueller Fall ist. Es offenbart freilich am stärksten die inneren Widersprüche der modernen bürgerlichen Ehe, aber es wird auch gezeigt, daß erstens diese Widersprüche keineswegs notwendig immer und überall in dieser selben Richtung auftauchen

[If there is a parallel plot in tragedy, it complements and underlines the main collision [. . .]. In the novel it is quite different. Tolstoy, for example, has several plots to parallel the tragic fate of Anna Karenina. The pairs Kiti–Levin, Daria–Oblonskii are only the big central complements to Anna and Vronskii; there are many others [. . .] In *Anna Karenina* the parallel plots stress that the heroine's fate, while typical and necessary, is yet an extremely individual one. Obviously her fate reveals the inner contradictions of modern bourgeois marriage in the most powerful terms. But what is also shown is first that these contradictions do not always necessarily take this particular path] (Lukács 1965: 171–72)

Lukács asserts Anna to have a tragedy, but stresses that it does not determine the nature of the narrative universe; one implication is that the eventual happiness of a character such as Levin does not need to be considered in direct relationship to that tragedy. Raymond Williams considered that in *Anna Karenina* as in *Women in Love*

an important relationship ends in tragedy, in a death given significance by the whole action [. . .] by the coexistence of these other relationships, the tragic relationship has been given a context. In this limited but important sense, a society has been formed, around the tragic experience. (1955: 122)

Certainly, the tragic experience is given a context — but arguably not a society, in the sense of something providing company.

The novel's complex ethics — condemning casual and earnest adulterers; suggesting that Anna is responsible for her own death, and is the victim of her circumstances; presenting Levin as a spiritual and ethical contrast to her, and undermining that contrast; according to Anna an iridescent tragic status which shines or is dull as the light is shone by herself or by any other character — are complicated still further by Oblonskii. Whereas *Daniel Deronda* has only two main domains, *Anna Karenina* has a third important domain consisting of Moscow (the Boston *Literary World*'s review of *Anna Karenina* tellingly described the novel as 'two or three novels in one') (quoted in Knowles 1978: 341). In several respects Moscow lies half way along the scale which connects Saint Petersburg and the country; the Shcherbatskii wife and husband, and Oblonskii husband and wife, represent Saint Petersburg weaknesses and Russian virtues respectively. However, Oblonskii is also the novel's equivalent of Daniel — its major mediator. He is Anna's brother, Vronskii's friend, Levin's friend, Kiti's brother-in-law, and a kneader of social dough who can make Saint Petersburg celebrities and country-dwellers mix at a party in his house, is present when Vronskii meets Anna and Kiti accepts Levin, and persuades Levin to meet Anna. He is also, as Alexandrov noted, 'oddly and largely guiltless (even as he dissipates the family's wealth)' (2004: 211). That is, he is satirized in a manner which amuses and endears, for emotionally and financially hurting a wife who embodies the virtues which Anna lacks, and for practicising some of the vices which epitomize her domain. Shestov wrote that:

> Все действующия лица 'Анны Карениной' разделены на две категории. Одни следуют правилу, правилам и вместе с Левиным идут к благу, к спасению; другие следуют своим желаниям, нарушают правила и, по мер смелости и решимости своих действии, подпадают более или менее жестокому наказанию.

> [All the characters in *Anna Karenina* are divided into two categories. Some keep to the rules, and along with Levin find paradise; the others serve their own desires, break the rules, and, in proportion to the audacity and decisiveness of their actions, suffer a more or less cruel punishment.] (Shestov 1907: 4)

Yet Oblonksii is merely the most prominent example of the majority of the characters in the latter category who are permitted to satisfy their own desires without suffering any kind of punishment. Although he is not the adulterer in the novel most directly comparable to Anna (those are Betsi amongst women and Vronskii amongst men), both his actions and his speech point to Anna's scapegoating by society. On the other hand, the fact that his presentation makes him more 'oddly and largely guiltless' than Gascoigne or than Brooke of Tipton (with whom Tolstoi was familiar from *Middlemarch*) might be considered to contribute to Anna's scapegoating by her text. A further possibility is that he be considered as a comedic source of resistance to the novel's values as represented by Levin, Dolli, and Platon, rather as Lucio functions as an ethical wild-card in Shakespeare's *Measure for Measure*. Bayley states that 'there could be no place for Stiva in Tolstoy's moral vision, for the mere existence of Stiva makes it impossible for that vision to achieve its ideal reality' (1960: 23). The result is that the vision does not in fact achieve its ideal reality: Oblonskii's dismissive treatment by Koznyshev and the Princess at the end of the novel is hardly as decisive as Henry V's dismissal of Falstaff. Had he lived in Anna's domain, his role in enforcing her scapegoating by the text might have been more pronounced. As it is, from his base in the Moscow domain he offers a perspective which does not condemn Anna, and sees no necessary tragedy in her situation. He represents the liberal future in which women are ever less likely to commit suicide if they behave as Anna does. Yet he is also more ready than Levin to acknowledge that tragedy can result from illicit love. The troubles of his marriage to Dolli fit with the fact that she represents values which he and Anna lack; the durability of that marriage because of Dolli's forgiveness of Oblonskii's adultery, and their shared sympathy for, admiration of, and refusal to condemn Anna, work in Anna's favour. In addition, Dolli represents that lack of self-assertiveness which is implicitly criticized both in Varenka and in Sonia of *War and Peace*; even in the more conservative *Anna Karenina*, Tolstoi declines to help women who will not help themselves. Dolli's sense that she is worn out through child-bearing, child-rearing, and conjugal loyalty — culminating in a moment of jealousy of Anna — is left as a troubling element in the text, like a fainter version of Alcharisi's criticisms of Jewish patriarchy. On balance, therefore, both Oblonskiis function to Anna's benefit within the text. Oblonskii himself is not a privileged third point such as Fontenelle's narrator wishes for between the Moon and the Earth, from which to view the two main domains ('Qui serait entre la lune et la terre, ce serait la vraie place pour les bien voir' [Whoever was between the earth and the moon would be in the right place to see them both well]) (Fontenelle 1955: 81). Rather, he disrupts the ethical axis as imperfectly constituted by those domains — a disruptive function argued by Saussy to be common to third points in comparative literature (2003: 336, 340).

Levin's own relevance to Anna is limited. Whereas Daniel and Gwendolen are connected by an imperfectly successful attempt to comfort and advise, Levin and Anna have no such relationship, and his thoughts have limited applicability to her. Happily married, but otherwise unhappy, he is concerned with why to live under any circumstances; whereas Anna, unhappily married, is concerned with how to live under her own particular circumstances. Wasiolek argues that 'Levin's searching and finding are insubstantial' if they do not 'confront [. . .] Anna's physical passion' (1978: 162). The faith which Levin finds in his epiphany would be of help to Anna were she capable of attaining it — but Levin, who has had a religious upbringing, himself only reaches it after her death, and as an escape from a different kind of despair. Levin's limited relevance to Anna may be considered to exacerbate her scapegoating, since it weakens the implied ethical contrast which would justify the divergence of their fates. However, the sense more strongly emerging from the novel is that they are two individuals, living in different types of society, who with different spiritual resources confront different kinds of problem, and die or thrive accordingly. Saussy noted that 'Some literary scholars have a penchant for the preposition *in*, some for the conjunction *and*'; 'Comparative literature is largely a discipline of the *and* type' (2003: 338). To the extent to which this sense is felt, *Anna Karenina* constitutes comparative literature of the *and* type, and functions less at Anna's expense, than at that of the interpretative unity of the novel.

The instability of their relationship, as in the case of Gwendolen and Daniel, is revealed in their ambivalent and distanced personal relations. The novel opens with their failure to meet. Despite the fact that Levin has been friends with Oblonskii for much longer than he was friends with the young Prince Shcherbatskii — with whose three sisters he fell in love in turn — he has never met Oblonskii's younger sister before the novel begins. When it does begin, Anna and Levin neither meet, nor are mentioned, to one another. The plot as written gives the impression that they both leave Moscow soon after the ball, but in fact Anna arrives in Moscow on the morning that Levin leaves it, using stations at opposite sides of the city. Schultze considers that Tolstoi, who rewrote this section many times, intended this hidden near-coincidence (1982: 32). Wasiolek points out that Tolstoi 'dares risk only the briefest of encounters between' Anna's and Levin's 'two worlds' (1978: 162). Zarkhi's 1967 film adaptation] expands this scene to a discussion between Anna and Levin on the subject of suicide — but their feelings on this subject have little in common. In the novel, Levin dwells first on Anna's portrait and then on her person; a chapter break gives resonance to his wonder (AK IX: 278). He is 'совершенно побеждён' [completely won over] by her grace, urbanity, intelligence, wit, beauty, and 'правдивость' [truthfulness]; feels that he has judged her 'прежде так строго' [so severely hitherto]; and feels 'нежность и жалость, удивившие его самого' [a tenderness and pity which surprised himself] (AK IX: 283, 282, 283). The rhetoric of this and the two following scenes is ambivalent: Levin's feelings are qualified by his drunkenness, he begins to feel guilty even before rejoining Kiti, and reconciles himself with her by accusing Anna — whom Kiti calls 'ету гадкую женщину' [that nasty woman] — of bewitchment' (AK IX: 285). This accusation is partly supported by the subsequent revelation that 'она бессознательно [. . .] целый вечер делала все возможное для того, чтобы возбудить в Левине чуство любви к себе' [she had unconsciously the whole evening done everything in order to arouse in Levin a feeling of love for her] (AK IX: 285). The inauthenticity of Anna's behaviour is suggested by the naïve tone and apparent contradictions ('не только естественно, умно, но умно и небрежно' [not merely naturally and cleverly, but cleverly and carelessly]) of the narration as focalized by Levin (AK IX: 279). On the other hand, this very focalization gives the reader no clear grounds for judgement. Levin's repentance to Kiti is only partly sincere. The scene is finely balanced: Levin's persisting admiration and pity for Anna, which is consistent with finding her tragic, carries as much force as Kiti's denial of the validity of his response. The singularity of the meeting, and Levin's disadvantages of inebriation and admiration, implicitly acknowledge Levin's inability fully to contrast with or to contextualize her. Rachinskii commented to Tolstoi:

> How I enjoyed the acquaintance of Levin. You must agree that this is one of the best episodes of the novel. Here the opportunity presented itself to tie together all the threads of the story and to provide a unified conclusion. But you did not want this. (quoted in Schultze 1982: 14)

By refusing a 'unified conclusion' the narrative permits latitude in the interpretation of Anna, and on balance the effect on Anna of Levin's existence in the novel is benign.

Muted Tragedy

Anna has the honour of the novel's title, whereas *Daniel Deronda* makes its successful protagonist metonymic of the whole (rather as *Wuthering Heights* and *Howards End* name the component to which the novels' values more closely correspond). Even after Levin's role had expanded between the third and the fifth drafts to fill over half of the text, including the whole of the last of the novel's eight parts, the title continued to name the heroine alone. The subtitle too emphasizes Anna, since a *роман* [novel] is also euphemistically a love affair. The title *Anna Karenina* is unusual for Tolstoi, whose titles both before and after this novel tended to consist of abstract nouns rather than protagonists' names, and to reflect the structure of those works which are organized around comparison — for example *Два гусара* [*The Two Hussars*] (1856), 'Три смерти' ['Three Deaths'] (1859), *War and Peace* (1863–69), 'Два старика' ['The Two Old Men'] (1885–86), *Хозяин и работник* [*Master and Man*] (1895), 'Три старца' [*The Three Hermits*] (1886), *И свет во тьме светит* [*The Light Shines in the Darkness*] (1880s–1902), and an early draft of *Anna Karenina*, which was entitled *Два Брака* [*Two Marriages*]. The title *Anna Karenina* encourages interpretation of Anna as 'the fact of the novel', and requires no alteration for those film adaptations which largely exclude Levin (Bayley 1966: 202). However, its full poignancy is felt only in the fact that *despite* the novel's contents, it points to Anna alone. The title and subtitle hang above the novel rather as Pilate's epithet hangs above Christ on his cross, stating the crime of the man he has condemned to death (in Anna's case having a *роман*) in a manner indeterminately accusatory, ironic, and honouring. Within the novel Tolstoi, Pilate-like, both condemns Anna's society for condemning her, and imposes the death penalty (which that society did not possess) for the sake of a higher cause than that society conceives of. Yet the novel also contains a figure who partially resembles Tolstoi, and who partially alleviates Anna's scapegoating by his similarities to her, irrelevancies to her, and ambivalent contact with her. Girard describes 'persécuteurs naïfs' [naïve persecutors] who '*ne savent pas ce qu'ils font*' (1982: 17). Unlike *Daniel Deronda*, *Anna Karenina* is not a novel which is fully aware of its contradictions, and to the extent to which it is not, such persecution as it practises is naïve.

This may be explored in the transitions between the stories. When Anna, Vronskii, and Golenishchev enter Mikhailov's studio, they first survey the studio at will. The artist directs their attention to the painting of Christ before Pilate, but presently they turn away to a portrait of two boys fishing (AK IX: 42–46). The novel's artist has more control over his readers than does Mikhailov over his viewers; the reader has no possibility of watching Levin's rather than Anna's domain at this point in the narrative. As in *Daniel Deronda*, the unhappy *fabula* appears to be followed by the happy one. Levin's return to the country occurs and is narrated before Anna's return to Saint Petersburg, and Anna opens only one of the novel's eight parts. However, from Part II onwards her *siuzhet* runs in advance of Levin's, and also hurries ahead of his chronology (by nine months at the point when Anna has sex with Vronskii 'almost a whole year' after meeting him) (Schultze 1982: 24–25). Here too, then, there is a sense that the hero's *siuzhet* catches up with and avoids the mistakes of the heroine's.

Tolstoi, who fitted Levin's expanding story into Anna's older but still-evolving story, performed a function part-way between Eliot's (who wrote her novel in the order as presented), and that of a splicing editor. In *Daniel Deronda* the fact that the novel's first readers always started a new instalment, and sometimes a new chapter, in the story which they had last read, suggested the close relationship and common reality of the two *siuzhets*. By contrast, over half of *Anna Karenina*'s segment boundaries coincide not only with chapter boundaries (none occur within chapters), but with part or instalment boundaries. All but one Part (III) and two Instalments (VI and X) end with a segment, and a third of the instalments contain only one segment. No parts, and only four out of fourteen instalments, are based on the juxtaposition of one Anna segment with one Levin segment; five instalments are composed of only one segment, and three are composed of scarcely more than one. The remaining two instalments, which open the novel, contain multiple, complex, segment transitions (Schultze 1982: 44–47). Whereas in *Daniel Deronda* segment transitions tend to be semantically rather than structurally reinforced, in *Anna Karenina* the reverse is true. In *Anna Karenina* there is only one chapter epigraph, and the segments (and therefore the books and instalments) tend to be paratactically juxtaposed — either achronously, or with unobtrusive reorientation in time: 'После бала, рано утром, Анна Аркаьевна' [After the ball, early in the morning, Anna Arkadevna] (AK VIII: 106). Such transitions implicitly attribute to the *fabulae* a greater degree of independence. One effect is to confine Anna to her own domain by formal partitions. However, a stronger effect, and one which mitigates the scapegoating mechanism, is to suggest independent realities, neither of which attempts to contextualize the other. As Schultze notes, 'With so few installments based on the principle of juxtaposition, it is no wonder that readers originally thought of *Anna Karenina* as two loosely linked novels' (1982: 47).

Chapter 2 introduced three types of finalization suggested by Bakhtin in his essay on speech genres. The first type, finalization by semantic exhaustiveness, is found more often in *Daniel Deronda* than in *Anna Karenina*. In *Anna Karenina* some segments end with Levin's spiritual breakthroughs or impasses ['так-то и я! Ничего. . . Все хорошо' (that's what I'll do! It's OK. . . Everything's alright]), and one ends with the extinguishing of Anna's light 'навсегда' (AK VIII: 106; AK IX: 353). Such endings conform to the contours of the individual *fabulae*, but more of *Anna Karenina*'s segments end without obvious semantic justification, as for example at an inconclusive point in Levin and Oblonskii's conversation during their hunting (AK VIII: 184). The last paragraphs of several of the novel's segments contain a swift transition from a scene to a summary of geographical movement. For example, Dolli and Kiti's painful conversation about Vronskii and Oblonskii is separated from the end of a segment by two sentences, during which the sisters nurse Dolli's six children through scarlet fever, and in the last clause of which 'Щербацкие уехали за границу' [the Shtcherbatskiis went abroad] (AK VIII: 135). The apparent arbitrariness of such endings suggests independently existent *fabulae*, of which the narration may be interrupted and resumed at any point (Bakhtin 1979: 255). In this sense Anna is accorded greater freedom of independent action than is Gwendolen.

Bakhtin's second type of finalization corresponds to the termination of a segment by the will of the character dominating its action. Gwendolen more than Anna is the victim of the termination of her segments by another person's will. Karenin uncharacteristically terminates one of Anna's segments with his dictation of how they will live together: 'Вот все, что я имею сказать вам. Теперь мне время ехать. Я не обедаю дома. Он стал и направился к двери. Анна стала тоже. Он, молча поклонившись, пропустил ее' ['That's all I have to say to you. Now it's time for me to go. I'm not dining at home'. He stood and went over to the door. Anna got up too. He, bowing silently, let her pass before him] (AK VIII: 341). Unlike Gwendolen, however, Anna has the power to end her own segments. After telling Karenin about her affair she has to wait three hours for Vronskii, but she is never shown in this position of passivity because she closes her segment and the third instalment with the thought 'слава богу, что с ним все кончено' [thank God, it's all over with him] (AK VIII: 227). She and Vronskii several times choose to move location and, in the process, out of the narrative's focus; at the end of Part IV 'Алексей Александрович остался один с сыном на своей квартире, а Анна с Вронским уехала за границу, не получив развода и решительно отказавшись от него' [Alexei Alexandrovich was left alone with his son in his flat, whilst Anna and Vronskii went abroad, not having obtained a divorce and having decisively refused one] (AK VIII: 461). Anna's implied freedom reduces the sense of her scapegoating in the text (since she is free to move whither she pleases), and either increases or diminishes her scapegoating by the text, depending on how her implied responsibility for her own actions is regarded. The third kind of finalization is what Bakhtin calls 'typical compositional and generic forms of finalization' — as for example at moments of high tension (1986: 77). *Daniel Deronda* makes more use of such endings than does *Anna Karenina*. In the latter a segment ends when 'она просыпалась с ужасом' [she awoke in horror] from Anna's iterated dream that she has two husbands (AK VIII: 161). On the other hand, the sixth instalment ends not with Vronskii having shot himself, but with his irritation at his own inaccuracy, and with the arrangements then made for his nursing (AK VIII: 443). *Anna Karenina* more than *Daniel Deronda* refrains from prolonging characters' suspense across a segment boundary.

Bakhtin argues that an utterance, as opposed to a sentence, is distinguished by addressivity (1986: 95, 71). At certain of the novels' segment transitions one *siuzhet*'s speaker responds to what the other has said by providing corresponding information or describing a related phenomenon. Levin's return to Pokrovskoe is followed by an account of Anna's return to Saint Petersburg. After Anna perceives Kiti's dismay at Vronskii's behaviour towards her, and leaves the ball, Levin's segment opens with a more consciously articulated example of self-reproach: 'Да, что-то есть во мне противное, отталкивающее, — думал Левин, вышедши от Щербацких' ['Yes, there is something in me hateful, repulsive' thought Levin, as he came away from the Shtcherbatskiis] (AK VIII: 92). At the end of the latter segment Levin resolves how to lead a better life, whereupon Anna resolves to avoid the further company of Vronskii by returning to her family in Saint Petersburg (AK VIII: 106). Transitions based upon parallels between *fabulae* and characters are an obvious location for ethical comparison. Karenin is irritated by Dolli's exhortation to him to forgive Anna, immediately after Kiti has forgiven Levin for his entire history of fornication (AK VIII: 433). However, like *Daniel Deronda*, *Anna Karenina* tends to avoid such contrasts, and this is the more striking in *Anna Karenina* given the stronger parallels between its central *fabulae* and protagonists. As mentioned before, *What is Art?* condemned 'поразительность' [striking effects] as characterizing counterfeit art (WIA: 134). *Anna Karenina* already displayed an aversion to such effects. The strongest contrasts between Levin's and Anna's lives on the land exist between passages which are well inside the segments, rather than (as Bakhtin conceives it) facing external reality directly (1986: 74). The contrast between Levin's household of in-laws and Anna's household of servants and a self-serving aunt is mediated by Dolli's envy of Anna during her journey to the latter. That is, the novel tends to juxtapose problems in one domain with those of the other, rather than with solutions. Film adaptations, which do well at rendering the physical and atmospheric contrast between the indoor and country locations of the novel's domains, have tended to intensify the contrasts of action from what appears in the novel (whereas Andrew Davies in his 2002 BBC adaptation of *Daniel Deronda* manufactures no didactic contrasts at its segment transitions). Duvivier's 1937 adaptation alternates night shots of Anna climbing into a carriage bound for Italy with sunlit shots of Kiti climbing into her wedding carriage, in the manner of Eisenstein's simplest montage, in which 'The dialectic [. . .] exists in the sequencing of the ideas arising from the action' (Mitry 1998: 129). In the novel, the events to which these interpolated scenes most nearly correspond are separated by three chapters. In Zarkhi's 1967 adaptation Levin's euphoric sighting of Kiti passing in her carriage is followed by Vronskii's nightmare about a peasant; in the novel it is followed by an analysis of Karenin. In *Anna Karenina*, Tolstoi's reticence with regard to the contrast of the strories indicates also restraint with regard to the scapegoating of Anna.

Bakhtin's description of speakers with 'little mutual knowledge' applies well to certain of the segment transitions in *Anna Karenina* (1986: 114). At the end of the novel's third part and the fifth instalment Levin is oppressed by the thought of death: 'но именно вследствие этой темноты он чувствовал, что единственною руководительною нитью в этой темноте было его дело, и он из последних сил ухватился и держался за него' [just because of this darkness he felt that the one guiding clue in the darkness was his work, and he clutched it and clung to it with all his strength]. In the next segment, 'Каренины, муж и жена, продолжали жить в одном доме, встречались каждый день, но были совершенно чужды друг другу' [The Karenins, husband and wife, carried on living in the same house, met every day, but were completely estranged from one another] (AK VIII: 374, 375). All three characters are miserable, but for very different reasons. The effect is verisimilitudinous in the sense of presenting life as only partially coherent and only partially meaningful. At the end of the segment which contains Nikolai's death, 'возникла другая, столь же неразгаданная, вызывавшая к любви и жизни' [another [mystery] had arisen, just as insoluble, urging [Levin] to love and life]: Kiti's pregnancy (AK IX: 79). In the next segment Karenin is miserable and confused, having recently been left by Anna. The comedy of human reproduction which contextualizes Nikolai's death for Levin ('in the same moment the sickle is reaping and the seed is sprinkled') is unable to do the equivalent for Karenin (DD: 693).

The relations of tragedy and comedy in the novel are most palpable towards its end. Anna dies at the end of Part VII as surely as Antigonus dies on the sea coast of Bohemia. However, her body is neither amusingly commented upon, like his, nor misinterpreted, like Gwendolen's. In the original serialization 'затрещала, стала меркнуть и навсегда потухла' [the light [. . .] flickered, began to dim, and was forever extinguished] was followed by a note indicating that the novel was to be continued (AK IX: 353). Clearly, it was not Anna's life that was to be continued, and the very fact of continuity signalled that her death would be superseded by other action. This was not always Tolstoi's intention: the first draft had ended 'A day later her body was found in the Neva. Balashov went away to Tashkent, having handed the children over to his sister. Mikhail Mikhailovich continued his work in the civil service' (quoted in Turner 1993: 14). When Levin was introduced, and an eighth part was developed, this was first called an *эпилог* (epilog). Its final form, called *'Anna Karenina, Part Eight and Last'*, was not externally proleptic, but an integral continuation of the novel (Stenbock-Fermor 1967: 30). Tolstoi's will to continue the novel beyond Anna's death had grown strong enough to circumvent his editor Katkov's refusal to publish this part by publishing it privately.

Katkov not only disapproved of the attitude, evinced by this part, towards the Slavophiles, but considered the part extraneous to the novel's primary subject. In the paragraph summary of this part which he published a month after the instalment containing Anna's death, the 'in fact' is interpretative:

> with the death of the heroine the novel is in fact finished. According to the author a short epilogue, of about two sheets, is still needed; in it the readers would learn that Vronskiy, in confusion and grief after Anna's death, went as a volunteer to Serbia and that all the others were well and happy, and that Levin remained on his estate and was angry with the Slavic Committee and the volunteers. The author will perhaps develop these chapters in a separate edition of his novel. (quoted in Stenbock-Fermor 1967: 29)

Tolstoi parodied this summary's concentration on Anna in an unsent letter to *Новое Время* [*New Season*], in which he suggested that Katkov might have given the following summary, rather than troubling to publish the novel:

> There was a lady who abandoned her husband. Having fallen in love with Count Vronskiy, she started to get angry with various things in Moscow and threw herself under a railroad carriage. (quoted in Stenbock-Fermor 1967: 29)

Katkov reiterated his view in an article entitled 'What happened after the death of Anna Karenina', which described the eighth part as superfluous and ill-judged, since it provided no conclusion to the novel and was like 'additional musical motives that have no connection with the theme' (quoted in Stenbock-Fermor 1967: 30–31). As a result of this disagreement, 'Time' (fifteen months in real time and two months of fictional time) intervened between the publication of the thirteenth and fourteenth instalments. The involuntary delay may have allowed resonance to Anna's tragedy and to the 'навсегда' [forever] of her extinguishing (AK IX: 353). However, it may also have functioned like interval drinks, since by the time readers had read the final instalment the impact of Anna's death would have been dulled. The novel's scene moves from the railway tracks in spring to hot summer, Koznyshev's peaceful authorship of '*Опыт обзора основ и форм государственности в Европе и в России*' [*Towards a Survey of the Foundations and Forms of Governments in Europe and Russia*] (which makes no more impression on those for whose attention it is intended than do Gascoigne's articles) to the Levins' fecund '*тихим счастием вне течений в своем тихом затоне*' [peaceful happiness out of the flow in their quiet backwater] (AK IX: 354, 367). Anna is more thoroughly expunged from the novel during this part than is Gwendolen after the engagement of Daniel and Mirah; her name does not appear, Koznyshev and Vronskii avoid allusion to her, and only just before he leaves the novel does Vronskii remember her '*угрозу никому ненужного, но неизгладимого раскаяния*' [threat of a wholly useless, but indelible, remorse] (AK IX: 367). Dolli's mention to Levin of Koznyshev's meeting with Vronskii provokes only the response '*Это ему идет*' [That's the right thing for him], and a discussion of the Serbian question (AK IX: 391). Whereas Gascoigne's peaceful authorship characterizes an environment to which Gwendolen will return, that of Koznyshev has no connection with Anna. Her death, unlike Nikolai's, is treated not as a manifestation of the universal phenomenon of *смерть* [death], but as a particular ethical and spiritual disaster. The characters of Levin's domain have lived for two months since Anna's death, and by demonstrating the continuity of their interests in time beyond it, they induce in the reader (who may have lived for fifteen months, in the case of the novel's serial readers) the same. Overall, this transition permits more reverberation to the heroine's tragedy than does the equivalent in *Daniel Deronda*, but also more fully moves beyond it, in a world of plural, disconnected, interests. As Lukács comments on the novel:

> Wir sehen hier, daß die Beziehung der sich ergänzenden Parallelen und Kontraste untereinander im Drama eine viel engere ist als im Roman. Im Roman genügt eine äußerlich sehr entfernt scheinende Verwandtschaft des grundlegenden gesellschaftlich-menschlichen Problems, damit eine ergänzende Parallelhandlung zustande komme.

> [We see here that these complementing parallels and contrasts are much more closely related in drama than in the novel. All that is needed in the novel to justify a complementary plot is a mere affinity with the basic social-human problem, however remote it may seem.] (Lukács 1955: 172)

Overall, the apparent reality of the two novels' *fabulae* reflects the differences in the manner of the novels' compositions. The *fabulae* of *Anna Karenina* have greater imputed reality and independence than do those of *Daniel Deronda*, as suggested by their paratactic segment transitions, arbitrary segment endings, avoidance of finalization on a moment of high tension, and generation of a neutral common reality; only in its numbered divisions does *Anna Karenina* elevate *siuzhet* over *fabula*. For these reasons, and because of Anna's greater power to terminate segments, Gwendolen more than Anna is a scapegoat of her novel's segment boundaries. *Anna Karenina*'s contrasts of genre are milder, and lack the tension which belongs to the connection of Gwendolen and Daniel. *Daniel Deronda* cannot outlast this connection, whereas *Anna Karenina*, in which no such connection exists, outlives Anna by nineteen chapters. *Daniel Deronda* therefore ends by exposing some of the factors which are involved in the scapegoating of Gwendolen, whereas *Anna Karenina* successfully redirects interest both from Anna and from the nature of her death.

Mikhailov's neo-realist portrait of Pilate and Christ contains 'столько раз перемещаемые для соблюдения общего' [faces so many times transposed for the sake of the harmony of the whole] (AK IX: 43). By contrast, Levin finds that the *Fantasia of King Lear*:

> Беспрестанно начиналось, как будто собиралось музыкальное выражение чувства, но тотчас же разпадалось на обрывки новых начал музыкальных выражений, а иногда просто на ничем, кроме прихоти композитора, не связанные, но чрезвычайно сложные звуки. Но и самые отрывки этих музыкальных выражении, иногда хороших, были неприятны, потому что были совершенно неожиданны и ничем не приготовлены. Веселость, и грусть, и отчаяние, и нежность, и торжество являлись безо всякого на то права, точно чувства сумасшедшего.

> [It seemed as though a musical expression of feeling were constantly beginning, as if preparing itself. But as soon as it fell to pieces a new musical expression

would start up, or sometimes simply noting but the whim of the composer, disconnected, but exceedingly difficult sounds. But these same fragments of musical expression, though they were sometimes beautiful, were disagreeable, because they were completely unexpected and not prepared for by anything. Gaiety, and grief, and despair, and tenderness, and celebration, appeared without any apparent reason, like the emotions of a madman.] (AK IX: 266)[7]

In fact, Tolstoi objected not only to programme music but to *King Lear* itself for their incoherence. *What is Art?* also criticized Goethe in such terms:

Произведение, основанное на заимствовании, как, например, 'Фауст' Гете, может быть очень хорошо обделано, исполнено ума и всяких красот, но оно не может произвести настоящего художественного впечатления, потому что лишено главного свойства произведения искусства — цельности, органичности, того, чтобы форма и содержание составляли одно неразрывное целое, выражающее чувство, которое испытал художник.

[A work based on borrowing, such as Goethe's *Faust*, can be very well put together, filled with intelligence, and all kinds of beauty, but cannot make a true artistic impression, because it lacks the most important characteristic of art works — integrity, organicism, the combination of form and content in an indivisible whole, expressing the feeling felt by the artist.] (WIA: 136)

Tolstoi not only (like Eliot) used an organic metaphor for artistic coherence, but the structuralist metaphor of a labyrinth. Whilst working on Part v of *Anna Karenina* in April 1876, he wrote to Strakhov of 'бесконечном лабиринте сцеплении, в котором состоит и сущность искусства' [that endless labyrinth of connections which constitutes the very essence of art] (Donskov 2003 I: 268).

Во всем, почти во всем, что я писал, мною руководила потребность собрания мыслей, сцепленных между собой, для выражения себя, но каждая мысль, выраженная словами особо, теряет свой смысл, страшно понижается, когда берется одна из того сцепления, в котором она находится. Само же сцепление составлено не мыслью (я думаю), а чем-то другим, и выразить основу этого сцепления непосредственно словами никак нельзя; а можно только посредственно — словами описывая образы, действия, положения.

[In everything, or almost everything, I have written, I have been governed by the need to gather together ideas, which were interconnected as they were expressed, but each idea, expressed separately in words, loses its sense, and is terribly diminished, when it is taken out of that connection in which it is found. That same connection is made up not of an idea (I think), but of something else, and expressing the foundation of this connection directly in words cannot be done at all; it can only be done indirectly — with words describing characters, events, situations.] (Donskov 2003 I: 267).

The task of the critic is to guide readers through the labyrinth towards the laws that serve as the basis of these connections (Donskov 2003 I: 268). This metaphor better describes *Anna Karenina* than an organic metaphor. The stories seem to be linked by numerous connections, but to have little interdependence. Tolstoi also used an architectural metaphor of his work. In January 1878, half a year after the completion of *Anna Karenina*, Serge Rachinskii complained to Tolstoi about 'a basic deficiency in the construction of the whole novel: 'The book lacks architecture. Two themes not connected in any way develop side by side, and they develop magnificently' (TL 1: 311). Tolstoi responded on 27 January: 'Your opinion about *Anna Karenina* seems to me wrong. On the contrary, I am proud of the architecture — the arches have been constructed in such a way that it is impossible to see where the keystone is' (TL 1: 311). Between April 1876 and January 1878 Tolstoi's metaphor had shifted from the plural to the singular — from 'linkages' in an 'endless labyrinth' to 'an inner link' repeated in the 'arches' of a building. Stenbock-Fermor's *The Architecture of Anna Karenina*, which rests heavily on the latter metaphor of Byzantine architecture, does indicate real structures in the novel. However, as Mikhailov remarks to himself about Golenishchev's perception of 'выражения лица Пилата как чиновника' [the expression of Pilate as a civil servant], 'это соображение было одно из миллионов других соображений, которые, как Михайлов твердо знал это, все были и верны' [this reflection was just one of millions of reflections, which, as Mikhailov knew for certain, were all true] (AK IX: 44). The earlier metaphor, which is Byzantine in the sense of denoting infinite complexity without repetition, symmetry, or the force of gravity determining one shape rather than another, is more descriptive of the novel as a whole.

From the earliest reviews of *Anna Karenina* onwards critics have identified two tendencies in the novel, which create a conflict between what Bakhtin would term the monologic and the heteroglossic, and what Berlin called 'The Hedgehog and The Fox' (Berlin 1994: 22–81). Mikhailovskii's 1875 review of the first few episodes of the novel was entitled 'The Right Hand and the Left Hand of Count Tolstoi'; Wilson adopted the metaphor in describing the novel as 'the arena in which the dilemma between his right and left hands is being fought [. . .] both trying to write at once, with peculiar results' (quoted in Knowles 1978: 279; Wilson 1988: 278). Schultze wrote that:

> Tolstoi the hedgehog wanted to believe in life affirmation, as is shown in the story line, plot structure, symbolic structure, and the thematic and character structures in the novel. But Tolstoi the fox uses the same structures to show the presence of all that is contradictory and ironic in life as well. (1982: 157)

I have argued, however, that *Anna Karenina* makes little attempt to impose a single vision on both of its stories. In 1887 an American reviewer described Levin's story, with telling oxymoron, as a 'controlling sub-plot' (quoted in Knowles 1978: 351). Yet neither is it a subplot, nor does it attempt to exercise consistent contextualizing control over Anna's story. The ending of *Anna Karenina* is unstably dramatic rather than confidently narrative, and has no direct relation to Anna.

Overall, the disjunction of domains in *Daniel Deronda* is the greater. Two models for the division of fictional reality into different domains are offered by the contradictory meanings of the term *cleavage*. In that term's sense as unification (as a man leaves his parents and cleaves to his wife), profoundly different realities are closely juxtaposed; in its sense as division (as a cleaver cleaves meat) a reality is split into its components or tendencies. The word *cleavage*, as applied to the line between female breasts, might be thought to refer to the point at which two separate breasts cleave to each other — or else to the point where a hypothetical original sausage-like breast was cloven in two. In the first sense, the contrast is produced by selection; in the second, by intensification. The first more closely describes the division of *Daniel Deronda*; the second, of *Anna Karenina*. *Daniel Deronda* therefore more strongly suggests a pluralist ontology (although pluralism and *плюрализм* first reached dictionaries shortly after *Daniel Deronda* and *Anna Karenina* were finished). Nonetheless, it is worth noting that the novels' eponymous stories, which have opposite outcomes, have certain similarities in their relations with their partner stories. They appear to be more predetermined, are more cosmopolitan, and are more conscious of their artistic aspect. The outcome of this inverted correspondence is that in *Daniel Deronda* it is the tragedy which feels more realistic, whereas in *Anna Karenina* it is the comedy. Gwendolen could be considered to be punished for her reality, or alternatively could be considered as a free ethical agent, who is responsible for her own fate; Anna is the victim of her non-realistic decline.

In the Meyricks' parlour in *Daniel Deronda* hangs a collection of engravings including 'The Tragic Muse', 'Grand Melancholia', children at play, and other Classical, Christian, and secular icons (DD: 179). Were these engravings to be animated in Oblonskii's house, considered as representative of that novel's mixed domain, then the Tragic Muse would take hold of a girl's hand and hold it at times tightly, at others more loosely, but would lead her from the stage one act before the end of the play. Grand Melancholia would seize the hand of one of the boys, who would in vain appeal to the Prophets, Sibyls, and the School of Athens for protection. Sporadically he would pray to the Virgin, until in the final scene she appeared soaring amid her cherubic escort — spurning the School of Athens underfoot, and holding grand Melancholia in temporary subjection.

Notes to Chapter 3

1. The note does not survive; the list translated in Christian's edition is taken from a copy made by Tolstoi's daughter Masha.
2. The phrase *good life* is chosen to suggest εὐδαιμονία [*eudaimonia*] — a concept with which Tolstoi, who began reading Greek philosophers in the original in 1870, would have been familiar. The object of Levin's aspirations resembles *eudaimonia* by being an objective, rather than subjective, state of happiness, connected to both self-love and virtue. However, for him reason cannot constitute or give knowledge of this state, which fulfils the purposes of a creative principle or God.
3. Tolstoi does mediate Caucasian culture to Russian readers as a source of value in works written both before and after *Anna Karenina*: *Казаки* [*The Cossacks*] (1863) and *Хаджи-Мурат* [*Hadzhi-Murat*] (1896–1904).
4. Parts of the rest of this chapter also appeared, in different form, in Brown (2010a). I thank the editors of *Modern Language Review* for their kind permission to use this material, and for their editorial assistance with the article.
5. In this letter Tolstoi is referring to his first draft, written between 18 and 25 March 1873 (Tolstoi 1978 I: 258).
6. Whereas there is a sense that Gwendolen's domain is dying out, there is no such prophetic sense about Anna's, which within forty years would be destroyed far more completely. As Lawrence crowed in 1928: 'where now is the society that turned its back on Vronsky and Anna? [. . .] what is its condemnation worth, to-day?' (Verga 1928: 20)

7. Mirah shows greater tolerance for a similar performance from Hans, although this is deliberately comic:

> He passes from one figure to another as if he were a bit of flame, where you fancied the figures without seeing them [. . .] all in one minute Mr Hans makes himself a blind bard, and then Rienzi addressing the Romans, and then an opera-dancer, and then a desponding young gentleman — I am sorry for them all, and yet I laugh, all in one. (DD: 398)

CHAPTER 4

Women In Love

[It is] perversely arbitrary to assert that the movement of the action towards Gerald's death draws its significance and its power from its relation to a major and central drama of Birkin and Ursula.

F. R. LEAVIS 1955: 152

It is Birkin and Ursula who, as a pair, are played against Gerald and Gudrun (it is, of course, an interplay) in the total thought of Women in Love — the thought that completes itself in Gerald's death in the snow-world.

F. R. LEAVIS 1976: 84

Lawrence's World

Rather than following Eliot and Tolstoi in visiting Weimar, Lawrence sent the degenerate Gudrun and Loerke thither: 'It was a sentimental delight to reconstruct the world of Goethe at Weimar' (WL: 453). He also connected Goethe to Gerald, who discusses him with the German Professor (WL: 231). Yet Lawrence, like Eliot and Tolstoi, had formerly admired Goethe. He first encountered his works in the same 'International Library of Famous Literature' in which he was introduced to *Anna Karenina*, and by 1909 was using his poems to teach Helen Corke German (Sagar 1982: 72). In his 1913 essay on Thomas Mann he contrasted Goethe favourably with Mann, for living life as well as art (Arnold 1961: 35). But by the time he had finished *Women in Love* he had turned against him, more decisively than he had turned against *Anna Karenina*, and no less than Tolstoi had turned against Goethe twenty years before that (Sagar 1982: 91). In October 1919 Lawrence sent Catherine Carswell his copy of De Quincey, whose essay on Goethe he had been re-reading with approval: 'I like [De Quincey] because he also dislikes such people as Plato and Goethe, whom I also dislike' (LL III: 407). Lawrence and Tolstoi agreed that Goethe was not a religious writer: Mr Noon's description of Goethe's lyrics as 'cold, less than human, nasty and functional, scientific in the worst sense' connects Lawrence with those who found the author of *Wilhelm Meister* to write 'like a passionless Mejnour, to whom all things are interesting only as objects of intellectual contemplation' — and therefore distances him from Eliot, who explicitly repudiated the latter judgment (Lawrence 1984: 293; Ashton 1992: 129). But whereas *What is Art?* criticized Goethe for lacking moral content, Krockel suggests that Lawrence objected to Goethe's combination of liberal individualism with that doctrine of submission to the needs of society which connects *Die Wahlverwandschaften* with *The*

Mill on the Floss, and which he himself repeatedly repudiated (MN: 230; Krockel 2007: 6). On the other hand, whereas Eliot had defended 'The Morality of *Wilhelm Meister*' on the grounds that it also contained 'the salt of some noble impulse, some disinterested effort, some beam of good nature', Lawrence condemned Goethe's treatment of sexuality as perversely explicit and conscious, and in the same year as completing *Lady Chatterley's Lover* accused Goethe of intellectualizing the phallic consciousness: '*Wilhelm Meister* is amazing as a book of peculiar immorality, the perversity of intellectualised sex' (Ashton 1992: 131; LL VI: 342). Since this was a concern which he may well have felt about his own novel, the comment suggests that he used some of his criticism of Goethe as he used his criticism of Tolstoi, and as Birkin uses his criticism of Hermione — to distance himself from contradictions and rejected implications of his own thought (LL VI: 342).

Like Eliot and Tolstoi, Lawrence left no record of his response to the idea of *Weltliteratur* — in Goethe's or any other sense — but elements of what would have been his likely response may be inferred. As mentioned in Chapter 1, Lawrence not only generalized about humanity as a whole, but also about such groups as women, men, people of Arctic tendency, people of African tendency, the race-old, the race-young, Australians, Etruscans, Russians, and Jews. The fact of human division itself did not trouble him. Unlike Klesmer, who 'looks forward to a fusion of races', he preferred 'the sacred and ineradicable *differences* between men and races: the sacred gulfs'; in 1921 he wrote to Louis Golding concerning his book about Jews, *Babylon*:

> What is there at the bottom of the soul of a Jew which makes him a Jew? That's what I want to know [. . .] a Jewish book should be written in terms of *difference* from the Gentile consciousness — not identity with it. [. . .] I am tired of sympathy and universality. (DD: 413; LL III: 690)

Daniel Deronda, one may note by way of comparison, is not tired of *sympathy*, but it agrees with Lawrence in valuing Jewish distinctness. Lawrence specifically criticized the ideal of universal brotherhood which, in caricatured form, he attributed to Tolstoi, 'the philosopher with a very nauseating Christian-brotherhood idea of himself [. . .] That, really, was Tolstoi. That, even, was Lenin, God in the machine of Christian-brotherhood, that hashes men up into social sausage-meat'. 'He wanted to *be* absolute: a universal brother. [. . .] He wanted to puff, and puff, and puff, till he became Universal Brotherhood itself, the great gooseberry of our globe. Then pop went Leo! And from the bits sprang up bolshevists' (STH: 184; 187). Insofar as these comments apply to *Anna Karenina* it is to Levin, the wisdom of whose epiphanic vision is specifically repudiated in the character of his contemporary Mr Crich. Both men struggle to justify to themselves their wealth, resist the ruthless modernization of their working practices, feel their men to be their spiritual superiors, and cling to the Christian faith which they believe the latter to possess. Levin's epiphany occurs under the cosmic light of the Milky Way, whereas Mr Crich's faith in his old age is likened to 'beautiful candles of belief, that would not do to light the world any more' (WL: 229). Nowhere did Lawrence advocate a literature which would appeal broadly to humanity — one popular meaning of *Weltliteratur*. On the contrary, he considered that any given work of literature either appealed to an individual, or it did not. The narrator of *Mr Noon* opines:

> If I try to write down what I see — why not? If a publisher likes to print the
> book — all right. And if anybody wants to read it, let him. But why anybody
> should read one single word if he doesn't want to, I don't see. Unless of course
> he is a critic who needs to scribble a dollar's worth of words, no matter how.
> (PUFU: 65)

To which a critic can only respond '*touché*'. That novel was written without any
definite expectation of any readers at all, and the same was true of *Women in Love*
— *The Rainbow* having been suppressed in 1915, and the first version of *Women in
Love* 1916–17 having been rejected for publication. There was an unsuccessful plan
to have it published in Russia (where it was first translated only in 2007), and a
successful one to have it published in America (where it was published in 1920), but
there is no sign or likelihood that Lawrence modulated his novel in order to appeal
to either of those peoples, or — in Goethean spirit — to mediate English culture
to them.

Nonetheless, Goethe's idea of *Weltliteratur* as fostering understanding between
different peoples did have an echo in a comment in *Study of Thomas Hardy*: 'what
is refinement? It is really delicate sympathy. What then is the mission of Art? To
bring us into a sympathy with as many men, as many objects, as many phenomena
as possible' (STH: 227). *Women in Love* fulfils this ideal negatively — by shunning
any preference for one psycho-geographic division of humanity over any other, and
therefore avoiding any lack of sympathy for less-favoured groups. Its misanthropy
is indiscriminate: all of humanity is summoned up in order for its destruction to be
fantasized, twice by Birkin, and once by Gudrun and Loerke. Whereas Goethe's
ideal of *Weltliteratur* did not entail the abolition of nations, merely their mutual
mediation, *Women in Love* places no value on nationhood at all. It makes none
of the confident delineations of national character which characterize Lawrence's
travel writings, including *Twilight in Italy*, written when *Women in Love* was
started. Countries' differences are presented as insignificant in comparison to the
similarities which make them jointly worthy of destruction, and commercially
and spiritually competitive nationalism is one of these similarities. A rare point
of agreement between Birkin and Hermione is their criticism of nationalism at
Shortlands, and when they later disagree about the country of which the 'coming
to national consciousness' interests Hermione (and which is an example to Zionism
in *Daniel Deronda*) Birkin complains: 'I hate Italy and her national rant' (WL: 298).
On the other hand, the two novels resemble each other and differ from *Anna
Karenina* in their rejection of their native country: the one exception to *Women
in Love*'s impartiality is its expression of the particular animus against England
which Lawrence, at the time of writing, was experiencing whilst being kept under
surveillance with a German wife within it. This is one mode in which the novel
opposed the current war, and, as was the case with Book 8 of *Anna Karenina*,
was one reason for publication being refused. *Women in Love* is certainly 'keine
patriotische Kunst' [no patriotic art] (Goethe 1972: 539).

The novel's strongest cultural division is not between psycho-geographically
defined peoples, but between those who are *growing tips*, and the rest of humanity.

Lawrence used this botanical metaphor both before and after *Women in Love* in order to refer to those individuals and groups who develop themselves into the unknown. In *Study of Thomas Hardy* he argued that:

> we have the necessity to work, more or less, according as we are nearer the tip or further away. Some men are far from the growing tip. They have little for growth in them, only the power of repeating old movement. (STH: 36)

In the Epilogue to *Movements in European History*, written whilst he was finishing *Women in Love*, he argued that

> Mankind is like a huge old tree [. . .] In its roots and its massive trunk, the tree of mankind is undivided [. . .] each branch has its own growing tip. In every race, the growing tip is the living idea [. . .] But as every branch of mankind has its own growing tip, so the whole tree of Man has one supreme travelling apex, one culminating growing tip [. . .] For a thousand years, surely, we may say that Europe has been the growing tip on the tree of mankind [. . .] But our spirit and manhood began to weaken. Our idea and our ideal began to peter out. So the War came, and blew away forever our leading tip, our growing tip. Now we are directionless. (MEH: 256–57)

Yet even within this blasted Europe, certain individuals constitute new developments for good and ill, and it is with such individuals that *Women in Love* is concerned: Birkin, Gerald, Ursula, Gudrun, Hermione, Winifred, and Loerke. All of these are weighty, and all command certain kinds of admiration, although they may also be condemned. The Brangwen parents, Laura, Tibs, Diana, Marshall, Mrs Salmon, Mrs Kirk, the level-crossing labourers, the miners, Halliday, Hasan, Libidnikov, and the Pussum, are 'of no account' (Lawrence used this phrase to denote spiritual triviality, for example in his acquaintance David 'Maxim' Litvinov, a model for Libidnikov) (LL ii: 629). Whereas in *Anna Karenina* Levin's parents are absent but signifying something, in *Women in Love* Ursula's parents are present, but signifying nothing. Insofar as Lawrence is writing for anyone, it is for those who are or have the potential to be growing tips, in order to try to distinguish for them between positive and negative directions of growth. He is not writing to mediate such people to the rest of humanity, or vice versa.

Posnett's description of 'the gradual expansion of social life, from clan to city, from city to nation, from both of these to cosmopolitan humanity, as the proper order of our studies in comparative literature' describes also the 'Widening Circle' which characterizes Ursula's consciousness in *The Rainbow* (Posnett 1886: 86). In *Women in Love*, its continuation, all of the growing tips are distinguished from the rest of humanity by their familiarity with several languages and cultures. However, just as being a growing tip is not in itself a guarantee of healthy development, multicultural knowledge is of no more value in itself than it is in *Anna Karenina*. Breadalby, with its *Contessa* and *Fräulein*, and the Pompadour, with its young Russian, are cosmopolitan in clientele and consciousness, but are not sites of positive growth; the limited murderess Hermione is a 'Kulturträger, a medium for the culture of ideas' (WL: 16). The novel's emphasis is on rootlessness, not cosmopolitanism, and the gaining of knowledge of different cultures is entailed by an itinerant life, but is not its object. Whereas *Daniel Deronda* pointedly fails to gloss its French and German, *Women in Love* takes care not to exclude anyone unfamiliar with its languages; only Hermione's Italian, which irritates Ursula by excluding her, is left untranslated out of sympathy. When Gudrun and Loerke strengthen their relationship through multinational historical reconstructions they use a pidgin based on French modulated by German and English — a linguistic correlative of Goethe's idea of *Weltliteratur* as mediatory. Daniel Deronda's religious ecstasy at the Hebrew liturgy in Frankfurt is parodied by Gudrun's reaction to Loerke's presentation of Cologne dialect: 'Gudrun could not understand a word of his monologue, but she was spell-bound, watching him' (WL: 406). The novel's rejection of nationalism, then, does not entail an embrace of supranationalism. Gerald suggests that Birkin means '"that *nationally* all Englishmen must die, so that they can exist individually and — " "Super-nationally" — put in Gudrun, with a slight ironic grimace, raising her glass'; at the ensuing chapter ending the novel raises its own glass and grimaces (WL: 397).

Unlike *Daniel Deronda*, which looks to a Zionist Israel, and *Anna Karenina*, which looks to a Christian Russia, *Women in Love* has no place to which it aspires. Indeed, if *Daniel Deronda* implicitly casts Jews as inhabitants of the moon, who have a perspective on Gentile earthlings, the only perspective gained on the earth in *Women in Love* is posited by Gudrun and Loerke in their Swiftian parody of an apocalypse:

> As for the future, that they never mentioned except one laughed out some mocking dream of the destruction of the world by a ridiculous catastrophe of man's invention: a man invented such a perfect explosive that it blew the earth in two, and the two halves set off in different directions through space, to the dismay of the inhabitants. (WL: 453)

Paris offers no more than an alternative Bohemia; a superficially attractive Hindu is swiftly dismissed as insignificant. Even the Alps, which have a landscape as strange as that of the moon, constitute no source of value, but function as a dividing line which separates the couple which can escape to Italy (Ursula and Birkin) from the couple which cannot.

Those countries in which Lawrence was most interested at the time of writing the novel offer no hope at all. Libidnikov the Russian is made as attractive as possible, but ultimately constitutes only the most civilized aspect of Bohemia. Gudrun's plan to go to Saint Petersburg (since 'The emotional, rather rootless life of the Russians appealed to her') recommends that city somewhat less to the reader than does Klesmer's plan to go there in *Daniel Deronda*. America is present only as the source of the machines with which Gerald mechanizes his mines (the same, negative role that it serves for Levin in *Anna Karenina*). Throughout the year in which *Women in Love* was completed Lawrence thought of visiting Palestine, but of this country there is no mention in the novel beyond Birkin's momentary allegorical perception of Beldover as Jerusalem. His desire to reach an archetypal promised land ('Oh, do [David Eder] take me to Palestine, and I will love you for ever') makes the novel's refusal to contemplate such a land the more striking (LL III: 353). Germany is ambivalent in its presentation. The novel contained features that allowed certain German critics of the Nazi era to perceive it as pro-German (for example, Kurt

Weineck in his 1938 *Deutschland und der Deutsche im Spiegel der englischen erzählenden Literatur seit 1830* [*Germany and the German in the Mirror of English Narrative Literature Since 1830*] (Jansohn and Mehl 2007: 49). There is certainly 'no sign of the vile and barbaric Hun then being demonized in the British wartime press', nor of the dehumanizing Prussian army described for example in Lawrence's August 1914 article 'With the Guns'; the German guests in the Tyrol are, with the exception of Loerke, relatively positively presented (Bradshaw 1998: xxvi). Germany mediates between nations, as it did for Goethe, for Eliot, and to a smaller extent for Tolstoi: it is in Heidelberg that Birkin gets to know the Japanese man who taught him jiu-jitsu; Gerald, like Daniel, has shunned an Oxbridge education in order to study in Germany. However, that country is no longer the source and icon of a liberal education: Mordecai's drinking of knowledge from many sources has been replaced by Gerald's desire 'to see and to know, in a curious objective fashion, as if it were an amusement to him'. The ineffectuality of his education is suggested by the sentence which follows: 'Then he must try war' (WL: 222). Gudrun perceives that the wind blows 'towards Germany' just before Gerald half-kills her, and Dresden is the home not only of Loerke but of Dalcroze, whose eurhythmics, as David Bradshaw has pointed out, are negatively connected to the social-mechanistic theories of F. W. Taylor via their shared advocacy of control over the body by the will (Bradshaw 1998: xxxvi–xxxvii). One consequence of the novel's generalized misanthropy is that it demonstrates no Eurocentrism; the Arctic extreme is not preferable to the African (nor the reverse, in contrast to *The Plumed Serpent*, in which Mexico promises to supersede a degenerate Europe). Indeed, the novel is far less concerned with the distinction between Europe and anywhere beyond it than is *Daniel Deronda* or *Anna Karenina*, although it resembles both in its refusal to extol Europe as a source of value. It is to Gerald's mind, 'curious and cold', that 'the savage was duller, less exciting than the European', and 'On the whole' 'harmless', 'not born yet', and 'over-rated' (WL: 222, 66). Since there is no promised land, and since imaginary worlds are themselves mistrusted (for example those of Gudrun and Loerke), and since the idea of living in a commune is only once and tentatively put forwards, the solution for Birkin and Ursula is to wander.

In this respect at least Lawrence identified himself as a Jew, claiming in December 1919 that 'I am turned into a wandering Jew' (LL III: 435). However, the secular, emancipated, cosmopolitan Jew, represented positively by Klesmer in *Daniel Deronda*, is negatively represented by Loerke (the two mildly mocking, commercially minded Jews of *Anna Karenina* being part way between the two). In both of the English novels Jews are presented as *growing tips*, but they are growing in different directions. Differences between Eliot's and Lawrence's attitude towards Jews (the word 'anti-Semitism' had entered English between the former's death and the latter's birth) are one among many differences between them on which critics have remarked: 'His seriousness [. . .] hasn't her touch of solemnity'; Lawrence is more direct and inward than Eliot in his treatment of people's needs for each other; where Eliot is ethical, Lawrence is religious (Leavis 1955: 91, 101, 114). As early as 1908 Lawrence had declared of Eliot 'I am very fond of her, but I wish she'd take her specs off, and come down off the public platform' (LL I: 101). On the other hand, he considered Eliot to have pioneered the writing of psychological interiority; Jessie Chambers recalls him telling her:

> You see, it was really George Eliot who started it all [. . .] And how wild they all were with her for doing it. It was she who started putting all the action inside. Before, you know, with Fielding and the others, it had been outside. Now I wonder which is right? [. . .] You know I can't help thinking there ought to be a bit of both. (1965: 105)

He particularly admired *Adam Bede* (as did Tolstoi) and the first half of *The Mill on the Floss* ('The Virgin and the Gypsy' indicates his critique of the second half), and he was planning to reread both when starting *The Sisters* (Chambers 1965: 98). Gudrun contemplates 'the Arthur Donnithornes, the Geralds of this world. So manly by day, yet all the while, such a crying of infants in the night' (WL: 466). Although he thereafter hardly mentioned Eliot, he never turned decisively against her. *Women in Love* and *Daniel Deronda* are rendered comparable by, amongst other factors, the many characteristics which the authors share: as recorders 'of essential English history', inheritors of a Protestant ethical tradition, and critics of English culture (Leavis 1955: 110). Since it is not known whether Lawrence ever read *Daniel Deronda*, *Women in Love* can only implicitly and hypothetically be read as a response to it.

The same is not true of *Anna Karenina*, to which *Women in Love* makes a strongly implied response; as a result the novels *interanimate* one another, to use Steiner's term (1975: 436). Rather as Eliot and Lewes had taken refuge in Goethe during their first, adulterous tour of Germany in 1854–55 ('Their own personal situation gave an edge to their defence of Goethe's greatness against the still widespread charges of immorality and irreligion that had been leveled at him'), so Lawrence and Frieda took refuge in *Anna Karenina* in 1912 (Shaffer 1996: 7). The task of comparing *Women in Love* to *Anna Karenina* must take account of the fact that Lawrence was, in part, *constructing* a comparison. Like Tolstoi's comparison of Levin and Anna, this is acknowledged at the level of detail. Levin and Kiti's wedding is delayed, to the rising discomfiture of the assembled company, by Levin's search for a clean shirt; Laura and Lupton's wedding is similarly delayed, by the groom's search for a button-hook. Vronskii's mare Frou-Frou, who is killed by Vronskii's ineptitude during a race, symbolizes womankind in a manner reprised by Gerald's terrified mare at the level-crossing, and made explicit in Birkin's comment on the incident, 'woman is the same as horses' (WL: 141). The steam train, which in *Anna Karenina* is associated with nightmares, horror, and death, is in *Women in Love* 'like a disgusting dream that has no end' (WL: 111). On the largest scale, both novels contrast a relatively happy married couple with an unmarried couple of which one partner commits suicide.

Double-barrelled affair

Even more obviously than either Eliot or Tolstoi, Lawrence liked to construct his works around comparison. Several of his works contain two contrasting prot-agonists — often sisters, who are comparable by virtue of being of the same sex, the products of similar nurture (thus minimizing a variable which is irrelevant in the comparison of their natures), and often seen together. Works which juxtapose sisters include 'Second Best', 'The Christening', 'Daughters of the Vicar' (first called 'Two Marriages', as was an early draft of *Anna Karenina* [Два брака]), *Women in Love* (until 1919 called *The Sisters*), 'You Touched Me', 'The Virgin and the Gypsy', and *Lady Chatterley's Lover*. In the last four of these seven cases, written between 1913 and 1928, the sisters are all only two years apart in age, thus minimizing the differences in their nurture and maturity. Gudrun is born when Ursula is three, but the opening of *Women in Love* presents them as two years apart, perhaps in order to make them the more comparable. Since Lawrence's sisters do not remain single, his works also compare couples; in this he took Eliot as his precursor. Shortly before beginning *The White Peacock* he told Jessie Chambers:

> The usual plan is to take two couples and to develop their relationships [. . .] Most of George Eliot's are on that plan. Anyhow, I don't want a plot, I should be bored with it. I shall try two couples for a start. (Chambers 1965: 103)

The 'most of George Eliot's' might have included *Adam Bede*, *The Mill on the Floss*, *Middlemarch*, and *Daniel Deronda*; he himself went on to compare couples in *The White Peacock*, *Daughters of the Vicar*, *Women in Love*, *Aaron's Rod*, and *The Plumed Serpent*. Hirai and Trotter have noticed this as part of a more general phenomenon, and the latter cited Gissing, Forster, and Lawrence in his observation that 'Whereas the new women novelists tended to pair different types of degeneracy, the hoggish and the hysterical [. . .] their successors tended to pair a couple seeking regeneration with a couple [. . .] doomed to degeneracy' (Hirai 1998: 129; Trotter 1993: 124).

Although *Women in Love* uses words associated with comparison and contrast with only a tenth of the frequency of *Daniel Deronda*, its narrator makes explicit comparisons, for example noting on the first page that Gudrun's 'look of confidence and diffidence contrasted with Ursula's sensitive expectancy', and contrasting Gerald's and Birkin's physiques during their wrestling (WL: 8). The narrator's comparison of Mr Crich and Gerald is summarized by the crossing-keeper's observation that 'They're as different as they welly can be, Gerald Crich and his father'; indeed, Gerald *constructs* himself as a contrast to his father. Overall, the central characters and couples are considerably more aware of their similarities and differences than are those of *Daniel Deronda* and *Anna Karenina*: 'Gerald waited for the Ursula–Birkin marriage. It was something crucial to him'; he contemplates making it 'a double-barrelled affair', and proposes the joint holiday (WL: 350). After the marriage, Gerald comments to Ursula on her and Birkin's obvious happiness: 'She was very sensitive to suggestion. She asked the question he wanted her to ask. "Why don't you be happy as well?" she said. "You could be just the same"'; she then recommends that he marry Gudrun (WL: 370). Birkin, on the other hand, describes Gudrun as a born mistress and Gerald as a born lover, in contrast to himself and Ursula. Gudrun, like Gerald, is jealous of the other couple's happiness; on rejoining them after her first destructive sex in the Tyrol, '"How good and simple they look together" Gudrun thought, jealously. She envied them some spontaneity, a childish sufficiency to which she herself could never approach' (WL: 403). Whereas Lawrence usually uses singular titles for his works (*The White Peacock*, *The Trespasser*, *The Rainbow*, *Aaron's Rod*, *Kangaroo*, *The Plumed Serpent*), or else titles which denote a contrast rather than making an invitation to comparison (*The Virgin and the Gypsy*, 'New Eve and Old Adam'), *Women in Love* is rare in referring to comparable characters without comparing them: other examples include 'Daughters of the Vicar' and 'Two Blue Birds'. Here, the results of comparison are not forecast.

Of course, the comparison of either the sisters or the couples is complicated by the novel's likeness to 'a real quartet, not two duets' (Ford 1963: 97). Not only do many episodes involve the men, or the women, together, but they can include any combination of these characters, with or without Hermione. Of the novel's forty-one segments, five belong to the sisters, seven to the men, and six to all four characters. In only half of the segments do the couples appear in isolation from one another: thirteen for Ursula and Birkin, and nine for Gudrun and Gerald, of which all but two appear in the last two-thirds of the novel. The title appears to stress the female axis rather than the couples, but is of course ambiguous, since the women are defined in their relations to men (there is a similar ambiguity in the title of *Lady Chatterley's Lover*, which names her but denotes him). This fits with the fact that most of the chapters in which at least three of the central characters meet begin with the sisters, but end with their separation. The tensions involved in the title extend to jibing at *The Rainbow*'s suppression for depicting lesbianism; jibing at lesbianism itself (since the women are precisely *not* mutually in love); honouring love over war ('If I love, then, I am in direct opposition to the principle of war'); satirizing the novel's characters for having at least as much to do with hate; and satirizing the idea of being in love (although the mistranslated German title, *Liebende Frauen* [*Loving Women* rather than the accurate *Verliebte Frauen*] is no more appropriate to the novel) (LL II: 424; Jansohn and Mehl 2007: 56). Bradshaw notes that 'This is the only novel Lawrence wrote with a title which is not transparent' — it does at least, however, acknowledge the novel's quartet, by alluding to three of its constituent couples (1998: xiv). Another respect in which the novel differs from *Daniel Deronda* and *Anna Karenina* is that its space is not divided into domains. The social distinction between the families of the women and of the men is shrunk to triviality by the younger generation. A few geographical locations, such as Sherwood Forest and Paris, are briefly associated with one or other of the couples, but most of the novel's space is as neutral with regard to character as it is in *Sense and Sensibility* or *Howard's End*, where sisters conduct contrasting relationships with contrasting men in the same social and physical space. Narrative time is equally homogeneous. Sometimes, as often in *Daniel Deronda* and *Anna Karenina*, analepsis points to the simultaneity of the *fabulae* ('Meanwhile Ursula had wandered on'); more frequently, time drifts forwards between segments and chapters in gaps neither emphasized nor precise (only half of the chapters end with action continued immediately in the next) (WL: 123). The fact that Birkin, Hermione, and Gudrun are all connected by disappearing from the Beldover region for an extended period of time during the action of the novel is not felt by most readers, actions in time being far less important than the characters' congregation in space. These differences to the two earlier novels affects the mode of their comparison.

Inquest

One point on which they are comparable, however, is the fact that they all contain characters which invite investigation as possible scapegoats of their texts. *Women in Love* does not use the word *scapegoat*, although Lawrence, whose familiarity with the Old Testament is as evident in this novel as in anything he wrote, was certainly familiar with the concept. In *Women in Love* it is most obviously applicable to Gerald. He dies cast out from humankind, making his way through a wilderness, unredeemed by the archetypal scapegoat sacrifice represented by the Crucifix which he passes. Yet his death has multiple potential causes, which singly and in combination only partly fit the interpretation of him as a scapegoat; this section will consider them in turn, by way of inquest. First, Gerald lacks the personal qualities necessary in order to sustain life in the society in which he finds himself. Second, he dies because of Gudrun's treatment of him. Third, he dies because he refuses *Blutbrüderschaft* with Birkin. In the first case he may be seen as a scapegoat of his text only insofar as qualities which are not certainly culpable, or which he is not responsible for possessing, are being representatively punished by the novel. In the second case he is a victim *within* his text but not of it. In the third case he is a scapegoat of his text insofar as the connection between his rejection of Birkin and his death is imposed, from outside the narrative's logic, in order representatively to punish this rejection. In this novel, as in most of Lawrence's works, good living is generally its own reward, and bad living its own punishment. This contrasts, for example, with Tolstoi's works, in which many of his characters are able to achieve worldly success because they have the right relationship to life: in *War and Peace* Kutuzov achieves military victories *because* he uses intuition rather than Prussian military theory, and Levin finds that he knows why to live, is happy, and makes the best decisions on his estate, *because* he has found belief in God. Correspondingly, most of Lawrence's deaths serve no form of implied justice — for example, those of Mrs Morel, Tom Brangwen, or Mr Crich. Deaths such as Gerald's, which appear connected to the novel's values, are rare, and deserve particular scrutiny. The three types of cause of Gerald's death will be taken in turn.

The conditions for living as a growing tip are more demanding in this novel than in anything else Lawrence wrote. These circumstances can be contrasted not only with those of *The Rainbow*, but with those of *The First 'Women in Love'* (a novel of more humour and less destructiveness), and with those of *Anna Karenina*.[1] I will look at the last. Levin and Gerald are comparable as young, physically powerful landowners and masters of men who try to reform their estates, have a family history of traumatizing deaths (a protracted example of which they witness at first hand), exhaust the pleasures of casual sexual relations, sense the meaninglessness of their own lives, and fear their own impetus towards annihilation. Unlike Levin and his contemporary Mr Crich, however, Gerald

> did not inherit an established order and a living idea. The whole unifying idea of mankind seemed to be dying with his father [. . .] Gerald was as if left on board of a ship that was going asunder beneath his feet. (WL: 221)

Gerald's own contemporary Konstantin Dmitrich Levin would, had he existed, have experienced this sensation in a still more extreme form in Russia during the period in which *Women in Love* was written. Gerald represents what Levin might have been if denied the possibility of faith (with the addition of Vronskii's level of lust, taste for strong women, and military background, and Oblonskii's scepticism of his best friend's excesses). The comparison is stressed by the migration of a metaphor — the *пузырек* [bubble] — from Levin to Gerald. After attaining happiness in marriage Levin has a horror of life's finitude: 'В бесконечном времени, в бесконечности материи, в бесконечном пространстве выделяется пузырек-организм, и пузырек этот подержится и лопнет, и пузырек этот — я' [In infinite time, in infinite matter, in infinite space, is formed a bubble-organism, and that bubble lasts a while and bursts, and that bubble is — me] (AK IX: 375). After succeeding in the mines Gerald looks at his eyes in a mirror and 'was not sure that they were not blue false bubbles that would burst in a moment [. . .] and be a purely meaningless babble lapping round a darkness' (WL: 232). A different metaphor migrates to Gerald from the ending of Tolstoi's *Исповедь* [*A Confession*] (although, since the latter was not translated into English until by Aylmer Maude in 1921, this migration occurred without Lawrence's awareness unless someone such as Kotelianskii had told him of the passage). Tolstoi has a dream in which he is lying, as he thinks, in bed, but then realizes that he is suspended by ropes. He tries to adjust the ropes for comfort, but as he does so he begins to slip out, and realizes that he is suspended over a bottomless abyss. His terror is relieved only when he looks into the immensity of sky above, and realizes that he is firmly held (Tolstoi 1963: 92–94). After his father's death, Gerald 'was like a man hung in chains over the edge of an abyss' — but, unlike Levin, he is unable to look upwards, or to feel any such comfort in the existence of a 'creative mystery' as Birkin later feels whilst contemplating Gerald's own corpse (WL: 337; 478). When his relationship with Gudrun becomes overwhelmingly destructive, he has no reason to live (the greater importance which Lawrence places on relationships compared to Tolstoi may be seen in the fact that Levin wants to commit suicide *after* finding happiness with Kiti). Trotter summarizes: 'Gerald, unlike Birkin, cannot create an alternative to degeneracy. His failure propels him [. . .] into the final spiral of the degeneration plot' (1993: 127).

To a certain extent Gerald is condemned by spiritual bad luck in the sense of Bernard Williams's *moral luck*: his death gives resonance to his tetchy and wayward infancy, arctic nature, assertion of a 'family failing' of being 'curiously bad at living', being 'set apart, like Cain', a sense that 'he belonged naturally to dread and catastrophe', and his mother's warning 'You're hysterical, always were' (WL: 205, 172, 179, 327). His failed attempt to kill Gudrun is presaged as early as his time with the Pussum: 'Gerald was on the point of knocking-in Halliday's face; when he was filled with sudden disgust and indifference, and he went away' (WL: 81). To Birkin's questioning of whether Gerald is 'fated to pass away in this knowledge, this one process of frost-knowledge, death by perfect cold? Was he a messenger, an omen of the universal dissolution into whiteness and snow?' the novel answers in the affirmative (WL: 254). Hirai's description of Gerald's death as 'ruthlessly and yet sympathetically related as inevitable' resembles several critics' descriptions of Anna Karenina's death (1998: 210).

On the other hand, Gerald's failings, such as they are, are interpretable in terms of the novel's overarching values, such as *they* are. The novel excludes no-one from happiness on grounds of ethnicity or artistic talent (as *Daniel Deronda* might be considered to exclude Gwendolen). Daleski comments that: 'It is almost as if Lawrence carries out an autopsy on the still-breathing form of pre-war society' — yet in contrast to *Daniel Deronda* and *Anna Karenina*, which perform something similar, that society has almost no palpable presence in the novel; the cast of minor characters who are 'of no account' hardly figures. One result is that whereas Gwendolen and Anna are presented as the victims as well as examples of their societies' faults, Gerald represents negative extremes of a society which has no substantial presentation, and of which he is therefore not palpably the product.

A reading of Gerald as scapegoat is also supported by the fact that he suffers more than other characters whose characteristics are condemned by the novel's rhetoric at least as much, or more than, his. The characters 'of no account' play such small roles in *Women in Love*, like clowns in a tragedy, that their comparative lack of suffering is of no ethical relevance to Gerald (in contrast to, for example, Betsi Tverskaiia in relation to Anna). However, Loerke is last seen 'sitting ludicrously in the snow', knocked down in a come-uppance befitting the villain of a farce rather than of a tragedy (WL: 471). Hermione is strongly censured by Birkin and the novel's rhetoric, but is last seen in the novel 'assuming her rights' in Birkin's room, and enjoying power over the Mino (WL: 300). Thereafter, like a scapegoat in the Jewish sense of a wandering outcast, she is dismissed from the novel and not seen again. But her last conversation with Ursula has suggested that she will survive the news of a marriage between Birkin and Ursula, and that she will not be left as desolate as Gwendolen at the end of *Daniel Deronda*. Her dismissal from the novel is therefore more charitable than punitive (although it also, as will be seen below, frees the novel from a troubling ethical presence). The rest of the novel, by contrast, builds towards what is at least in part a punitive action against Gerald.

The interpretation of Gerald as Gudrun's victim, like the equivalent interpretation of Vronskii, must confront the fact that it is he who pursues her — albeit not with Vronskii's insistence, nor with his obstacles to overcome. One effect of the novel's episodic form is that the central characters seem to have the freedom to rearrange themselves without friction and at will, for tea, a walk, a meal, or a holiday, splitting off as soon as they weary of the company, and wholly free to establish whichever combination satisfies him or her the most. At the time of writing, Lawrence was making such trials (albeit with less freedom), by bringing Philip Heseltine, John Middleton Murry and Katharine Mansfield, Esther Andrews and Robert Mountsier, and Cecil Gray, into combination with himself and Frieda in Cornwall. Not only does Gerald choose Gudrun, but she is in certain respects *his* victim. Their sex, from the Beldover bedroom to the Tyrol, is consistently presented as more destructive of her than of him. In *The First 'Women in Love'* he is gentler: when inspecting Gudrun's wound in 'Rabbit', rather than being connected to the 'forever unconscious, unthinkable red ether of the beyond, the obscene beyond',

'He wanted to touch the exquisite, silken soft skin of her arm. But he had not the courage at this moment. They looked at each other with half-smiling eyes of unconfessed knowledge, as if recognizing a blood-brotherhood' (WL: 242; 1WL: 223). Birkin is less 'cold and damning' of Gudrun after Gerald's death in the final version (1WL: 438).

On the other hand, Lawrence has reversed the gender pattern from *Anna Karenina*, in which it is the woman who commits suicide and the man who is left desolate (although Gudrun's move to Dresden hardly matches Vronskii's move to Serbia). Before the most difficult phase of his relationship with Jessie Chambers, Lawrence had held that women were more vulnerable in relationships than men. This idea is voiced without significant repudiation in the 1910 short story 'A Modern Lover' when the Lawrence-figure, Cyril, tries to convince the Jessie-figure, Muriel, to have sex with him; she responds: 'but you know — it's much harder for the woman — it means something so different for a woman' (Lawrence 1987a: 47). However, Lawrence modified this perspective after Jessie had recoiled from their first sex, and after his friend Helen Corke's married lover had committed suicide after spending an illicit holiday with her on the Isle of White. In both cases the woman's revulsion from sex with him caused the man considerable distress. Lawrence told Jessie: 'I have always believed it was the woman who paid the price in life. But I've made a discovery. It's the man who pays, not the woman' (LL: 155). This altered perspective is apparent in *The Trespasser*, which was based on both Helen's relationship and his own. Of course, Gudrun has far more sexual appetite than Helen or Jessie: the obscene knowledge over her wound is shared; and it is not made known, as though this were unimportant, whether or not she is a virgin when Gerald comes to her. Since she has spent several years as an artist in London, it is possible (if on balance unlikely) that she should have had a lover or two, as Hilda and Constance Chatterley do before their respective marriages. Despite this, like Helen and Jessie she feels violated by sex in a way which damages the man who gives it to her; unlike them, she desires revenge. In this she resembles Lawrence's interpretation of Anna Karenina, Hester Prynne (in *The Scarlet Letter*), and Sue Bridehead (in *Jude the Obscure*), of whom he wrote that 'these women are never satisfied till they have shattered the man who responded to them' (SCAL: 249). Even the young doctor who tries to rescue Diana Crich dies at the hands of the woman to whom he reaches out — the only successful strangling in the novel. It is Gerald who remarks: 'She killed him' (WL: 189).

Several passages of the novel suggest that Gudrun will vanquish Gerald. When she strikes him on the island during the Water-Party:

> 'You have struck the first blow,' he said at last, forcing the words from his lungs, in a voice so soft and low, it sounded like a dream within her, not spoken in the outer air. 'And I shall strike the last,' she retorted involuntarily, with confident assurance. He was silent, he did not contradict her. (WL: 171)

He does not include this detail in his later account of the incident to Birkin, but the reader is reminded of his failure to mention it. When Gudrun realizes what she perceives to be Gerald's essentially polygamous nature,

The deep resolve formed in her, to combat him. One of them must triumph over the other. Which should it be? Her soul steeled itself with strength. Almost she laughed within herself, at her confidence. It woke a certain keen, half contemptuous pity, tenderness for him: she was so ruthless. (WL: 413)

In *Anna Karenina* Anna is increasingly tormented by the fear that Vronskii will leave her — a fear without cause. In *Women in Love* it is Gerald who fears that Gudrun is withdrawing from him, and this time with cause. When Gudrun kneels at the window of their Alpine room Gerald senses not only her withdrawal, but her worship of what will become the medium and environment of his death:

> She was gone. She was completely gone, and there was icy vapour round his heart. He saw the blind valley, the great cul de sac of snow and mountain peaks, under the heaven. And there was no way out. The terrible silence and cold and the glamorous whiteness of the dusk wrapped him round, and she remained crouching before the window, as at a shrine, a shadow. (WL: 401)

Whereas Gerald's sex is usually felt as destructive by Gudrun, Gudrun's sexuality is sometimes described as such by the narrator: 'A strange black passion surged up pure in Gudrun. She felt strong. She felt her hands so strong, as if she could tear the world asunder with them. She remembered the abandonments of Roman licence, and her heart grew hot' (WL: 287). Admittedly, Birkin suggests that Gerald's victimhood might be voluntary: when Gerald tells him, before the latter leaves for Verona, that 'There's something final about this. And Gudrun seems like the end, to me. [. . .] It blasts your soul's eye [. . .] and leaves you sightless', Birkin responds: 'Yet you *want* to be sightless, you *want* to be blasted, you don't want it any different' (WL: 439). The implicit contrast is made with Birkin himself, who had the life-instinct to resist the second blow from the piece of lapis-lazuli, and tells Hermione: 'It isn't I who will die' (WL: 106). On balance, then, the novel does not suggest that either Gerald or Gudrun is overwhelmingly responsible for the destructiveness of their relationship. Nor, on the other hand, does it suggest that she is either actively or passively an overwhelming or sufficient cause of his death.

The third line of interpretation connects Gerald's death not with his relationship to Gudrun but to Birkin — or rather, the absence of a *final* one. Birkin himself seems to consider that had Gerald accepted *Blutbrüderschaft* with him, then he might not have committed suicide — the connection being either one of correlation (the kind of man capable of committing himself in friendship to Birkin would not have entered into such a destructive relationship), or else one of causation (Gerald's commitment to Birkin would have prevented him from developing such a relationship). Birkin therefore differs from Daniel and Levin, in that he places considerable blame on the novel's least successful character. At their last meeting, ' "I've loved you, as well as Gudrun, don't forget" said Birkin bitterly. Gerald looked at him strangely, abstractedly. "Have you?" he said, with icy scepticism. "Or do you think you have?" [. . .] Something froze Birkin's heart, seeing them standing there in the isolation of the snow' — rhetorically connecting the failure of their relationship with Gerald's fate (WL: 440). On the other hand, Birkin also feels that had Gerald committed to him, then death would not have mattered. Those who die, and dying still can love, still believe, do not die. They live still in the beloved. Gerald might still have been living in the spirit with Birkin, even after death. He might have lived with his friend, a further life. But now he was dead. (WL: 480)

Birkin's interpretation meets with Ursula's scepticism, but with no alternative interpretation or narrative scepticism (WL: 480).

Blutbrüderschaft was an important concept for Lawrence at the time of writing; in March 1916 he had written to Murry and Mansfield: 'Let it be agreed for ever. I am Blutbruder: a Blutbruderschaft between us all' (*sic*) (LL II: 570). The discarded Prologue to the novel, written in the following month, describes how Gerald and Birkin became friends, and stresses Birkin's 'passion of desire for Gerald Crich, for the clumsier, cruder intelligence and the limited soul, and for the striving, unlightened body of his friend' (WL: 493). However, Birkin's offers of *Blutbrüderschaft* were not introduced until the final version of the novel, written between March 1917 and September 1919. Here, his sexual attraction to Gerald is almost excluded, and the concept has reverted to its usual denotation of exclusively male friendship (in contrast to its use both in the letter of March 1916, and in another of November 1918, in which he wrote to Mansfield: 'I believe the same way in friendship between men and women, and between women and women, sworn, pledged, eternal, as eternal as the marriage bond, and as deep') (LL II: 302). Rather, Birkin's approaches to Gerald resemble those of Lawrence to Middleton Murry. Ursula's lack of an equivalent desire, Birkin and Gerald's closest union in the intimacy of wrestling, and Ursula and Gudrun's closest union in a shared picnic and social contempt, fit with views expounded by Lawrence both before and during the writing of *Women in Love* (WL: 352). In *Study of Thomas Hardy* he placed women at the axle and men at the rim of a metaphorical wheel, and in 'Education of the People' (late 1918) argued that men should make spiritual explorations in intimate mutual friendship (STH: 60; RDP: 166). Lawrence's interest in the attempts of men to achieve relationships may be one reason why he is relatively uninterested in blood brothers, whose relationship is already established. Indeed, brothers in his fiction are typically undistinguished wastrels or tyrants, such as Alfred's brothers in 'Daughters of the Vicar', Mabel's brothers in 'The Horse Dealer's Daughter', and Teresa's brothers in *The Plumed Serpent*. The proposal of *Blutbrüderschaft* is first made and rejected in 'Man to Man'. Then, after their wrestling, Gerald asks: ' "[. . .] Is this the Bruderschaft you wanted?" "Perhaps. Do you think this pledges anything?" "I don't know," laughed Gerald' (WL: 273). The narrative does not insist on knowing, at this point, but the subject is brought up again reproachfully by Birkin at the end of 'Continental', and finally in 'Exeunt'. Although slightly more of the novel's space is given to Gerald and Birkin than to Gudrun and Ursula, 'contacts between the men fall off more dramatically, and earlier in the novel, than they do for the sisters' (Blanchard 1980: 205). The last time that the men appear alive together for a scene is in 'Marriage or Not', and for only two and a half pages — 'a dramatic structural indication of the failure of that brotherhood' (Blanchard 1980: 205).

Of course, Birkin does not speak with a monologic voice; Lawrence himself considered that 'Every art has a morality, but must also criticise it'. Wright is one of several critics who have described *Women in Love* as a 'genuinely polyphonic novel', in which Ursula in particular makes successful challenges to Birkin (RDP: 380; Wright 2000: 131). Bell considers that 'it is not so much that Birkin is ironised as that he is used to explore, sometimes through rhetorical extremes, possibilities of feeling and attitude to which the novel is not necessarily committed even as it supports the emotional quest' (Bell 2001: 190). The same comment also could be applied to Levin, and indeed Mills found that 'Levin showed Lawrence how to treat Birkin humorously' (Mills 1996: 57). Nonetheless, the episode in the Pompadour Café, in which Birkin's style is parodied, is intended to work in his favour, and his ideas are considerably more supported by the narrative rhetoric than are Levin's. Birkin's position is never as exposed as is, for example, Levin's in the Anglia Restaurant concerning the impossibility of tragedy for impure women. Birkin, not Levin, is supported by the narrative when they argue for opposite positions concerning the value of education — an issue on which both novels broadly agree.[2] When Levin disputes the value of educating peasants on the grounds that educated peasants make inferior workers, Levin feels 'нравственно припертым к стене' [morally pinned against a wall] by Koznyshev (AK VIII: 260). Koznyshev's challenge that if education is 'хорошо для тебя, то и для всякого' [a good thing for you, then it's a good thing for everyone] is echoed in Birkin's question: 'Would you rather, for yourself, know or not know, that the little red flowers are there [. . .]?' (AK VIII: 260; WL: 40). More importantly, the events of the novel support Birkin's ideas far more than is the case for Levin. This is particularly true in relation to Gerald.

When Gerald is presented as doomed, it is often through Birkin's eyes, and the events of the novel subsequently bear his perspective out. After Gerald's first rejection of him:

> They lapsed both into silence. Birkin was looking at Gerald all the time. He seemed now to see, not the physical, animal man, which he usually saw in Gerald, and which usually he liked so much, but the man himself, complete, and as if fated, doomed, limited. This strange sense of fatality in Gerald, as if he were limited to one form of existence, one knowledge, one activity, a sort of fatal halfness, which to himself seemed wholeness, always overcame Birkin after their moments of passionate approach, and filled him with a sort of contempt, or boredom. It was the insistence on the limitation which so bored Birkin in Gerald. Gerald could never fly away from himself, in real indifferent gaiety. He had a clog, a sort of monomania. (WL: 207)

Birkin is also privileged among the four central characters in his focalization of free indirect speech. When Gerald asks Birkin 'what sort of way?' there is to go after death, the narrator's perspective displaces Gerald's in description which has the grammatical form of free indirect speech for Birkin: 'He seemed to press the other man for knowledge which he himself knew far better than Birkin did' (WL: 204). In the narrator's description of Gerald's thoughts on marrying Gudrun, Gerald is displaced without acknowledgement by Birkin as the focus of free indirect speech:

> He was ready to be doomed. Marriage was like a doom to him. He was willing to condemn himself in marriage, to become like a convict condemned to the mines of the underworld, living no life in the sun, but having a dreadful

subterranean activity. He was willing to accept this. And marriage was the seal of his condemnation. He was willing to be sealed thus in the underworld, like a soul damned but living forever in damnation. But he would not make any pure relationship with any other soul. He could not. Marriage was not the committing of himself into a relationship with Gudrun. It was a committing of himself in acceptance of the established world, he would accept the established order, in which he did not livingly believe, and then he would retreat to the underworld for his life. This he would do. The other way was to accept Rupert's offer of alliance, to enter into the bond of pure trust and love with the other man, and then subsequently with the woman. If he pledged himself with the man he would later be able to pledge himself with the woman: not merely in legal marriage, but in absolute, mystic marriage. Yet he could not accept the offer. There was a numbness upon him, a numbness either of unborn, absent volition, or of atrophy. Perhaps it was the absence of volition. For he was strangely elated at Rupert's offer. Yet he was still more glad to reject it, not to be committed. (WL: 353)

Insofar as Birkin not only resembles Lawrence, but is privileged in the mode of narration of the novel, he is implicated in the writing of the novel in which Gerald dies. This gives to the death the aspect of punishment for having disappointed him, as though Birkin were simultaneously *Blutbruder manqué*, grieving friend, coroner, and hanging judge. In this respect Gerald differs from that other Lawrencian scapegoat, Jill Banford in *The Fox*, who is killed in the revised ending of November 1921 not only representatively for her qualities, but structurally, for standing in the way of a relationship. 'The Woman who Rode Away' (1925) is killed representatively, but wholly impersonally (Girard, not Lawrence, recognizes the victims of Aztecs as scapegoats). Gerald's death is personal; Birkin demonstrates the irritation of a refused partner, as well as of a reluctant adviser, in answering Gerald's enquiry as to whether he should marry: 'If I were you I would *not* marry: but ask Gudrun, not me. You're not marrying me, are you?' (WL: 351). Blanchard's comment that 'One might call it a book of retaliation, almost of revenge' refers to this dynamic, although it exaggerates it (Blanchard 1980: 185). Gerald seems particularly helpless insofar as he is presented as not understanding Birkin's wishes any more than Oblonskii understands Levin's ideas: 'In the Train' 'Gerald watched him with curious eyes. He could not quite make him out' (WL: 57). I concur with Murry that Lawrence 'puts his finger in the balance' in favour of Gerald's death, although Murry expresses this as primarily a punishment for choosing Gudrun, rather than for rejecting Birkin (he is near-quoting Lawrence's 'Morality and the Novel': 'When a novelist puts his thumb in the scale, to pull down the balance to his own predilection, that is immorality') (Murry 1931: 121; STH: 528).

In *The First 'Women in Love'*, in the chapter part of which becomes 'Man to Man', the love of the men is described in the following terms:

For the present, there was only Gerald who had any connection. Gerald and he had a curious love for each other. It was a love that was perhaps death, a love which was complemented by the hatred for woman. It was a love that tore apart the two halves, and brought universal death. It tore man from woman, and woman from man. [. . .] But if this was so, it was so. There was the love between him and Gerald and the other was denied, all other was denied. Then there must be death. Unless Ursula would yield. [. . .] No man can create life by himself. It needs a man and a woman. And if the woman refuse, then the life is uncreated, and death triumphs. (1WL: 185)

The final version reverses this perspective, and yet the connection between male love and death remains. In *The First 'Women in Love'* Kaiser Wilhelm's lament about the First World War, 'ich habe es nicht gewollt' [I didn't want it], appears in a pessimistic speech by Birkin at the end of the episode which becomes 'Excurse' (1WL: 293). In the final version, it appears in Birkin's thoughts before Gerald's corpse. Hirai comments:

When Ursula is reminded of the Kaiser's statement on the anniversary of the outbreak of war, she is struck with horror at Birkin's possibly fatal emotional involvement in Gerald's death [. . .] While registering the universal failure, Birkin, far from exempting himself from it, identifies himself as an *unconscious* killer-victim, personally, emotionally as well as historically involved. (1998: 210)

Indeed, throughout his relationship with Gerald, Birkin had shown considerable self-consciousness. Like Daniel in relation to Gwendolen, he is a spiritual guide who makes little impact on Gerald's outward life other than occasionally making him feel temporarily 'soothed', and providing the example, which is not followed, of marriage (WL: 266). But he is considerably more reluctant and diffident in the role than Daniel, and responds agnostically to Gerald's requests for advice about the Pussum or Gudrun. When Gerald, in 'Gladiatorial', says that he wants 'something abiding, something that can't change' with a woman:

Birkin looked at him, and shook his head. 'I don't know,' he said. 'I could not say.' Gerald had been on the *qui vive*, as awaiting his fate. Now he drew back in his chair. 'No,' he said, 'and neither do I, and neither do I.' 'We are different, you and I,' said Birkin. 'I can't tell your life.' 'No,' said Gerald, 'no more can I. But I tell you — I begin to doubt it!' 'That you will ever love a woman?' 'Well — yes — what you would truly call love — You doubt it?' 'Well — I begin to.' There was a long pause. 'Life has all kinds of things,' said Birkin. 'There isn't only one road'. (WL: 276)

Birkin's answer echoes Anna Karenina's answer to Betsi Tverskaia's question as to whether adultery has potential advantages: 'Я думаю, — сказала Анна, играя снятою перчаткой, — я думаю. . . если сколько голов, столько умов, то и сколько сердец, столько родов любви'. ['I think,' said Anna, playing with the glove which she had taken off, 'I think. . . if there are so many people, so many minds, then there are so many hearts, so many kinds of love'] (AK VIII: 148). The relativism of her answer indicates to the listening Vronskii that he can hope to gain her, and the novel ultimately condemns both it and her. Birkin is denying that there is 'only one road' to successful living, whilst the novel suggests literally and metaphorically that 'the great Imperial road leading south to Italy' is the only one which offers at least some hope, and would, had he found it, have saved Gerald (WL: 478).

Like Daniel, Birkin is troubled by any imputation of responsibility for his advisee's fate. Gerald's mother tells him at the wedding reception:

'I should like him to have a friend,' she said. 'He has never had a friend.' 'Am I my brother's keeper?' he said to himself, almost flippantly. Then he remembered, with a slight shock, that that was Cain's cry. And Gerald was Cain, if anybody. Not that he was Cain, either, although he had slain his brother. (WL: 26)

During their first scene together in the novel, then, Birkin pre-emptively tries to disclaim responsibility for killing his metaphorical brother. His thought 'Not that he was Cain, either' might be thought also to absolve Gerald pre-emptively of any responsibility for hurting Birkin. Yet Gerald is saddled — through accident, through narrative design, or through his own deliberate fault — with the childhood murder of his biological brother, and is 'set apart, like Cain' (WL: 172). Cain himself bears a complex relationship to the concept of the scapegoat. Unlike a scapegoat, he has committed a crime, and has done so because (as Girard points out) he himself unjustly holds Abel responsible for God's preference for Abel's sacrifice. Like a scapegoat, on the other hand, he is condemned to wander for all his days — not being killed, merely shunned. He is also representative of, and cursed on behalf of, all murderers, since he is the first amongst them. Gerald's murder of his brother is also ambivalent: it can either be considered an early indication of his destructive nature (Ursula considers it not to have been an accident), or else as an accident or ancestral curse to which he is perforce passive (Birkin is unsure). Either way, Birkin's confused reference to Gerald as Cain connects Gerald in the reader's mind with a figure who is ambivalently an offender and victim, immediately after Birkin has disclaimed responsibility for him in a way which connects *himself* with that figure. This is the closest Birkin comes in the novel to recognizing his potential implication in Gerald's scapegoating.

Yet Birkin's feelings for Gerald never resemble Cain's for Abel. He feels for Gerald all the muted, conflicted attraction and pity which Daniel feels for Gwendolen, and the admiration and tenderness which Levin momentarily feels for Anna. It was mentioned in Chapter 2 that critics have found a related contrary motion of love and retribution in Tolstoi's treatment of Anna, which might explain why Anna's beautiful face is left untouched by the train which kills her. The description of Gerald's final moments is still more tender, since his suicide passively removes him from a torment, rather than being its culmination; there is the softness and cleanness of snow in the words with which he is put to sleep in it: 'he slipped and fell down, and as he fell something broke in his soul, and immediately he went to sleep' (WL: 474). In *The First 'Women in Love'* the echo of *Anna Karenina* is still closer. Anna dies as follows (the translation given is the Constance Garnett translation with which Lawrence was familiar; Garnett moves *forever* from the penultimate word to the end):

И свеча, при которой она читала исполненную тревог, обманов, горя и зла книгу, вспыхнула более ярким, чем когда-нибудь, светом, осветила ей все то, что прежде было во мраке, затрещала, стала меркнуть и навсегда потухла.

[And the light by which she had read the book filled with troubles, falsehoods, sorrow, and evil, flared up more brightly than ever before, lighted up for her all that had been in darkness, flickered, began to grow dim, and was quenched forever.] (AK IX: 353; AK G: 910)

In *The First 'Women in Love'* Gerald dies as follows:

> But he wandered on unconsciously, till he slipped and fell down, and immediately went to sleep for ever. (1WL: 436)

In that version Birkin is still more loving, since he does not reproach Gerald for his rejection: 'he strove to say' 'We will love you — you won't be cold' 'we needn't all be like that. All is not lost, because many are lost. — I am not afraid or ashamed to die and be dead' (1WL: 440). Almost the last line of *The First 'Women in Love'* is Birkin's thought that: 'All is not lost, because many are lost' (1WL: 443). This draft of the novel, at least, ends, like *Daniel Deronda*, with sombre Miltonic optimism. In the final version, the tenderness is tempered with blame, because Birkin had had far more need of Gerald than Daniel had of Gwendolen, or Levin of Anna.

A challenge to Birkin's ethical hold on the novel is presented by Hermione, not so much in what she says to him as in how she functions in the novel's structure. Even numerically she is *de trop*, once the 'Prologue' chapter (which presented the original trio of which she was part) had been discarded. In the first two thirds of the novel she presents a challenge by complicating the quartet into a quintet; after the 'Man to Man' chapter, which concerns Birkin and Gerald, the reader expects that 'Woman to Woman' will concern the sisters, but Hermione appears in Gudrun's place — as unexpected to the reader as unwelcome to Ursula. Her character becomes more stylized and attacked in the changes from the first to the final *Women in Love*, and from the Prologue in which she partly resembles Jessie Chambers. In the final version she serves the function of parodying Birkin, drawing the criticism which might otherwise be levelled at his ideas, and purging Birkin of responsibility for aspects of Lawrence's ideas which troubled Lawrence himself. But both the fact of the proximity of their ideas, and the brutality of his denunciation of her, mean that she herself serves in part as a scapegoat within the text. More troublingly, she presents a parallel to him in being disappointed of a close relationship which she desperately desires. She inherits some of what Lawrence considered to be the faults of Anna Karenina, including her need for control over her lover, and her desperation to be 'so beautiful that he would be enchanted once and for all' (WL: 514). When Hermione realizes that Birkin is not in the church to which she arrives as a bridesmaid, her response resembles Anna's psychosis on receiving a curt reply to her last letter received by Vronskii: 'And then, he was not there. A terrible storm came over her, as if she were drowning. She was possessed by a devastating hopelessness. And she approached mechanically to the altar. Never had she known such a pang of utter and final hopelessness. It was beyond death, so utterly null, desert' (WL: 18). Unlike Anna, she is not deluded in the idea that her lover is leaving her, and despite this, she survives; Lawrence attributes to her greater dignity than does Tolstoi to Anna. However, insofar as Birkin is indirectly responsible for the death of the man he loves, he is merely more successful than is Hermione with her paperweight. Leavis's comment that: 'What Birkin denounces so brutally in Hermione is what he knows as a dangerous potentiality in himself' may be applied as much to his feelings towards Gerald, as to his thoughts on any other subject (1955: 178). Hermione is not presented as a scapegoat of her text any more than is Gerald, but unlike him she highlights Birkin's hypocrisy, and is a more actively troubling agent in the text.

Limits of Contrast

Gerald's fate should be considered not only in relation to Birkin, Gudrun, or Hermione, but in relation to his and Gudrun's *shared* relative failure as contrasted to Birkin and Ursula's relative success. Understanding of this divergence of fates is significantly complicated by the lack of clear distinctions between the novel's four central characters and, in particular, between the two central couples. This was less true of the couples in *The First 'Women in Love'*, in which Birkin and Ursula's relationship was markedly less sexual than that of Gudrun and Gerald (in 'Excurse' Birkin speaks against sex, rather than being narrated having it). In addition, Gerald — like Vronskii over successive drafts of *Anna Karenina* — is mentally and spiritually coarser than he becomes. There has been a tendency in criticism of the novel, from which this chapter is not exempt, to read back spiritual differences between the two couples from the differences of their endings.

Daleski considers that:

> Birkin and Ursula, clinging to the life preserver of their own 'unison in separateness', abandon ship, whereas Gerald and Gudrun, by trying to destroy each other, symbolically prefigure in themselves the desire for death of those who do not attempt to leave the ship. (1965: 127–28)

This sentence does not make clear the connection between 'unison in separateness' and 'abandoning ship', or 'trying to destroy themselves', and not leaving the ship — nor is the connection one which the novel convincingly establishes. Leavis considered that: 'In Birkin's married relations with Ursula the book invites us to localize the positive, the conceivable and due — if only with difficulty attainable — solution of the problem; the norm, in relation to which Gerald's disaster gets its full meaning' (1955: 174). The invitation is indeed made, but its acceptance presents difficulties. Leavis sounds both hesitant and somewhat forced when he later states:

> Actually, it seems to me, the position for which Birkin contends in his wooing of Ursula does emerge from the 'tale' vindicated, in the sense that the norm he proposes for the relations of man and woman in marriage has been made [. . .] sufficiently clear [. . .] to compel us to a serious pondering. (1955: 176)

Bell is scrupulously reserved in his statement: 'In a limited sense, to be sure, Birkin and Ursula are defined well enough by their very contrast to Gerald and Gudrun' (1992: 118). George H. Ford concedes that 'We are in fact being asked to make very fine distinctions' (although 'The effort to find it is worth making'), Birkin being 'no White Knight', but 'a suffering character dramatically involved in extricating himself from a death-loving world to which he is deeply, almost fatally, attracted' (Clarke 1969: 185). In fact, the fineness of the distinctions concerned relies also on the condition that both the flux of creation and the flux of destruction are presented as necessary, and to be embraced and encouraged to varying degrees. As Lawrence writes in *Fantasia of the Unconscious* immediately after finishing *Women in Love*: 'Life itself is dual. And the duality is life and death. And death is not just shadow or mystery. It is the negative reality of life. It is what we call Matter and Force, among other things' (PUFU: 167). Tolstoi's notion that 'Good is only the opposite of evil, as light is of darkness, and just as there is no absolute light and dark, so there is no good and evil' is remarkably Lawrentian, which is to say more typical of Lawrence than of Tolstoi (Donskov 2003 I: 110). Chung likens Lawrence to 'Goethe, George Eliot or Virginia Woolf' in his acknowledgement of 'dualism in the individual' — but in the case of Lawrence, the dualism is not Faustian (Chung 1989: 74). Goethe's Faust confesses that 'Zwei Seelen wohnen, ach! in meiner Brust, | Die eine will sich von der andern trennen' [Two souls, oh! are housed in my breast, | And each wants to part from the other], but for Lawrence no such struggle should be necessary (Goethe 1967: 41). Health in *Women in Love* is therefore implicitly presented in terms of *proportion*: an excess of destruction, or of persecution of destruction, or of Arctic temperament, or of African temperament, is presented as unhealthy. The reader is implicitly asked to compare the two couples' proximity to an ideal balance which is with difficulty extrapolated from the text, even by its end.

Moreover, there are several ways in which the novel might have contrasted the couples, but refrains from doing so. The partners of the couples are more often placed in mutual juxtaposition than are the couples themselves. To return to Bakhtin's terms which were introduced in Chapter 2, the speakers representing the heterosexual partners respond relatively frequently to each other's utterances. Ursula hates Birkin at the end of 'Sunday Evening', whereupon 'He lay sick and unmoved, in pure opposition to everything' (WL: 198–99). Gerald decides that 'his *mind* needed acute stimulation, before he could be physically roused', whereupon 'Gudrun knew that it was a critical thing for her to go to Shortlands' (WL: 233–34). Such segment transitions are less often used to connect the two sisters, the two men, the men and the women, or the two couples. Examples of the last include Gerald and Gudrun's connection through Bismarck being followed by Birkin and Ursula's connection in opposition to the moon, and Gerald and Gudrun's visit to the Pompadour being followed by Birkin and Ursula's journey to the Continent. However, neither of these make a sharp contrast between the couples; the only such example is when Gerald and Gudrun's ice-like passion on arrival in the Tyrol is succeeded by Birkin and Ursula sitting with an air of 'childish sufficiency' and an appreciative interest in *Kranzkuchen* (WL: 354, 403). The contrasts between the couples are sharpened in Ken Russell's film adaptation (as the equivalent is done in film adaptations of *Anna Karenina*) (Russell 1969).

Admittedly, the couples are distinguished by timing. Gerald and Gudrun lag several chapters behind Birkin and Ursula in most stages of their relationship: namely, the man first looking properly at the woman (behind by four chapters), kissing (three chapters), sex (ten chapters, if it first occurs between Birkin and Ursula after the Water-Party), and marriage (Gerald and Gudrun never catch up). Whereas in *Anna Karenina* the unsuccessful couple runs ahead, in *Women in Love* it lags behind. However, because of the spatial rather than temporal orientation of this novel, these differences are not strongly felt. The similarity of the names of Gerald and Gudrun is, in the context of Lawrence's oeuvre (which includes Lottie and Leslie in *The White Peacock*), a faint warning, and the fact that Gerald is the only man in the novel to be called by his first name makes him the unnatural counterpart and forerunner of Banford and March (the writing of the first version of *The Fox* overlapped with that of *Women in Love*). Again, however, these details are tiny. The similarities are striking. Both couples have vicious arguments, disintegrative sex, and moments of being hotly in love. For many readers such similarities are the ground against which their differences appear, rather than, as with Levin/Kiti and Anna/Vronskii, the reverse being the case. This is also true of the two sisters, who have become far more alike since *The Rainbow*.

As a result, for many first-time readers, the couples' divergent fates are not predictable. Trotter considers that 'The Gudrun–Gerald Crich story is not in the least carnivalesque, and the "language" it incorporates, of degeneration theory, proves all too prophetic of its outcome. There plot endorses idiom, rather than revealing its limitations' (1993: 189). Yet this comment overestimates the difference in the language used to describe the two couples: the plot precisely does *not* follow the idiom, at least not predictably. In his review of the novel Murry denoted 'the Excurse experience' as *x* and 'Gerald and Gudrun' as *y*: 'we can see no difference between them [. . .] Yet *x* leads one pair to undreamed-of happiness, and *y* conducts the other to attempted murder and suicide [. . .] For Mr Lawrence they are the supreme realities, positive and negative, of a plan of consciousness the white race has yet to reach' (Clarke 1969: 71). The novel's inhabitants:

> writhe continually, like the damned, in frenzy of sexual awareness of one another [. . .] To him they are utterly and profoundly different; to us they are all the same [. . .] We should have thought that we should be able to distinguish between male and female, at least. But no! Remove the names, remove the sedulous catalogues of unnecessary clothing — a new element and a significant one, this, in our author's work — and man and woman are indistinguishable as octopods in an aquarium tank. (Clarke 1969: 68, 70)

Similarly, a Miss Macaulay, in her review for the *Westminster Gazette* of 2 July 1921, found 'Ursula and Gudrun [. . .] as indistinguishable in character and conversation as they are in their amours and their clothing' (WL: liii). The German critic Walter F. Schirmer made a similar point in his 1923 *Der englische Roman der neuesten Zeit* [The Contemporary English Novel] (Jansohn and Mehl 2007: 43). Certain critics have found Birkin and Ursula to be still less admirable than Gerald and Gudrun. Murry argued, a decade after his review of the novel, that 'Rupert and Ursula are a whole stage further on [than Gerald and Gudrun] in the process of damnation'; Pinkney gave a more moderate version of this view:

> It would be too much to say that a wholesale reversal of the paired lovers has taken place, but it is clear that the relationship the novel offered to us as a utopian alternative to a sick civilisation has in fact attracted to itself many of the most negative features of that very society. (Murry 1931: 131; Pinkney 1990: 93)

Raymond Williams modulated this position, arguing that 'it is Ursula and Birkin, who want to grow beyond this reduction, this disintegration and dissolution, who reach the most tragic position' (1966: 136). A minority of critics have found Gerald and Gudrun to be more positively admirable than Birkin and Ursula —

for example Kurt Weineck, who considered that Gudrun, 'vielleicht Lawrences höchstentwickelter Frauentyp findet in ihm [Gerald] den kongenialen Partner' [perhaps Lawrence's most highly developed female character, finds in him the ideal partner] (quoted in Jansohn and Mehl 2007: 49). Bradshaw agrees, at least, that 'it is the degenerate Gerald and Gudrun who steal the show' (1998: xxii).

Bell considered that:

> it is always important not to slip into seeing it [*Women in Love*] as the story of the 'good' Lawrencean [*sic*] couple contrasted with the destructive 'modern' couple. The book is rather a Dostoevskean psychomachia in which the major figures are potentialities of each other. (1992: 105)[3]

There is some force to this idea. Daleski points out that, in terms of the sex-classification of *Study of Thomas Hardy*, Birkin is female, because he stresses being rather than doing in the world; Gerald is therefore his active, masculine counterpart (Daleski 1965: 182). The single psyche being split between the male characters of *Women in Love* could also be considered to be Levin's. The similarities of Levin with Gerald and Mr Crich have already been noted; between Levin and Birkin there is a literal and metaphorical weak rhyme. They resemble their authors more nearly than any other character, are men of independent means in their early thirties, withdraw from the society to which they feel alien and superior, are contemptuous of organized politics, have no parents, believe a relationship between a man and woman to be one of the most important goals in life, and are imperfectly satisfied with such a relationship once they achieve it.[4] Like Levin, and unlike Vronskii, 'Birkin understands what is at stake internally but is largely ineffective in the outer world while Gerald has an outer effectiveness divorced from inner meaning' (Bell 1992: 105). Both partly alleviate their spiritual malaise by struggling into consciousness of the idea that human flourishing involves certain kinds of restriction on the power and remit of consciousness.

However, the splitting of Levin between Birkin and Gerald is imprecise, and the splitting of a single psyche — in Dostoevskian mode or otherwise — does not mean that judgement is not imposed. The discrepancy between the distinctness of the characters and of their fates is one factor which suggests that Gerald suffers unfairly. Rather as Shestov proposed that it was necessary for Tolstoi that Anna and Vronskii fail in order to provide a fulcrum through which Tolstoi could retain his spiritual equilibrium, so Gerald's disaster with Gudrun serves the purpose of furnishing a contrast with Birkin and Ursula, by magnifying such differences as exist between them (Shestov 1907: 3–4). Not only do the couples have important similarities with each other, but all four characters are dissimilar within themselves. As is the case with Anna's character in *Anna Karenina*, there are discontinuities in their presentation. Gerald's most destructive actions — his mining revolution, and his most aggressive sex with Gudrun — do not seem necessarily connected. When 'In the Train' Gerald is arguing that poor people ought to have their share of the world's goods, 'Birkin watched him narrowly. He saw the perfect good-humoured callousness, even strange, glistening malice, in Gerald, glistening through the plausible ethics of productivity' (WL: 56). Such good-humoured callousness is neither at this point nor at any other revealed by his action, it is merely asserted by Birkin; but since it receives no contradiction, it inevitably affects the reader's judgement. Such treatment of character appears also in *The Rainbow*; in the 'Shame' chapter Winifred Inger is introduced by the narrator as 'a rather beautiful woman of twenty eight, a fearless-seeming, clean type of modern girl [. . .] clever and expert in what she did, accurate, quick, commanding'. Yet once Ursula has turned against her, she has 'clayey, inert, unquickened flesh, that reminded her of the great prehistoric lizards', and 'the real mistress of Winifred was the machine' (R: 311; 325). As Keith Sagar notes, her transformation in Ursula's eyes lacks objective correlatives and is therefore unsubstantial for the reader: 'She is even physically transformed to account for Ursula's sudden nausea' (2008: 30). In the case of Gerald, the physical transformation is real — he becomes 'like clay' in Birkin's eyes — but that very actual transformation from life to death bears an aspect of judgement for certain faults which have been asserted in Birkin's thought more than vividly demonstrated by Gerald.

Leavis considers that in *Women in Love* (specifically in Hermione's attempt to murder Birkin) 'the powers of a great novelist manifest themselves in ways that offer nothing to baffle [. . .] the reader who comes to Lawrence from George Eliot and Tolstoy' (1955: 184). In fact, there is plenty to baffle such a reader. In a letter of June 1914 Lawrence defended the artistry of *The Wedding Ring* to Edward Garnett, distinguishing it from that 'In Turguenev, and in Tolstoi, and in Dostoievski'. He claimed to have a 'different attitude to my characters', and to be relatively uninterested in the 'old-fashioned human element — which causes one to conceive a character in a certain moral scheme and make him consistent' (LL ii: 182–83). He might as appropriately have said *inconsistent*, insofar as inconsistency is generated and explained by what Bell calls 'layers of sensibility within the one psyche [. . .] For Lawrence is less concerned now with the layers of sensibility within the one psyche and more concerned with the different ontological possibilities as between one kind of sensibility and another' (1992: 108). The change which Lawrence aims to effect in characterization is hinted at when Gudrun watches the guests at Laura Crich's wedding. Most of them she responds to as to characters 'In Turguenev, and in Tolstoi, and in Dostoievski', but then she sees the Crich family, and begins to take a 'different attitude':

> She saw each one as a complete figure, like a character in a book, or a subject in a picture, or a marionette in a theatre, a finished creation. She loved to recognise their various characteristics, to place them in their true light, give them their own surroundings, settle them for ever as they passed before her along the path to the church. She knew them, they were finished, sealed and stamped and finished with, for her. There were none that had anything unknown, unresolved, until the Criches themselves began to appear. Then her interest was piqued. Here was something not quite so preconcluded. (WL: 14)

The new mode of characterization is applied most of all not to the Crich family, however, but to Birkin. One of its effects is to mediate the contradiction which might otherwise exist in Birkin's conscious, verbal advocacy of unconscious, non-verbal spiritual experience, by allowing his experiences and statements on them to be two sides of the same coin. It is rendered a felt truth that both are made of the language with which the novel is written, and both refer to the non-verbal experience. They arrive with the same suddenness. When Birkin's argumentation gives way to his sexual activity — as when, at the end of 'Mino', he kisses Ursula and says 'I'm bored by the rest' — the change in his mode is less profound than that between Levin when he is interested in a debate, and when he abandons that debate in order to get engaged to Kiti (WL: 154). Levin abandons the argument; Birkin pursues it in another form. Moreover, he is, as the Contessa notes, a 'changer' (WL: 92). Not only can he switch mode abruptly from intensity to urbanity (this might be a feature of a more realistic character, such as Vronskii), but his ideas change abruptly and (in contrast to Levin) often without apparent external motivation. He changes from extolling sensuality 'and nothing else', to love between a man and woman as 'the be-all and the end-all', to rejecting love and people (after Hermione's attack), to demanding stellar equilibrium between 'man and woman', to kissing Ursula and agreeing that love is enough, to rejecting love (after being rejected by Ursula), to thinking of sex as polarization, to desiring *Blutbrüderschaft* (after a failure to connect with Ursula), to wanting 'a further sensual experience', or else 'snow-abstract annihilation', or the creative way of 'proud individual singleness', or marriage, to wanting 'To be free, in a free place, with a few other people!' (after the ecstasy of 'Excurse'), to wanting connection with a man (after Gerald's death) (WL: 43, 57, 152, 206, 252, 254, 316). Such a mode of characterization fits with the novel's episodic structure. Although *Women in Love* is marginally longer than *The Rainbow*, it has twice as many chapters, and 'The characteristic time-span of a chapter is a single vivid instant' (Pinkney 1990: 95). Moreover, unlike *The First 'Women in Love'* (which had only thirteen chapters) the final version has chapter titles which emphasize their episodic nature: 'Coal Dust', 'Sketch Book', 'An Island', 'Carpeting', and 'Mino' were formerly all one chapter. Their division makes the novel seem, as it were, cubist, with each chapter an internally coherent facet of truth, but at an angle to each of the others. The abrupt transitions between Birkin's positions, and the fact that these positions are repeated assaults on the same question of the spiritual-sexual good life (whereas Levin veers between metaphysical, emotional, and agricultural concerns) make the contradictions between them more noticeable. These contradictions are acknowledged by the narrative in Ursula's complaint that Birkin 'always contradicts himself', and Birkin's awareness of the same (WL: 294). For despite Lawrence's claim to Garnett, he could not, or did not wish to, leave 'the old-fashioned human element' entirely behind, and H. C. Harwood, in his *Outlook* review of the novel of August 1921, described Lawrence as having 'with difficulty disengaged himself from the realistic conventions overshadowing literature at the beginning of his career' (LL II: 182; WL: lv). Birkin is therefore split between an old-fashioned, layered character who is conscious of the contradictions between and within his arguments, and a character in which these contradictions are unimportant. There is some tension between these two modes. When Birkin asks himself: 'Was it really only an idea, or was it the interpretation of a profound yearning?' he may propitiate a reader's concern on precisely this question — or he may disturb her sense of the irrelevance of the distinction (WL: 252).

To some extent the above is true of all the growing tips of the novel. However, Birkin expresses far more fully Lawrence's new mode of characterization than does Gerald, who remains more of an 'old-fashioned' character, in two respects. First, Birkin talks more and his thoughts are more often narrated directly, rather than being summarized or commented upon by the narrator: he makes a far more 'passionate struggle into conscious being' than does Gerald (WL: 485–86, Foreword). The continuity between verbal and non-verbal action is therefore more apparent in his case. Secondly, Birkin's ideas are less conventional than Gerald's, and their very verbal expression makes his characterization heterodox (one common early criticism of the novel was that Birkin spoke as no one actually speaks, whereas Mr Crich was considered the best, because most conventionally, drawn character) (WL: lv). Of the central characters, 'Gerald, the last percipient of the four', is the most conservative, and one of his roles is to serve, less effectually than Oblonskii to Levin, as a sceptical foil to Birkin (Bell 1992: 116). There is therefore a large gap apparent between the conventional man of business, or host of the water-party, or 'Chanticleer' — and the man who controls his mare 'with an almost mechanical relentlessness', or shares with Gudrun 'mutual hellish recognition' (WL: 394, 111, 242). A further implication is that whereas (in the words of *The First 'Women in Love'*) 'Birkin was unsubstantial almost as an idea, as a piece of script', Gerald has a greater physical presence in the novel, quite apart from his more powerful physique (1WL: 246). He is in this respect the counterpart to Vronskii, who on his way to see Anna 'заложил одну на колено другой и, взяв ее в руку, ощупал упругую икру ноги' [crossed one leg over the other knee, and taking it in his hand, felt the springy muscle of his calf] (AK VIII: 333). Birkin notices Gerald's 'white-skinned, full, muscular legs, handsome and decided' (WL: 96). His more physical, less reflective, nature renders him less capable of acting upon himself. Whereas Birkin seems unified with and therefore responsible for his spiritual states, Gerald seems helplessly switched between his social and spiritual modes. In addition, he is relatively powerless to determine his own presentation, and is instead reflected upon by other characters — especially the two who have a grudge against him (Gudrun and Birkin). The net result is that Gerald seems more the victim of his own nature and presentation than are the more conscious characters, despite the stress placed by Birkin and the novel on the value of unconsciousness.

Bedient, who generally considers Eliot and Lawrence to be ethical and spiritual opposites, draws this parallel between them:

> Each became a novelist of Nemesis and inexorable law. The Bulstrodes, Melemas, and Grandcourts of George Eliot's pages have their counterparts in the Skrebenskys, the Criches, the Ricos of Lawrence's. In each *oeuvre* egoists are impaled by the stake of Inevitability, and either left squirming or finished off. Severely, each world gives support to only one way of life. To attempt a different way is to step into quicksand [. . .] [Lawrence's] 'vision of consequences' could be equally bullying. The great apocalyptic example of this, of course, is the 'dark' half of the plot of *Women in Love*, in which the whole of Northern Europe, brought to a demonic focus in Gerald Crich and Gudrun Brangwen, is burning itself out, spectacularly, in a 'black' ecstasy of destruction. Here, too, most men are recklessly 'shut out', in George Eliot's words, from a 'good

strong terrible vision,' because, in Lawrence's, they are 'hideous with egoism.' Hetty Sorrel is adrift from the community of Hayslope, whereas 'a Gerald and a Gudrun, incestuously locked upon themselves, are adrift from the great vital current of Being [. . .] Both writers constitute a sort of Terror or police of the soul [. . .] each became a Salvationist in his fiction, as if hoping, each time a new novel was begun, that *this* time he would himself be converted by his message. (Bedient 1972: 107–09)

I hope to have demonstrated the respects in which this is not true. Bedient's comment resembles Shestov's on *Anna Karenina*:

All the characters in *Anna Karenina* are divided into two categories. Some keep to the rules, and along with Levin find paradise; the others serve their own desires, break the rules, and, in proportion to the audacity and decisiveness of their actions, suffer a more or less cruel punishment. (1907: 4)

This is as true in the case of *Women in Love* as it is in that of *Anna Karenina*. It is only in a very loose sense of the term that (certain) *egoists* are made to suffer in Lawrence's writings. Moreover, Gerald and Gudrun are significantly less distinct from Birkin and Ursula than is Hetty from Dinah, Grandcourt from Daniel, or Anna and Vronskii from Levin and Kiti. The fact that the divergence of fates in *Women in Love* is not matched by the divergence of types of relationship is one factor which troubles ethical interpretations of the novel. One other such factor is the treatment of Winifred, who plays a similarly heterodox role in her novel, as do Alcharisi in *Daniel Deronda* and Oblonskii in *Anna Karenina*. She is not just a modern *growing tip*, in the sense in which Ursula is and her parents are not; she is if anything postmodern: perpetually unstable, detached, and ironic. The character whom she most resembles is Loerke, who is in his turn described as 'like a child, and like a troll, quick, detached' (WL: 405). She seems in considerable danger of being a negative growing tip. Yet in the judgement of Birkin (who praises her 'special nature'), and of the novel, she remains 'oddly and largely guiltless' (WL: 205; Alexandrov 2004: 211). In comparison to Oblonskii in *Anna Karenina*, however, her role, and disruptive capacity, is small.

Lawrence would have been as troubled as Eliot by Bedient's analysis. Like her, he disliked the idea of the 'so-called moral denouement, in which rewards and punishments are distributed according to those notions of justice on which the novel-writer would have recommended that the world should be governed if he had been consulted at the creation' (Ashton 1992: 130). He rejected *Dies Irae* and *The Latter Days* as possible titles for the novel — which would have contrasted the saved and the damned — in favour of a title which cuts across this schism (Letters II: 669; Wright 2000: 130). In addition, he had a conception of incomparability which undermined the possibility of making the discriminations necessary for the imposition of an eschatology. Whilst finishing *Women in Love* he wrote an essay called 'Democracy' in which he argued:

Each human self is single, incommutable, and unique. This is its *first* reality. Each self is unique, and therefore incomparable. It is a single well-head of creation, unquestionable; it cannot be compared with another self, another well-head, because, in its prime of creative reality it can never be comprehended by any

> other self [. . .] When I stand with another man, who is himself, and when I
> am truly myself, then I am only aware of a Presence, and of the strange reality
> of Otherness. There is me, and there is *another being*. That is the first part of
> the reality. There is no comparing or estimating. There is only this strange
> recognition of *present otherness*. I may be glad, angry, or sad, because of the
> presence of the other. But still no comparison enters in. Comparison enters only
> when one of us departs from his own integral being, and enters the material-
> mechanical world. Then equality and disquality starts at once. (RDP: 78, 80)

Six years later, in 'Reflections on the Death of a Porcupine', Lawrence declared it to
be part of 'the inexorable law of life' that 'Any creature that attains to its own fulness
of being' becomes a 'nonpareil' in 'the fourth dimension, the heaven of existence',
but 'At the same time, every creature exists in time and space' where 'it exists
relatively to all other existence, and can never be absolved. Its existence impinges
on other existences, and is itself impinged upon' (RDP: 358). At Breadalby, Birkin
insists to Hermione that:

> spiritually, there is pure difference and neither equality nor inequality counts
> [. . .] In the spirit, I am as separate as one star is from another, as different in
> quality and quantity. Establish a state on *that*. One man isn't any better than
> another, not because they are equal, but because they are intrinsically *other*, that
> there is no term of comparison. The minute you begin to compare, one man
> is seen to be far better than another, all the inequality you can imagine is there
> by nature. (WL: 103–04)

Birkin's version of the idea is more egalitarian than those expressed by the essays:
every person, not just one 'that attains to its own fulness of being', is on the spiritual
level a 'nonparail' (RDP: 358). It therefore avoids the contradiction inherent in
the essays' versions of the idea, since the criterion of 'fulness of being' can only
be judged by comparison with other, less-than-full, beings (the paradox which is
always involved in attributions of incomparability). Birkin's conception eases the
difficulties which arise in comparing the novels' characters owing to their internal
dissimilarities and mutual similarities. It also accords both with the respect which
the novel rhetorically pays to *all* of its four main characters, and with Birkin's love for
Gerald — a love based not on a comparative appraisal of his spiritual excellence, but
a yearning towards his quiddity, which arises from Birkin's own quiddity. However,
none of the expressions of Lawrence's idea of incomparability takes into account the
temporal dimension of narrative, or the fact of plot. The very structure of *Women
in Love* appears eschatological; Birkin and the narrator give indications of how the
characters and couples spiritually differ, and the plot encourages a hardening of the
perceived differences, in order to render the apparent eschatology comprehensible.
It does not follow that 'The minute you begin to compare, one man is seen to be
far better than another, all the inequality you can imagine is there by nature'; even
the most binary interpretations of the novel cited above, such as those of Bedient,
Daleski, and Leavis, do not find that 'all the inequality you can imagine is there
by nature' between Birkin and Gerald (WL: 103–04). Nor would Birkin himself
suggest this to be the case. But his assertion of spiritual incomparability does not
alter the fact that he is a privileged participant in a plot which finally impels its
readers towards an act of spiritual comparison.

Barren Tragedy

It is worth considering, in the light of these conclusions, whether or not Gerald is permitted to be tragic. As in *Daniel Deronda* and *Anna Karenina*, the novel's dominant society is banal, and is not itself tragic even though moribund. Lawrence was as horrified by banality as was Eliot; even Clifford Chatterley gives an echo to Mirah Lapidoth (in her complaint at the absence of 'grand meanings' from men's conceptions) when

> Herbert, the elder brother and heir, laughed outright, though it was his trees that were falling for trench props. But Clifford only smiled a little uneasily. Everything was ridiculous, quite true. But when it came too close and oneself became ridiculous too — ? At least people of a different class, like Connie, were earnest about *something*. They believed in something. (LCL: 11; cf. DD: 184)

Lawrence placed Eliot and Tolstoi in the same literary category when in 1928 he criticized a young Italian who slighted Verga: 'They find Tolstoi ridiculous, George Eliot ridiculous, everybody ridiculous who is not "disillusioned"' (Lawrence 2005: 148). He uses the terms *tragedy* and *tragic* in several ways in his writings, but one of them correlates, as it does for Mirah, to seriousness, purpose, and stature:

> If we really could know what we were fighting for, then the struggle might have dignity, beauty, satisfaction for us. If it were a profound struggle for something that was coming to life in us, a struggle we were convinced would bring us to a new freedom, a new life, then it would be a creative activity in which death is a climax in the progression towards new being. And this is tragedy. [. . .] If men are not more than implements, it is nontragic and merely disastrous. In tragedy the man is more than his part. (Preface to *Touch and Go*, Lawrence 1999: 238)

One indication of the banality of Beldover society is its misapplication of the term to the death of Laura Crich, which is presented as precisely *not* tragic: 'Such a tragedy in Shortlands, the high home of the district!' (WL: 190). Like Gwendolen's and Anna's stories, Gerald's story has resonances with Greek tragedy, although it should be stressed that these resonances are not references, such as *Daniel Deronda* is fraught with; *Women in Love* shuns not only contemporary society, but the society of past and present literature. Gerald is a proud and exceptionally sensitive man from a cursed dynasty who chooses wrong deliberately ('He was willing to be sealed thus in the underworld, like a soul damned but living forever in damnation'), and persists without an aim until the point of death ('He was weak, but he did not want to rest, he wanted to go on and on, to the end') (WL: 353, 472). Still less than Gwendolen and Anna does Gerald find any chorus in his society; moreover, this society is not counterbalanced by a positive one, such as that represented by the Meyricks and the Shtcherbatskiis. Raymond Williams's argument that in *Women in Love* and *Anna Karenina* 'an important relationship ends in tragedy, in a death given significance by the whole action [. . .] a society has been formed, around the tragic experience' applies still less to Gerald than to Anna (1966: 122). In Gerald's case the 'society' consists of Ursula and Birkin, who are themselves profoundly isolated, and the latter of whom interprets Gerald's death in relation to a possibly 'non-human' universe (WL: 478).

However, just as Ursula considers that 'illness is so terribly humiliating', and that 'it is degrading not to be happy', she admires animals for being 'incapable of soulfulness and tragedy, which she detested so profoundly' (WL: 244). Lawrence too disdained tragedy, of certain other kinds (WL: 125, 296). For example, his comment in *Study of Thomas Hardy* that 'The tragedy today is that men are only materially and socially conscious' turns the term tragedy against itself in a way which describes the pathetic (in both senses of the term) tragedy of, for example, *Death of a Salesman* (STH: 213). Williams rightly interpreted Lawrence's 'falling out' with *Anna Karenina* as part of his investigation into the nature of tragedy (1966: 123). Lawrence wrote that 'In Shakespeare and Sophocles the greater morality is transgressed and punished. In Hardy and Tolstoi the smaller. The greater is only passively, negatively transgressed' (STH: 30). But such tragedy is nonetheless destructive. Gerald's relationship with Gudrun resembles sex tragedy as described in the first (1919) version of Lawrence's essay on Nathaniel Hawthorne, in which he argues that sex may be creation, or else wrestling and struggle 'bringing tragedy' (SCAL: 268, 249). The end of *Women in Love* was written at the beginning of a period in which Lawrence increasingly condemned sex tragedy as restricting, restricted, and (as noted above) principally the woman's fault. Lawrence commended the fact that 'Tolstoi said No to the passion and death conclusion' of *Anna Karenina* — although he rejected Levin's alternative (PUFU: 200). But the narrator of *Mr Noon* emphasizes the banality of such an end:

> 'Man survives earthquakes, epidemics, the horrors of disease, and all the agonies of the soul, but as long as time lasts his most excruciating tragedy is, has been, and will be — the tragedy of the bedroom' [. . .] I am quoting the great Leo Tolstoi, who, in such matters [. . .] seems to me a quite comical fool. (Lawrence 1984: 190; Gorky 1920: 19)

Gerald's is therefore a barren tragedy. In a different spirit to Gudrun, the reader is invited to share her assessment of the tragedy: 'My God! this was a barren tragedy, barren, barren'; 'A pretty little sample of the eternal triangle!' (WL: 476, 477). The barrenness does not come of Gerald's *failure* to be Othello — to strangle the woman of whom he is jealous; Lawrence would judge Othello's to be a barren tragedy too.

A repudiation of tragedy of a different kind can be discerned in Gerald's resemblances to Captain Scott. These have been pointed out by Fjågesund, who notes that Lawrence was not only writing *Women in Love* in an England which was still extravagantly and communally mourning Scott (who died in 1912), but was personally connected to people who were connected to the Scotts, such as Gilbert and Mary Cannan. Like Gerald, Scott was 'a soldier, and an explorer'; both can ski and toboggan (Fjågesund 2008: 186). Moreover,

> both Gerald and Scott very nearly made it; the Scott myth is not least dependent on the cruel fact that he and his remaining companions were only a few miles from the nearest depot, which would have saved their lives and at least part of the national honour. (Fjågesund 2008: 192)

Birkin, on visiting the place where Gerald died, feels that 'Gerald might have found this rope. He might have hauled himself up to the crest', and might have found the Imperial Road into Italy (WL: 478). The Scott myth was also used to encourage volunteers for the First World War which, from Lawrence's point of view, was also a senseless and futile waste (Fjågesund 2008: 186). Lawrence therefore uses Gerald's mode of death in part as an attack on the myth of Scott, on his own country, on the war, and on barren tragedy; the first of these constitutes another possible reason for its rejection by publishers (Fjågesund 2008: 185, 191). Fjågesund notes that:

> In the popular imagination, polar death was seen as a clean, heroic and dignified death, with the dead apparently looking as if they had just fallen asleep. In the context of the undescribable terrors of gas attacks and trench warfare, this was an important and consoling element. (Fjågesund 2008: 192)

Gerald too is given a consoling death, rather than being killed in war, or otherwise horribly, in connection with his machine-like aspect or obscene knowledge. This could, as suggested above, have been done by Lawrence in accordance with Birkin's tender love for Gerald. Such a death is also the fulfilment of Gerald's Arctic aspect. Yet — to turn the anti-Scott critique of the novel against itself — it might in part also be done euphemistically, in order to sanitize a death for which Birkin is partially responsible.

Nonetheless, the emotional effect of Gerald's death on Birkin and on the reader *is* tragic. Bell, in describing *Women in Love* as a 'Dostoevskean psychomachia in which the major figures are potentialities of each other', rightly added that: 'If they do indeed grow apart it is by a tragic wrenching' (1992: 105).

> Terribly weary, Birkin went away, about the day's business. He did it all quietly, without bother. To rant, to rave, to be tragic, to make situations — it was all too late. Best be quiet, and bear one's soul in patience and in fullness.

The description of this patience and fullness is a stronger depiction of mourning, and of a sense of a tragedy having occurred, than anything in *Daniel Deronda* or *Anna Karenina* (WL: 479). In *The First 'Women in Love'* Birkin, whilst looking at Gerald's corpse, not only 'remembered a dead stallion he had seen', but thinks: '"That human stallion!" He remembered Dostoevsky's words about Vronsky' (WL: 480; 1WL: 438). The comparison makes apparent the fact that not only is Gerald more tragic than Vronskii but, unlike him, his tragedy has no competition. Gudrun explicitly repudiates tragedy, and because of this has none of her own, even though she is left hardly better off than Gwendolen at the end of *Daniel Deronda*.

Birkin and Ursula's comedy is, like the comedies of Daniel and Mirah, and Levin and Kiti, uncertain. It more resembles the latter, in the uncertainty concerning the future of the relationship — an uncertainty revealed in the cadences of the following sentences (just before they leave the Tyrol for Italy):

> She knew that, in spite of his joy when she abandoned herself, he was a little bit saddened too. She could give herself up to his activity. But she could not be herself, she *dared* not come forth quite nakedly to his nakedness, abandoning all adjustment, lapsing in pure faith with him. She abandoned herself to *him*, or she took hold of him and gathered her joy of him. And she enjoyed him fully. But they were never *quite* together, at the same moment, one was always a little left out. Nevertheless she was glad in hope, glorious and free, full of life and liberty. And he was still and soft and patient, for the time. (WL: 435–36)

The limitations of the peripatetic life are hinted by Birkin's hopeless thought, which reflects upon the entire action of *Women in Love*: 'Why strive for a coherent,

satisfied life? Why not drift on in a series of accidents — like a picaresque novel?'
(WL: 302). That novel, like *Daniel Deronda* and *Anna Karenina*, is the end of a phase;
Ursula and Birkin are not followed further, into Italy; rather Lawrence breaks
into a new phase. But Bradshaw goes too far in arguing that 'There seems to be
every likelihood that Birkin will lose Ursula as well as Gerald' (1998: xviii). Birkin
and Ursula's relationship has been repeatedly shown to be capable of containing
profound disagreement. That Ursula and Birkin end the novel neither permanently
settled in the country (like Levin and Kiti), nor making a confident movement into
the unknown (like Daniel and Mirah), but have their things 'ready to be sent off, to
whatever country and whatever place they might choose at last', suggests adaptability
more than fragility (WL: 380). Two predications of doom are defied by Ursula, and
the novel does not prove her wrong: Hermione feels that 'it would be perfectly
disastrous for you to marry him — for you even more than for him', and Ursula
overcomes her initial superstition about the opal ring which fits her in 'Excurse'
(WL: 22). Omens apply to Gerald, but not to Birkin and Ursula. Nonetheless, their
comedy does not provide a sharp contrast of brightness to Gerald's tragedy, nor does
it overshadow it. After Gerald's death no tragicomic transition is made, as from the
tragic first three acts of *The Winter's Tale* to the comedic Bohemian sheep-shearing
festival which opens the fourth. Nor is a tragicomic transition made, as from
Shylock's condemnation in *The Merchant of Venice* to the reconciliations of Bassanio,
Portia, Gratiano, and Nerissa. In contrast to *Daniel Deronda* and *Anna Karenina*, the
narration after the catastrophe opens with the retrieval of Gerald's body, and until
the end of the novel Birkin and Ursula's conversation relates to him.

This continuity fits with this novel's greater cohesiveness. *Women in Love* has
provoked none of the complaints of disjunction which have been levelled at the
two earlier novels, despite the fact that it was Eliot and Tolstoi, not Lawrence, who
explicitly advocated unity in works of art. Claims such as Tolstoi's to be 'proud
of the architecture' of *Anna Karenina* are parodied in Lawrence's 1926 story, 'Two
Blue Birds', in which the sympathetic, sardonic female protagonist overhears her
pompous husband dictating a magazine article about the modern novel:

> He was dictating a magazine article about the modern novel. 'What the modern
> novel lacks is architecture — ' Good God! Architecture! He might just as well
> say: What the modern novel lacks is whalebone, or a teaspoon, or a tooth
> stopped. (TL I: 311; Lawrence 1995c: 12)

Women in Love's cohesion is enforced not by arches or joints, but by its unity
of domain, emptiness of time, and fluid combinations of five and four central
characters. It is not, like *Daniel Deronda* and *Anna Karenina*, a double-headed
monster, about which the reader is impelled to enquire whether the two heads
converse, on what subject, and in what language. But neither is it entirely coherent;
it is related to *Daniel Deronda* and *Anna Karenina* as a tragi-comedy in which the
divergence of fates between the two central couples is imperfectly justified, and
in which the least successful protagonist is both a partial scapegoat of his text, and
ambivalently tragic. If the double-plotting of *Daniel Deronda* is based upon the
cleavage of combination (of disparate phenomena), and that of *Anna Karenina* upon
the cleavage of division (according to opposing tendencies), *Women in Love*, as befits

its more complex structure, contains both kinds. The sisters are eventually cleaved asunder as a result of cleaving to their respective partners; the men cleave to one another, but they are too unalike for their cleavage to be durable. The novel makes a far more urgent appeal to its readers to comprehend comparisons of its characters than is the case in *Anna Karenina* — a novel with which the novel as a whole asks for comparison. Raymond Williams claimed that Lawrence the critic of Tolstoi was sometimes put right by Lawrence the novelist, but in his doubly comparative, quadruple-plotted response to Tolstoi's double-plotted novel the two work by and large in harmony (B. Williams 1963: 641).

Notes to Chapter 4

1. Parts of this chapter which compare *Women in Love* to *Anna Karenina* also appeared, in different form, in Brown (2010b). I thank the editors of *Comparative Literature* for their kind permission to use this material, and for their editorial assistance with the article.

2. Sergei Karenin's perspective on education would make him an ideal candidate for university education according to the criteria of Lawrence's 'Education of the People':

   в душе его были требования, более для него обязательные, чем те, которые заявляли отец и педагог [. . .] Воспитатели его жаловались, что он не хотел учиться, а душа его была переполнена жаждой познания. И он учился у Капитоныча, у няни, у Наденьки, у Василия Лукича, а не у учителей.

   [in his soul there were demands, which were more binding on him than those which his father and teacher made [. . .] His teachers complained that he didn't want to learn, but his soul was filled with the hunger for knowledge. And he learned from Kapitonich, from his nurse, from Nadenka, from Vassili Lukich, but not from his teachers.] (RDP 98; AK VIII: 102)

3. Bell also argues that:

   another way of expressing the difference between *The Rainbow* and *Women in Love* is as a shift from the Tolstoyan to the Dostoevskean. For, like Dostoevsky, *Women in Love* uses a group of extraordinary, articulate, slightly perverse, yet representatively modern characters to conduct an in-depth psychological investigation of their own authenticity. It privileges the 'struggle into conscious being' rather than the Tolstoyan commitment to the traditionary and the unconscious. (Bell 2001: 190)

4. During the action of *Anna Karenina* Levin is thirty-two to thirty-four years of age; Birkin's age is not given, but Gerald is thirty-one at the end of the narrative's year. Levin is orphaned; Birkin's parents are not mentioned.

CHAPTER 5

Conclusions

How Literature was Compared

> I meant everything in the book to be related to everything else there.
> GEORGE ELIOT on *Daniel Deronda*; EL VI: 290

Comparison Reflects

> if as teachers of literature we teach reading, literature can be our teacher as well
> as our object of investigation.
> SPIVAK 2003: 23

This book has engaged with comparative literature in three senses of the term: in its common sense (as a type of academic practice historically based in the analysis of literature of more than one country); in the sense denoted if the terms *study of* are inserted between the adjective and noun; and in the sense denoted if the adjective is understood to qualify the noun (as literature which demands that the performance of comparison play a particularly important part in its appreciation). In relation to these three senses taken individually and collectively an infinite number of comparisons on an infinite number of conceptual levels could be conceived and described — but here I will confine myself to considering seven comparisons or relationships, existing on four conceptual levels. They are as follows. First, the comparison of stories in a double-plotted novel. Second, the comparison of the results of the first comparison as applied to three novels. Third, the comparison of the first and second kinds of comparison, considering them as respectively concerning things found together, and things placed together, by the comparer. Fourth, the comparison of the first and second kinds of comparison, considering them as respectively the comparison of two things and of three. Fifth, the comparison of comparisons involving one, and more than one, time period; equally, the comparison of studies which entertain a hypothesis of influence connecting the *comparanda*, and studies which entertain no such hypothesis. Sixth, the comparison of comparisons involving one, and more than one, country or language. Finally, the comparison of comparisons orientated on the axis of space, and those orientated on the axis of time.

Comparison, it was earlier observed, can denote not just a methodical process, but the unexamined impression which prompts it. The novels examined in this book impressed me as comparative literature — not by virtue of presenting significant contrasts, which most literature does, but by virtue of presenting parallels and divisions more sustained and ostentatious than those presented by other literature. Methodical comparison of their stories broke down into comparisons of the stories' components: characters, *fabulae*, *siuzhets*, and domains, of which the boundaries of all but the first were indistinct. Locating those boundaries for hermeneutic purposes relied not on conceptual definition, but on an intuitive sense of equivalent or comparable entities. Their coexistence in enduringly powerful works of verbal art entailed that their relations were particularly rich in implicature and emotive potential. In this respect the novels differ from the Hatter's riddle to Alice in *Alice in Wonderland*, 'Why is a raven like a writing desk?' (95). Neither the Hatter nor the March Hare has the 'slightest idea', and in this sense the riddle is anti-artistic (L. Carroll 1970: 97). Solutions can be and have been found; Carroll himself suggested, when asked: 'Because it can produce a few notes, though they are very flat; and it is never put with the wrong end in front!' (95). But these solutions do not, individually or collectively, indicate that ravens and writing desks are in Todorov's sense metaphors (constituted by the tension of difference and resemblance, separateness and communication) (1978: 226). Nor does their discovery entail much interpretative risk; the degree of validity and profundity of the answers to the riddle found is immediately obvious.

By contrast, discernment of the similarities, differences, and relationships of the parts into which the novels were discerned to fall entailed considerable risks of mis- and over-interpretation. In all of the novels, the third point from which the two stories could be viewed was found to be improvised and unstable: none of the novels contains a third character, domain, or discourse which provides a basis for interpretation of the main stories, nor does any clearly project a hypothetical standpoint from which to view them (as, for example, the narrator of *Vanity Fair* distances its readers from both the main characters, thus encouraging their dispassionate comparison). In *Daniel Deronda* the reader is encouraged to consider one domain from the perspective of the other, but the perspective gained on the heroine from the hero's domain is imperfect. In *Anna Karenina* the same is true, but it is also true of the reverse perspective. Some of its readers have been tempted to over-interpretation of the stories' connections, whereas others have been tempted not to proceed beyond a cursory comparison of the two stories; a more responsive course involves feeling for the limits of the stories' ethical coherence and mutual emotional relevance. *Women in Love* complicates performance of the comparison which its denouement invites by simultaneously urging other comparisons, and by inconsistencies of characterization. The inducement to over-interpretation of character contrasts is particularly strong in this novel, with its divergent fates occurring within a single domain, and its prominent binary structures. Yet the novel also does much to undermine such a reading, and in structure and characterization it is as though deliberately more complicated than novels such as those of Eliot and Tolstoi, to which it responds. All three novels shun obvious contrasts. None of them fully justifies the disparate fates which they depict, and which are left with some of the uninterpretability which disparate fates are often felt to have in life. Beyond the point at which understanding fails, the reader experiences what Docherty, summarizing Badiou, calls an *encounter* — although I would not, like him, liken it to love (2006: 34).

Comparison itself was an insufficiently precise topic of comparison, and the relations of the novels' stories needed to be more narrowly focused. My focus of choice — scapegoating — was chosen as a high common factor of interest of the double-plotting in all the novels. This, studied in relation to the novels' juxtaposed stories of disaster and success, brought as a concomitant another *tertium comparationis*, the genres of comedy and tragedy. These genres are no more mutually exclusive or logically opposed in literary history or theory than are the two stories in any of my novels, and in these novels they are brought into ethically complex juxtaposition. One implication of concentration on a single scapegoat figure was that the comparisons were rendered asymmetric: they opened with an analysis of that character's function in the novel, and moved on to a consideration of the effect upon her or him of the relatively comedic character, story, and domain. Nonetheless, wherever applicable, symmetric comparison was used — for example of the two central characters, and the narration of their stories. The comparison of the novels was still more asymmetric. *Daniel Deronda* was discussed largely alone, the discussion of *Anna Karenina* made some reference to it, and that of *Women in Love* made reference to both. *Women in Love* was therefore the beneficiary of two *comparanda*, whereas *Daniel Deronda* helped to determine many of the terms in which all three were discussed, and the approximate structure of their analysis. The fact that the latter had to be modified more for *Women in Love* than for *Anna Karenina* was itself an indication of the novels' relative comparability.

To return to the metaphor of conversation, this book aimed to bring together texts which were capable of conducting a focused conversation, which was worth overhearing. In this conversation, each speaker gave a monologue on a similar pattern, whilst the others made short interventions where relevant. Remak was right to observe that 'A comparative literature study does not have to be comparative on every page nor even in every chapter, but the overall intent, emphasis and execution must be comparative' (1961: 15). However, the length of utterance on the part of each *comparandum* has considerable implications for the type of comparison demonstrated. This book might have been differently arranged by allowing the novels to engage in rapidly responsive conversation; they would then have regularly been compared within a chapter, page, and sentence, and more often at the level of the sentences of juxtaposed quotations. This would have allowed them to be presented as close as possible together in space and time. It would also have enforced an oscillation of attention between the novels more resembling that of the novels between their stories — although all of the critical utterances would have been strictly relevant and clearly related to one another, unlike many of the novels' segments. In comparative literary studies, *comparanda* are often separated into adjacent analyses when the principal interest is less the results of the comparison *per se* than the several relations of each *comparandum* to the topic on which they are being compared. On the other hand, rapid responses between the *comparanda* limit the length and complexity of the points which they can make, and the amount of substantiation which they can provide for them. Moreover, the more *comparanda* are involved, the more complicated to perform and read such comparisons become; as Plato knew, exploratory conversations work best as dialogues.

Nonetheless, within the monologue structure some symmetric comparison was included. The one simply quantitative and repeatable comparison was the novels' frequency of use of words related to comparison. The degree of ontological cohesion of *Daniel Deronda*'s and *Anna Karenina*'s domains, and the degree to which scapegoating of their heroines took place, could be conceived on a single axis. Each of the novel's monologues made reference to the Bible, Shakespeare, Goethe, and Germany. The first two of these demonstrated the common religious, and overlapping literary, inheritances of England and Russia. The last two were used as temporary third points from which to compare the novelists and novels on their attitudes towards mediation, in which *Daniel Deronda* was most interested and *Women in Love* the least. The fact that Eliot, Tolstoi, and Lawrence did not know precisely the same parts of Goethe or Germany indicated that third points function less well when they are themselves complex objects. No response could be found on the part of my authors to the mediatory idea of *Weltliteratur*, which was taken as a comparative high ground from which all three novelists could be simultaneously, but hypothetically, viewed.

The interest of comparing any novels' component stories lies in perceptions of how those novels work. The interest of comparing these results with those for other novels lies in sharpening those perceptions through comparison, and in providing a new perspective on the novels' authors, periods, countries, genres, and highest common factors. A temperamental similarity between Eliot, Tolstoi, and Lawrence is underlined by the fact that all wrote novels which expressed both didactic and eschatological impulses, and an impulse, conscious or otherwise, to undermine those impulses, and to acknowledge 'all that is contradictory and ironic in life' (Schultze 1982: 157). The authors' differing attitudes to nationalism are underlined by the facts that Eliot used comparison to criticize her own nation in relation to another, Tolstoi used Levin's comparisons to question the relevance of comparing Russia to Europe, and Lawrence used Birkin to question the validity of contrasting any nationality to any other. Comparison of the novels' modes of comparison suggests an observation concerning Lawrence's differing mode of characterization which correlates with dominant narratives of developments in English and Russian prose fiction between the 1870s and 1910s. In depicting two contrasting couples, all three novels are part of a trend in the European novel which existed in this period, to the study of which my investigation has contributed three mutually defined models.

Comparison of its first- and second-order comparisons engages the puns of this book's title and subtitle. In the subtitle *How Novels and Critics Compare* the verb could in grammatical terms apply actively and passively to the novels and the critics — but I have only implicitly compared critics' views with my own and each other in my responses to them. The novels do not, of course, actively compare their stories; critics compare both them and novels. The comparison of the relations of stories in different novels multiplies the number of ratios being related; one could in theory compare it with a comparison of comparisons of a different literary feature (such as triple-plotting, or rival tragedies), and so on *ad infinitum* — although such higher-order comparisons would quickly loose comprehensibility and interest. Yet even the supposedly first-order comparison, of the novels' stories, involves comparing such ratios as the relationship between Anna and her domain, and Levin and his. Writers are able to create and arrange novels' stories as the artist paints a painting such as *Bright Pear* (or as Willa Cather put 'on the table a green vase, and beside it a yellow orange' as she wrote) (Bohlke 1986: 24). In the case of *Bright Pear*, the artist has selected fruits rather than anything else, two tangerines and one pear, the pear slightly to the rear between the two tangerines, and the light shining from the left. The critic is in the more passive position of, for example, Daniel and Levin, who are faced with the conjunction of two worlds, and obliged to work out how they should relate to them and how they relate to each other. By concentrating more on comparing the stories than the novels, this book presents as it were three novels side by side on a table, and invites its readers to investigate their relations. Of course, I was not *entirely* 'out of it' (as Cather claimed), and did make some description of the novels' relations (Bohlke 1986: 24). In this respect the novel which my book most resembled was *Daniel Deronda*, which showed the most conscious concern for the degree of communication existing between its stories, and of which the domains constituted more a juxtaposition of different entities than the splitting of a unity into different tendencies. However, my analyses are not art, and the comparison of their arguments is a far less complex practice than the comparison of aesthetic objects. The two kinds of comparison are approached with different assumptions: art is approached with an assumption of the coherence of its parts; different novels — especially those produced by different writers in different countries and times — are approached with an assumption of disjunction. Precisely because detailed similarity is not expected of novels, their similarities and differences are not in *tension* — except when a hypothesis of influence is entertained, as between *Anna Karenina* and *Women in Love*.

The two kinds of comparison performed in this book were also distinguished as comparing two and three objects respectively. The novels' binary structures generated certain tensions which the minor, disruptive, third points in each novel (Alcharisi, Oblonskii, Hermione, and Winifred) served as much to emphasize as to mitigate. The three novels, by contrast, had similarities and differences which allowed them to work well as a trio, since each of the three pairs were comparable on certain points to the exclusion of the third. Or, to adopt the balletic metaphor of Ed Ahearn and Arnold Weinstein who claimed that 'A new Dickens emerges when pirouetted in the light of Balzac and Dostoevsky', this book aimed to pirouette each of its novels in the light of the other two, with the three positioned at the points of an equilateral triangle (Bernheimer 1995: 80). For example: *Daniel Deronda* and *Anna Karenina* present two domains of imperfect mutual relevance, of which the more favourably presented embraces the traditions and religion local to its people, and of which the other possesses faults for which a female character acts as a scapegoat; *Women in Love* is distinct from both these novels in its single domain, quartet structure, and characterization. *Anna Karenina* and *Women in Love* are connected by the similarities of Levin, Birkin, and Gerald, their concentration on sexual ethics, and their relatively small trust in history, art, or the history of art. In other respects the two novels by lower- to middle-class provincial Protestant English novelists are most closely connected. They are less realistic and baggy, in James's sense, than *Anna Karenina*, and their scapegoats are more the victims of their counterpart *fabulae* than is the case in *Anna Karenina*. They not only criticize, but present a successful escape from, the dying, native societies which they depict; Daniel, Mirah, Birkin, and Ursula all escape from England, and Gerald and Grandcourt return to rest in it as corpses. The comparison of three rather than two novels prevented any single axis from emerging between them; they presented no Fontenellian moon and earth in relation to each other. Nor, on the other hand, did they generate any sense that the triangle was closed, and that three fundamental models of double-plotting were being presented. There could have been four points — a Russian novel of the 1910s being added — or any greater number.

National difference did not obtrude itself as a problematic variable, nor was it examined as a significant one. Attitudes towards nationalism and patriotism were one of the characteristics on which the novels were compared, but not in relation to national tendencies: Eliot and Lawrence were no more presented as typical of England (or even of their own oeuvres) in their criticisms of England than was Tolstoi presented as typically Russian in such patriotism as *Anna Karenina* demonstrates. The comparability of the cultural *realia* of the two languages and periods was occasionally striking: trains function similarly in *Anna Karenina* and *Women in Love*, both as a quotidian means of transport and a mechanical source of horror, relative to the difference between the relative modernity of the Moscow–Saint Petersburg railway at the time of the former, and the familiarity of Nottinghamshire railways at the time of the latter (they were opened in 1851 and 1839 respectively). Gwendolen, Anna, and Gudrun have parallel fantasies about being able to do what men do (hunt tigers, speak in Parliament, and swim naked in lakes). *Women in Love* looks back to the previous generation, which more closely resembles that of *Anna Karenina* than that of *Daniel Deronda*. My book as a whole therefore does not so much mediate nations as attempt to transcend them; this was the easier task, given the abstract, second-order, nature of my topic of comparison.

The difference between comparisons in which a time difference is involved, and ones in which it is not, is not the same as the difference between synchronic and diachronic comparison within the novels, because two types of time are involved. The first type corresponds also to events not directly connected to the novels, whereas the second type is the otherwise empty medium in which narrative takes place; comparisons of novels of different periods therefore tend to make reference to the changes which have occurred in the intervening period, whereas all the information directly relevant to understanding the relations of succeeding portions of a novel is contained in the novel itself. Despite this, there may be certain similarities: in *Daniel Deronda* the relationship of the *siuzhets* suggests that Daniel's story follows, and avoids the problems of, Gwendolen's; *Women in Love*, when read in comparison to *Anna Karenina* (even apart from the probability of influence between them) has the aspect of avoiding some of the latter's problems. Moreover, if the past is, as L. P. Hartley suggested, another country, then another country can also seem to correspond to a different time. England in *Anna Karenina* represents not only luxury but also modernity, in a way which is borne out by differences between the societies depicted in that novel and in *Daniel Deronda*. In the latter's England there are, as Levin supposes to be the case in England, no major controversies about ownership of land, no duels (the bloodless duel between

Mrs Glasher's Irish husband and Grandcourt took place twenty years before the time of the novels' writing), and women can choose their marriage partners, as Gwendolen and Catherine Arrowpoint do and Anna Karenina does not (*Anna Karenina* also associates England with croquet, billiards, the phrase *not in my line*, and *pluck*, all of which are mentioned or used in *Daniel Deronda*). One might add that in England Jews are considerably more emancipated than in *Anna Karenina*'s Russia. Even contemporary novels, then, can be read as responding to each other. The sentence in *Daniel Deronda* 'Most of those who remembered the affair now wondered what had become of that Mrs. Glasher, whose beauty and brilliancy had made her rather conspicuous to them in foreign places, where she was known to be living with young Grandcourt' could be read in response to Anna Karenina's story, demonstrating the possible differences of treatment of confessed adulteresses in the two novels' respective countries (DD: 287).

Counter-historical studies of response employ the hypothetical mood, as Leavis does frequently in his comparisons of Eliot and Lawrence when speculating what Eliot *would have* made of Lawrence (which he does far more than considering what Lawrence would have made, or left evidence that he indeed made, of her). This hypothetical mood was sparingly used in this book; rather, the certainty that Lawrence had read and responded to *Anna Karenina* encouraged an interpretation of all of its salient differences to *Women in Love* in terms of conscious or unconscious responses on Lawrence's part. Such comparisons of two novels using the hypothesis of influence may be likened to the comparisons which were drawn between the final version of a novel, and its drafts. The final version could be interpreted in terms of the authors' criticism of the earlier versions, alongside the retention of characteristics which rendered the final characters inconsistent. The psychological connection of the earlier and later drafts' characters in the author's mind could be analogically displaced onto the characters themselves: just as actual people are formed from the people whom they have been, largely without conscious memory of this process, so one might say that Anna Karenina has forgotten that she was once a plump, plain, seductive coquette, Karenin that he was a sympathetic Christian, Birkin that he was once strongly sexually attracted to Gerald and happy with Hermione, and Gudrun that she was raped by Gerald (Bayley 1966: 219; Turner 1993: 21; IWL: liii). The reader's knowledge of these histories may provide a context in which the characters appear more rather than less intelligible, just as knowledge of Lawrence's non-fictional responses to *Anna Karenina* make *Women in Love* more rather than less comprehensible.

The fact that Lawrence's responses to Tolstoi's novel are the only extant records of any of the three authors' responses to each others' novels fits with the fact that his perspective is closest to my own as an English person with some knowledge of Russian literature living later than Eliot and Tolstoi. However, since he did not read Russian, the translation which he read was on a few occasions compared to Tolstoi's novel. Such comparisons, at the level of juxtaposed sentences, were also occasionally made between the novels themselves, although only in the latter case was my concentration at least as much on similarity as on difference. Since English was the language in which my investigations were conducted, related issues pertained to the applicability of my terms to Tolstoi's novel, as to the equivalence of Garnett's terms to Tolstoi's. My uses of *fabula* and *siuzhet* hardly redressed the balance, particularly since they have become naturalized, via their reception by French structuralism, into English; Bakhtin's terms were used largely in translation. Even referring to *Anna Karenina* as a *novel* as opposed to a *роман* is problematic, and Mrs Glasher's sin of adultery is not quite Anna's of *прелюбодеяние*. Nonetheless, this study, like all comparative literature in the traditional sense of that phrase, placed faith in the principal of equivalence (maximum and significant similarity) at several levels. Adultery is not *прелюбодеяние* any more than Mrs Glasher is Anna, but they are comparable within their respective systems, rather as *comparing apples and oranges* is the equivalent of the French *comparer des pommes et des poires* [comparing apples and pears]. Gwendolen and Anna and Gerald were compared as equivalent characters; Gascoigne's and Koznyshev's compositions were compared with each other and with the opening of *The Winter's Tale*'s sheep-shearing festival as equivalent scenes in their respective works. The similarities of equivalents function as the significant context for their differences, without which the latter would lack meaning, and in this respect equivalence underlies any comparison; a broader but otherwise synonymous term is *comparability*.

As we have seen, in literary comparison space and time are not discrete categories, and their superimposition may reveal their similarities. Moretti is reminded of

> Gide's reflections on the form of the novel at the time he was writing *The Couterfeiters*: granted that the novel is a slice of life, he muses, why should we always slice 'in the direction of length', emphasizing the passage of time? why not slice *in the direction of width*, and of the multiplicity of simultaneous events? Length, plus width: this is how a tree signifies. (2007: 90–91)

— and it is also a way in which this book signifies. The fact that my novels formed a right-angled triangle in space and time allowed the two dimensions to be compared with a minimum of points. On the other hand, the dimension of space would have been more fairly compared to time had a Russian novel of the 1910s been added (for example, Belyi's *Петербург* [*Petersburg*], 1913 revised 1922, although this is not double-plotted). Rather than the book resembling a love triangle, it would in that case have resembled a quartet, like that of *Women in Love*, with each of the couples asserting its own qualities. As it was, the novel which interacted more intensively with the two others than they did with each other was not, as might be expected of its right-angular position, *Daniel Deronda*, but *Anna Karenina*. In *Limits to Interpretation* Vladimir Alexandrov claimed to use *Anna Karenina* as a case study for the approach for which he argued because the novel's breadth of complexity suits it to this purpose. For the same reason it is suited to its role in this book. The placing of the chapter on *Anna Karenina* second may have had its own effect on the mode of comparison, by juxtaposing that novel to both of the others; this suited the fact that Tolstoi mediated between the other novelists in time; and yet, had *Women in Love* been discussed second and *Anna Karenina* last, time and space might more fairly have been compared.

Comparison's Limits

> I have been studying how I may compare
> This prison where I live unto the world
> And for because the world is populous,
> And here is not a creature but myself,
> I cannot do it; yet I'll hammer it out.
>
> WILLIAM SHAKESPEARE, *Richard II*, V. 5. 1–5

The order of discussion of *comparanda* is particularly influential when their number is small. A study of a few *comparanda* imposes particular limitations with regard to generalization: more confident generalizations about double-plotting and literary comparison would have been generated by a study of more novels. The claim at the end of the statement that 'The terms *контрасть* [contrast], *сопоставление* [contrast], *противоположность* [opposition], and *противоположение* [opposition] are used with half the frequency of *contrast* in *Daniel Deronda* — which is still a relatively high rate' was only *demonstrated* to be true in relation to the tiny sample taken of nine English Victorian novels. Most of my other comparative statements were demonstrated to be true only in relation to the still smaller sample of three novels. On the other hand, although my discussions favoured certain critical positions rather than others on matters of critical controversy in relation to the novels taken individually, the novels' comparisons generated no serious challenge to such broad critical orthodoxies as the differences between the presentations of character in Tolstoi, Lawrence, and their respective periods. I did not come to abolish the law, but to nuance it.

Despite the fact that one of the justifications of a small number of *comparanda* is the prioritization of accuracy, I often found the level of detail of my descriptions to be less than I would have wished for. A reader with greater interest in one of the novels may have been irritated at the lack of detail in the descriptions made of it, whilst accepting the conversion of the others into stable comparators (as Anna uses a neighbouring photograph of Vronskii to peel a photograph of her son out of an album, in order to look at the latter more closely) (AK IX: 115). The first chapter found 'salmons' (such as Fluellen finds in the rivers of Macedon and Monmouth) in all three authors, and even more salmons in each of the two pairs of authors — although the implicit claim was merely that the novels were comparable, rather than a justification of a critical equivalent of conquering France (*Henry V*, IV. 7. 21–31). The level of critical detail of the analysis was restricted not only by factors of space and time. Description of difference in relation to the other is one aim of comparison, but description of difference in relation to the self is not. The very wish to compare produces several attendant impulses: to stabilize at least one of the *comparanda* rather than to pay attention to the instabilities of all simultaneously; to limit the length of investigation of each story and novel, in order to maintain contact between them; and to limit the potentially infinite discovery of difference in thick description and, therefore, of non-comparability. The self must be gathered, as Birkin might have said, before it can enter into pure relationship with an other.

In addition, the arts, unlike the sciences, are infrequently able to use quantitative units in comparison (although they might do so more often than they do), but rely on a crude vocabulary of identity, opposition, equilibrium, and comparatives, modified by intensifiers and qualifiers. Most of the comparative cadences used in this book asserted either identity or difference: 'In contrast to *Daniel Deronda* neither domain of *Anna Karenina* demonstrates much faith in art'; 'Unlike *Daniel Deronda*, which looks to a Zionist Israel, and *Anna Karenina*, which looks to a Christian Russia, *Women in Love* has no place to which it aspires'. Most comparatives were ungraded: '*Daniel Deronda* makes more use of such endings than does *Anna Karenina*'; 'Overall, however, the disjunction of domains in *Daniel Deronda* is the greater'; '*Daniel Deronda* therefore more strongly suggests a pluralist ontology'. 'Degrees of coherence' were compared, but this is metaphoric language; coherence is not measured in discrete degrees, and nor is scapegoating. The vague term *relatively* was used to indicate a relatively small difference of degree: 'The insecurity of Daniel's ending is relatively superficial by comparison'. The phrases *just as* and (more conscientiously) *rather as* covered a range of degrees and types of similarity; *whereas* covered a range of differences; *however, but*, and *on the other hand* served to give greater weight to difference than similarity; the current discussion is no more precise than what it describes. Or little more. Or hardly more. It is relatively easy to describe the relations of different qualities, but hard to describe degrees of possession of a quality. Levin suggested that 'A noncomparing comparatist might be compared with a violinist who disdains to use a bow and thereby limits his performances to a sequence of *pizzicati*' (Levin 1972: 75). In terms of comparative description, however, the difficulty lies in obtaining a slide. The description of most things by any single adjective means that it is considered so in comparison to the most relevant *comparanda*. A consideration of the limits of language in relation to comparison is therefore a useful potential approach to a consideration of the descriptive limits of language in general.

However, in explicitly comparative work the degree of descriptive detail attained is particularly decisive, since it determines what is described as a similarity and what as a difference. Any two novels are similar by virtue of their genre, and different in the selection, order, and punctuation of their words. Between these outer extremes of critical scale, similarities and differences may be arranged interchangeably in bands. For example, the difference that *Daniel Deronda* and *Anna Karenina* were written in different languages gives way to the similarity that they are both double-plotted, which itself gives way to difference, and to other similarities, when described in greater detail. The similarities between what I described as the two major domains of *Anna Karenina* gave way to the differences by which I distinguished them, which in turn gave way to similarities of detail. All of the seven types of comparison discussed so far in this chapter started with assumptions of difference, which yielded to certain perceptions of likeness, until and unless a greater level of descriptive detail was attained. The scale of comparison undertaken tends to be governed by the type of results which are desired; in general, obvious large-scale and obscure small-scale similarities and differences are of less critical interest than are those of an intermediate scale, such as the distinction of domains. I at times attempted to operate at a critical scale which would allow both similarities and differences to be described; however, in practice the transition from the former to the latter often involved a slight increase in the level of critical detail. It is salutary to be reminded of the flexibility of such terms as *similarity* and *difference*, which are such heavily used tools of thought, and are generally supposedly antonyms; similarity is merely difference on a relatively small scale.

Theophrastus asserted that:

> To discern likeness amidst diversity, it is well known, does not require so fine a mental edge as the discerning of diversity amidst general sameness. The primary rough classification depends on the prominent resemblances of things: the progress is towards finer and finer discrimination according to minute differences. (Eliot 1994: 143)

Lawrence's perception of the incomparability of two beings on a spiritual level is also congruent with the incomparability of any two things at the level of quiddity:

> When I stand with another man, who is himself, and when I am truly myself, then I am only aware of a Presence, and of the strange reality of Otherness. There is me, and there is *another being*. That is the first part of the reality. There is no comparing or estimating. There is only this strange recognition of *present otherness*. I may be glad, angry, or sad, because of the presence of the other. But still no comparison enters in. (RDP: 80)

Six years before, H. V. Routh had written that comparative literature had too long stressed 'resemblances and parallels. But if the student were to turn his attention to differences and contrasts, he would be amazed to find how quickly his researches were leading him behind the scenes' (1913: 3). However, the salient 'differences and contrasts' to which he is referring exist not just at the level of detail, but can exist at any scale. In reading each of my novels in relation to the concept of *Weltliteratur*, one task was to identify the nature of the most important *division* in each work — for example, between growing tips and the rest of humanity in *Women in Love*.

Yet the perception of similarity continues to distinguish much comparative literary work; Aristotle considered metaphor a sign of genius, 'since a good metaphor implies an intuitive perception of the similarity in dissimilars' (Aristotle, 1970: 61). Eliot's Theophrastus opined:

> Yet even at this stage of European culture one's attention is continually drawn to the prevalence of that grosser mental sloth which makes people dull to the most ordinary prompting of comparison — the bringing things together because of their likeness. The same motives, the same ideas, the same practices, are alternately admired and abhorred, lauded and denounced, according to their association with superficial differences, historical or actually social. (Eliot 1994: 143)

In a specifically literary context, Ahearn and Weinstein described comparison as:

> a shaping venture that ceaselessly reconfigures its materials and proffers pattern and gestalt where there had been discrete entities. This undertaking draws every bit as much on the fashioning powers of synthesis as the critical procedures of analysis, and its respect for particularity, indeed for Difference, is compatible with its commitment to field pictures and transnational groupings. (Bernheimer 1995: 89)

Still, as discussed above, differences and similarities are not always and only the product of different kinds of perception; they can be alternative ways of expressing the perception of a certain degree of difference. I was constantly aware of the element of choice in the presentation of my findings, and that according any greater degree of detail to the similarities would abolish them as such. Either differences or similarities could be subsumed in a *nonetheless*, in order to stress the other as more important. My analysis of scapegoating frequently invoked the rhetoric of the texts it studied, but it also employed its own rhetoric; those who disagree with my analyses might consider my arguments to have persecuted the novelists concerned. Crudely performed or described comparison can exaggerate either difference or likeness to create critical *поразительность* [striking effects] in order to justify an asserted contrast, or else to enforce *Blutbrüderschaft* between reluctant partners, in order to make both jointly collaborative in the desired interpretation. Masson-Oursel was aware of these dangers:

> The methodologist will find no difficulty in remarking that everything more or less resembles or differs from everything else in accordance with the disposition or ingenuity of the observer; and that the most capricious similitudes and unexpected differentiations present themselves to our gaze, provided we know how to vary appropriately the angle of vision from which the fact is perceived. (1926: 38–39)

Comparisons (using the term to denote perceptions or assertions rather than systematic procedures) have long been associated with rhetoric, not to mention odiousness: 'Odyous of olde been comparisonis, | And of comparisonis engendyrd is haterede' (OED *c.* 1430, Lydgate). In Shakespeare's works comparison is repeatedly described as the act of comparing, quibbling, equivocation, jibing allusion, and scoffing analogy. Rosaline in *Love's Labour's Lost* disparages Berowne as renowned as 'a man replete with mocks; | Full of comparisons and wounding flouts'; Beatrice predicts that Benedick will 'but break a comparison or two on me; which, | peradventure not marked or not laughed at, strikes him into melancholy'; Falstaff complains of Hal as 'the most comparative, rascalliest, sweet young Prince' (*Love's Labour's Lost*, v. 2. 30–31; *Much Ado About Nothing*, II. 1. 136–68; *Henry IV Part 1*, I. 2. 80–81). Of course, comparative literary critics are relatively unlikely to deserve the insult 'vain comparative' applied by Henry IV to Richard II; their systematic comparisons are rarely undertaken with the aim of disparagement, although they may use comparisons to enforce a value judgement. Leavis uses both Lawrence's similarities to, and differences from, Eliot, to the former's advantage (*Henry IV Part 1*, III. 2. 67). The nature of the three novels discussed determined that many of my discussion's findings were explicit ethical judgements, but I have tried to avoid making my conclusions 'a distribution at the last of prizes, pensions, husbands, wives, babies, millions, appended paragraphs, and cheerful remarks' (James quoted in Kermode 1967: 22; Ashton 1992: 130). Still, critics do wish to find results which justify the undertaking of the comparison; when the Hatter and the March Hare tell Alice that they have no idea why a raven is like a writing desk, 'Alice gave a weary sigh. "I think you might do something better with the time," she said, "than wasting it in asking riddles that have no answers"' (L. Carroll 1970: 97). This desire can exert a pressure towards the clear delineation of similarity or difference. Whereas experimental scientists tend to start with a hypothesis which they hold open to empirical confirmation, falsification, or modification, the comparative critic may start without a hypothesis, but has the goal of eventually enunciating a clear thesis. I meant everything in this book to be related to everything else there, but some of my likenesses, for example between the different types of comparison, may have seemed forced, or reliant on the possibility of applying the same terms in different senses to them. It is in the nature of comparison that less substantiation for perceptions of the individual *comparanda* is given than in studies of single works; the critic's reader is therefore all the more reliant on her scrupulousness.

Comparison's Fruits

> What needs propagating is the comparative reflex, the comparative way of thinking.
>
> SAUSSY 2006: 5

There are several justifications for Saussy's assertion, despite all of the above. Bassnett notes that 'Comparative literature people have always asked themselves "How can comparison be the object of anything?"' (1993: 2). Taking the term *object* to mean purpose, comparison can for several reasons be the object of a practice. It was noted at the beginning of this book that comparison is intrinsic to thought and willed action. Given this, it is worth sharpening one's acuity at it, and consciousness of its pleasures and dangers, in the intellectually challenging but pragmatically sheltered environment of literary criticism. Such criticism cultivates sensitivity, since comparison of a limited number of objects requires empirical openness to the precise location of the centre of gravity which permits a balance of separateness and communication between them (Daniel's father believed 'that the strength and wealth of mankind depended on' this balance) (DD: 619). This in turn relies upon feeling for a point of balance between particularity and generality, and it is in precisely this realm between the real and the ideal — as between history and philosophy — that art and art criticism are located; Masson-Oursel noted that 'The scheme of intelligibility proper to the comparative method consists neither in identity nor in distinction', which would lead respectively to 'a science or a history' (1926: 44).

Still, the perspective afforded by comparison is as necessary to a kind of objectivity in art as it is in philosophy or history. Masson-Oursel stresses that 'philosophy, which ought to be comparative, should not take man, or human reason, but the different types of humanity or reason, for its subject [. . .] philosophy cannot achieve positivity so long as its investigations are restricted to the thought of our own civilization'; 'our Western faiths have no meaning at all except in terms of a comparative theory of civilization' (1926: 33; 205). Becker agrees that 'Those who persist in comparative study point to the promise of fresh and illuminating perspectives on the central ethical issues of their home traditions, including the issues of ethical relativism' (Becker 1992: I 272). Posnett thought that Greek thought was restricted because the Greeks refused to perform historical comparison:

> Groups, like individuals, need to project themselves beyond the circle of their own associations if they wish to understand their own nature; but the great highway which has since led to comparative philosophy was closed against the Greek by his contempt for any language but his own [so] the Greeks made poor progress in comparative thinking, as a matter not merely of unconscious action but of conscious reflection. This conscious reflection has been the growth of European thought during the past five centuries, at first indeed a weakling, but, from causes of recent origin, now flourishing in healthy vigour. (Posnett 1886: 74)

The term *comparatively* is related to *relatively*, with the latter understood not just in its connection to relativism (which is not a necessary concomitant of comparative thought), but to relationships — to the understanding of any phenomenon in its relevant contexts, and in the light of potential alternatives.

Of course, comparativism can risk giving the illusion of impartiality. F. G. Crookshank, in his introduction to Masson-Oursel's *Comparative Philosophy*, considered that the latter's 'method is one which may be said [. . .] to be designed to attain the positive by way of the comparative, for he would secure objectivity by the due appreciation of relativity' (Masson-Oursel 1926: 2). Cheah warns that 'The very act of comparison, as in comparative literature, can seem to signal a liberation from insularity and national prejudice into the one true judgment' (Cheah and Robbins 1998: 248). Any number of *comparanda* for a literary work will fall short of constituting its whole context, and the conclusions drawn will be true only of those *comparanda*. Rather, the comparative approach should militate against any sense of possessing a whole or sufficient context. The idea that George Eliot was responding to German literature opens the possibility that she was also responding to French, and Italian, and Spanish, and Hebrew literature, which literatures were themselves influenced by each other, and so on: 'Virgin literatures, like the virgin land, are a myth. Comparatists are the people trained to bring us this critical news' (Bernheimer 1995: 79). A similar myth is virginal reception, beyond one's earliest childhood reading; simultaneous recollection of works which one has read is involved in all reading.

At an ethical and political level, the willingness to compare one thing or oneself with an other or others undermines absolutism, and permits competing voices to be heard. In this respect 'Comparative Literature has an ideology of inclusion of the Other', and is indeed historically, in its American manifestation, 'a result of European intellectuals fleeing "totalitarian" regimes' (Spivak 2003: 3; Tötösy de Zepetnek 1998: 13). Levin remarked that in the Soviet Union the charge of comparing Russian with Western literatures was like a charge of treason — although one suspects that he himself was not unaffected by rhetorical intent in making the comment (Levin 1972: 71–72). It is not necessarily the case that, as Lawrence asserted, 'Comparison enters only when one [. . .] enters the material-mechanical world. Then equality and disquality starts at once', and it is not wholly irrelevant that Lawrence was not attracted to liberalism or democracy (RDP: 80). The first and second Citizens in *Julius Caesar* hint at the connection of comparison to democratic choice in agreeing to hear Brutus and Cassius speak and to 'compare their reasons, | When severally we hear them rendered' (*Julius Caesar*, III. 2. 9–10). Comparison can also undermine prejudice. The narrator of *Daniel Deronda* advises that:

> a little comparison will often diminish our surprise and disgust at the aber-
> rations of Jews [. . .]. this evening Deronda, becoming more conscious that
> he was falling into unfairness and ridiculous exaggeration, began to use that
> corrective comparison [of considering aberrant Christians]. (DD: 309–10)

The connection of comparison to tolerance is whimsically suggested in Shakespeare's
Sonnet 35, which enjoins its addressee to 'No more be griev'd at that which thou
hast done: | Roses have thorns, and silver fountains mud [. . .] All men make faults,
and even I in this, | Authorizing thy trespass with compare' (Sonnet 35 1–2, 5–6). In
polycultural societies, according to Linda Hutcheon, 'difference is both constitutive
of identity and something to be constantly negotiated' (Saussy 2006: 227). It is an
ethically and emotionally sound principle of human interaction for individuals to
respect their own and each other's quiddity, whilst reaching to find maximum
common ground. Finally, ethical analyses may be assisted by comparative reference
to moral benchmarks: far from inducing ethical relativism, their use forbids it. The
Nazi Holocaust can serve to indicate the potential evil of aims or methods which
resemble its own — for which reason Norman G. Finkelstein was right to remark
that: 'Only those using a benchmark evil not as a moral compass but rather as an
ideological club recoil at such analogies. "Do not compare" is the mantra of moral
"blackmailers"' (2003: 149).

Since comparison is involved in all thought, thought about comparison is
necessarily self-reflexive. This is one reason why analysis of the use of comparison in
literary criticism should form part of literary theory, and why comparative literature
can serve as a home for literary theory. Literary comparison in the narrower sense of
the term risks several potential problems, including unwarranted deductions from
limited sample sizes, lack of detail, and exaggeration to rhetorical effect or in self-
justification. It has the compensatory virtues of demanding empiricism, openness,
and integrity, extending awareness of similarities, and revealing the structures
underlying much literary-critical, and practical, thought. The difference of degree
rather than kind between similarity and difference, the mind's tendency to seek out
equivalents, and the limited attention paid to any individual object being compared,
apply also to comparison more broadly understood, from which comparison in
the narrower sense is distinguished as much by degree as by kind, and which is
unconsciously performed in everything from understanding linguistic *différance*,
to reading *Anna Karenina* in relation to all of the novels which one remembers, to
choosing one's lover.

The pun in *The Art of Comparison* is still less valid than that of the book's subtitle.
There is, as I have argued, literature which is by its nature comparative, but its
analysis, and indeed comparison of any kind, is not an art, nor does comparative
criticism constitute art. Of the metaphors for connection in works of art mentioned
in this book, Eliot's organic metaphor fits the book itself insofar as its parts are
aware of each other and aim to support each other. Tolstoi's metaphor of repeating
arches is less appropriate, since not even my three central chapters, let alone all five,
have sufficiently similar structures or arcs of thought. The reader of this book is
not, in the metaphor of the anonymous reviewer of *Anna Karenina*, thrown from

side to side of a train on a winding route, since three rather than two *comparanda* were concerned, and their analyses were successive rather than interspersed. The most fitting metaphor is Tolstoi's alternative metaphor of the 'endless labyrinth of connections', which denotes asymmetricality and complex contacts between all of its parts (Donskov 2003 I: 268). The book is not art, but criticism, with all of the complex relations to creativity and objectivity which pertain to the latter. But it is particularly worth exercising the comparative faculty *on* art, because of its potential for complexity, and to teach and reflect on comparison. I have for this reason treated double-plotted novels as what Martin Swales calls 'a heuristic tool, a grid which allows the critic to select a number of novels for analytical and comparative purposes', and as capable of shedding light on my method (1979: 92).

This study has been guided by a hope that, even if no such revolution in university organization as proposed in my opening chapter occurs even in the slightest degree, the perceptions which underlie the proposals will inform the work both of those who consider themselves to work in comparative literature, and of those who do not. All literary critics might benefit by becoming more conscious of the nature of literary comparison, more aware of the analogies of this comparison to those demanded and performed in life at large, and correspondingly perceptive of the extent and limits of similarity of art and life, both of which may be perceived alternatively in terms of the conjunction of disparate elements, and the splitting of a hypothetical unity into its component tendencies. Comparison helps give us a sense of where art fits into life; how it relates to it; how it compares to it.

BIBLIOGRAPHY

ALDINGTON, RICHARD. 1951. *Portrait of a Genius, But... The Life of D. H. Lawrence, 1885–1930* (London: Heinemann)

ALDRIDGE, A. OWEN. 1969. *Comparative Literature: Matter and Method* (London: University of Illinois Press)

ALEKSANDROV, A. 1879. *Польный англо-русский словарь* (Санкт Петербург: печатано в тип. морскаго министервство)

ALEXANDROV, VLADIMIR E. 2004. *Limits to Interpretation: The Meanings of 'Anna Karenina'* (Wisconsin: University of Wisconsin Press)

APPIAH, K. ANTHONY. 1995. 'Geist Stories', in *Comparative Literature in the Age of Multiculturalism*, ed. by Charles Bernheimer (Baltimore: Johns Hopkins University Press), pp. 51–57

APTER, EMILY S. 2006. *The Translation Zone: A New Comparative Literature* (Princeton: Princeton University Press)

ARISTOTLE. 1970. *Poetics*, trans. by Gerald F. Else (Ann Arbor: University of Michigan Press)

ARNOLD, ARMIN. 1961. 'D. H. Lawrence and Thomas Mann', *Comparative Literature*, 13 (1): 33–38.

ARNOLD, MATTHEW. 1893. *Literature and Dogma* (London: Smith, Elder, & Co.)

——1895. *Letters of Matthew Arnold 1848–1888* (London: Macmillan)

——1903. 'Count Leo Tolstoi', in *Essays in Criticism Second Series* (London: MacMillan), pp. 253–300

——1965. *Culture and Anarchy with Friendship's Garland and Some Literary Essays* (Michigan: University of Michigan Press)

ARNOPOULOS, PARIS. 1998. *Cosmopolitics: Public Policy of Outer Space* (Toronto: Guernica)

ASHTON, ROSEMARY (ed.). 1992. *George Eliot: Selected Critical Writings* (Oxford: Oxford University Press)

——1996. *George Eliot: A Life* (London: Hamish Hamilton)

AUERBACH, ERICH. 1946. *Mimesis: Dargestellte Wirklichkeit in der abendländischen Literatur* (Bern: Francke)

——1967. 'Philologie der Weltliteratur', in *Gesammelte Aufsätze zur romanischen Philologie*, ed. by Fritz Schalk (Bern and Munich: Francke Verlag), pp. 301–12

——1968. *Mimesis* (Princeton: Princeton University Press)

BAKER, WILLIAM. 1975. *George Eliot and Judaism* (Salzburg: Institut für englische Sprache und Literatur, Universität Salzburg)

——1977. *The George Eliot–George Henry Lewes Library: An Annotated Catalogue of Their Books at Dr. Williams's Library, London* (New York and London: Garland Publishing)

——and J. C. ROSS. 2002. *George Eliot: A Bibliographical History* (London: British Library)

BAKHTIN, MIKHAIL. 1963. *Проблемы поэтики Достоевского* (Москва: Советский писатель)

——1979. *Эстетика словесного творчество* (Москва: Искусство)

——1981. *The Dialogic Imagination*, trans. by Caryl Emerson and Michael Holquist (Austin: University of Texas Press)

——1984. *Problems of Dostoevsky's Poetics*, trans. by Caryl Emerson (Manchester: Manchester University Press)

—— 1986. *Speech Genres and Other Late Essays*, trans. by V. W. Mcgee (Austin: University of Texas Press)

BARING, MAURICE. 1960. *Landmarks in Russian Literature* (London: Methuen)

BARRETT, DOROTHEA. 1989. *Vocation and Desire: George Eliot's Heroines* (London and New York: Routledge)

BASSNETT-McGUIRE, SUSAN. 1993. *Comparative Literature: A Critical Introduction* (Oxford: Blackwell)

BAYLEY, JOHN. 1960. *The Characters of Love: A Study in the Literature of Personality* (London: Constable)

—— 1966. *Tolstoy and the Novel* (London: Chatto and Windus)

BECKER, LAWRENCE C. and CHARLOTTE B. BECKER. 1992. *Encyclopedia of Ethics* (New York: Garland Publications)

BEDIENT, CALVIN. 1972. *Architects of the Self: George Eliot, D. H. Lawrence, and E. M. Forster* (Berkeley, Los Angeles, and London: University of California Press)

BEER, GILLIAN. 1983. *Darwin's Plots: Evolutionary Narrative in Darwin, George Eliot, and Nineteenth-Century Fiction* (London: Routledge and Kegan Paul)

—— 1986. *George Eliot* (Brighton: Harvester Press)

BELL, MICHAEL. 1992. *D. H. Lawrence: Language and Being* (Cambridge: Cambridge University Press)

—— 2001. 'Lawrence and Modernism', in *The Cambridge Companion to D. H. Lawrence*, ed. by Anne Fernihough (Cambridge: Cambridge University Press), pp. 179–98

BENNETT, JOAN. 1948. *George Eliot: Her Mind and her Art* (London: Cambridge University Press)

BERGHAHN, KLAUS L. 2001. 'Patterns of Childhood: Goethe and the Jews', in *Goethe in German-Jewish Culture*, ed. by Klaus L. Berghahn and Jost Hermand (New York: Camden House), pp. 3–15

BERLIN, ISAIAH. 1978. *Russian Thinkers* (London: Penguin)

—— 1994. 'The Hedgehog and the Fox: An Essay on Tolstoy's View of History', in *Russian Thinkers*, ed. by Henry Hardy and Aileen Kelly (London: Penguin)

BERLIN, MIRIAM H. 1982. 'George Eliot and the Russians', in *George Eliot: A Centenary Tribute*, ed. by Gordon S. Haight and Rosemary T. Vanarsdel (London: Macmillan)

BERNHEIMER, CHARLES (ed.). 1995. *Comparative Literature in the Age of Multiculturalism* (Baltimore: Johns Hopkins University Press)

BILLIG, MICHAEL. 1995. *Banal Nationalism* (London: Sage)

BIRDWOOD-HEDGER, MAYA. 2006. *Tension between Domestication and Foreignization in English-Language Translations of Anna Karenina* (Edinburgh: University of Edinburgh Press)

BLANCHARD, LYDIA. 1980. 'The "Real Quartet" of *Women in Love*: Lawrence on Brothers and Sisters', in *D. H. Lawrence: The Man Who Lived*, ed. by Robert B. Partlow, Jr., and Harry T. Moore (Carbondale: Southern Illinois University Press), pp. 199–206

BLUMBERG, EDWINA JANNIE. 1971. 'Tolstoy and the English Novel: A Note on *Middlemarch* and *Anna Karenina*', *Slavic Review*, 30: 561–69

BODENHEIMER, ROSEMARIE. 1994. *The Real Life of Mary Ann Evans: George Eliot, Her Letters and Fiction* (Ithaca and London: Cornell University Press)

BOHLKE, L. BRENT (ed.). 1986. *Willa Cather in Person: Interviews, Speeches, and Letters* (Lincoln and London, University of Nebraska Press).

BONAPARTE, FELICIA. 1979. *The Triptych and the Cross: The Central Myths of George Eliot's Poetic Imagination* (Brighton: Harvester)

BOOTH, WAYNE C. 1988. *The Company We Keep: An Ethics of Fiction* (Berkeley, Los Angeles, and London: University of California Press)

BRADSHAW, DAVID. 1998. 'Introduction', in *Women in Love*, ed. by David Bradshaw (Oxford: Oxford University Press), pp. vii–xxxviii

BRADY, KRISTIN. 1992. *George Eliot* (Basingstoke: Macmillan Education)

BREWSTER, DOROTHY. 1954. *East–West Passage: A Study in Literary Relationships* (London: Allen and Unwin)

BROOKS, PETER. 1995. 'Must We Apologize?', in *Comparative Literature in the Age of Multi-culturalism*, ed. by Charles Bernheimer (Baltimore and London: Johns Hopkins University Press), 97–105

BROWN, CLARENCE. 1935. *Anna Karenina*. MGM.

BROWN, CATHERINE. 2009. '*Daniel Deronda* as Tragi-Comedy', *Essays in Criticism*, 59: 302–23

—— 2011. 'Scapegoating, Double-Plotting, and the Justice of *Anna Karenina*', *Modern Language Review*, 106.1 (179–94)

—— 2010b. 'The Unconscious Good Life in *Anna Karenina* and *Women in Love*', *Comparative Literature*, 63.1 (Winter 2011), 25–46

—— 2010c. 'Why Does Daniel Deronda's Mother Live in Russia?', *George Eliot–George Henry Lewes Studies*, 58–59 (September 2010), 26–42

BROWN, MARSHALL. 2006. 'Multum in Parvo; or, Comparison in Lilliput', in *Comparative Literature in the Age of Globalization*, ed. by Haun Saussy (Baltimore: Johns Hopkins University Press), pp. 249–61

BRUNEL, PIERRE, CLAUDE PICHOIS, and ANDRÉ MICHEL ROUSSEAU. 1983. *Qu'est-ce que la littérature comparée?* (Paris: Armand Colin)

BURGESS, ANTHONY. 1985. *Flame into Being: The Life and Work of D. H. Lawrence* (London: Heinemann)

CARROLL, DAVID (ed.). 1971. *George Eliot: The Critical Heritage* (London: Routledge and Kegan Paul)

—— 1992. *George Eliot and the Conflict of Interpretations* (Cambridge: Cambridge University Press)

CARROLL, LEWIS. 1970. *The Annotated Alice* (Harmondsworth: Penguin)

CARSWELL, CATHERINE. 1981. *The Savage Pilgrimage: A Narrative of D. H. Lawrence* (Cambridge: Cambridge University Press)

CHAMBERS, JESSIE, 'E.T.'. 1965. *D. H. Lawrence: A Personal Record*, 2nd edn (London: Frank Cass)

CHANDLER, FRANK W. 1936. 'Comparative Literature: Is It Dead?', in *Books Abroad*, 10.2: 136–38

CHEAH, PHENG and BRUCE ROBBINS. 1998. *Cosmopolitics: Thinking and Feeling beyond the Nation* (Minneapolis and London: University of Minnesota Press)

CHESTERTON, G. K., G. H. PERRIS, and E. GARNETT. 1903. *Leo Tolstoy* (London: Hodder and Stoughton)

CHUNG, CHONG-WHA. 1989. 'In Search of the Dark God: Lawrence's Dualism', in *D. H. Lawrence in the Modern World*, ed. by Peter Preston and Peter Hoare (Cambridge: Cambridge University Press), pp. 69–89

CLARKE, COLIN. 1969. *D. H. Lawrence: 'The Rainbow' and 'Women in Love'* (London: Macmillan)

CLEMENTS, ROBERT J. 1978. *Comparative Literature as Academic Discipline: A Statement of Principles, Praxis, Standards* (New York: Modern Language Association of America)

CORNWELL, NEIL. 1998. *Reference Guide to Russian Literature* (London and Chicago: Fitzroy Dearborn Publishers)

CREEGER, GEORGE R. (ed.). 1970. *George Eliot: A Collection of Critical Essays* (New Jersey: Prentice-Hall)

CROSS, JOHN WALTER. 1885. *George Eliot's Life as Related in her Letters and Journals* (Edinburgh and London: Blackwood)

CULLER, JONATHAN. 1981. *The Pursuit of Signs: Semiotics, Literature, and Deconstruction* (London and Henley: Routledge & Kegan Paul)

——2006. 'Comparative Literature, at Last', in *Comparative Literature in the Age of Globalization*, ed. by Haun Saussy (Baltimore: Johns Hopkins University Press), pp. 237–48

CURTIUS, ERNST ROBERT. 1953. *European Literature and the Latin Middle Ages*, trans. by Willard R. Trask (London: Routledge & Kegan Paul)

DAL´, VLADIMIR. 1955. *Толковый словарь живого великорусского языка*, 2nd edn (Москва: Терра)

DALESKI, H. M. 1965. *The Forked Flame: A Study of D. H. Lawrence* (Evanston: Northwestern University Press)

DAMROSCH, DAVID. 2003. *What Is World Literature?* (Woodstock: Princeton University Press)

DAVIE, DONALD. 1965. *Russian Literature and Modern English Fiction: A Collection of Critical Essays* (Chicago: University of Chicago Press)

DAVIS, GABRIELE A. WITTIG. 1983. 'Novel Associations: Theodor Fontane and George Eliot within the Context of Nineteenth Century Realism', *Stanford German Studies*, 19: 59–72

DENTITH, SIMON. 1986. *George Eliot* (Brighton Harvester Press)

DICKENS, CHARLES. 1966. *Oliver Twist* (Oxford: Clarendon Press)

DIEDERICH, NICOLE A. 2003. 'The Art of Comparison: Remarriage in Anne Bronte's *The Tenant of Wildfell Hall*', *Rocky Mountain Review of Language and Literature*, 57 .2: 25–41

DIERDRE, DAVID (ed.). 2001. *The Cambridge Companion to the Victorian Novel* (Cambridge: Cambridge University Press).

DOCHERTY, THOMAS. 2006. 'Without and Beyond Compare', *Comparative Critical Studies* 3: 1–2

DONSKOV, A. A. (ed.). 2003. *Л. Н. Толстой–Н. Н. Страхов польное собрание переписки* (Ottowa, Slavic Research Group at the University of Ottowa)

DOSTOEVSKII, F. M. N.D. *Дневник писателя за 1877 год* (Paris: YMCA-Press)

DOYLE, MARY ELLEN. 1981. *The Sympathetic Response: George Eliot's Fictional Rhetoric* (London: Associated University Presses)

DRYDEN, JOHN. 1964. *Of Dramatick Poesie: An Essay* (London: Oxford University Press)

DUREY, JILL FELICITY. 1993. *Realism and Narrative Modality* (Tübingen: Narr)

DUVIVIER, JULIEN. 1947. *Anna Karenina*. Twentieth Century Fox

DYER, GEOFF. 1997. *Out of Sheer Rage* (London: Abacus)

EAGLETON, TERRY. 1978. *Criticism and Ideology: A Study in Marxist Literary Theory* (London and New York: Verso)

ECKERMANN, JOHANN PETER. 1948. *Gespräche mit Goethe* (Zurich: Artemis Verlag)

EGGERT, PAUL, and JOHN WORTHEN (eds). 1996. *Lawrence and Comedy* (Cambridge: Cambridge University Press)

EIKHENBAUM, BORIS. 1974. *Лев Толстой: семидесятые годы* (Ленинград: Художественная литература)

ELIOT, GEORGE. 1954–78. *The George Eliot Letters* (London: Oxford University Press)

—— 1976–80. *Some George Eliot Notebooks* (Salzburg: Institut für Anglistik und Amerikanistik Universität Salzburg)

——1980a. *Adam Bede* (London: Penguin)

——1980b. *Felix Holt, the Radical* (Oxford: Clarendon Press)

——1980c. *The Mill on the Floss* (Oxford: Oxford University Press)

——1984. *Daniel Deronda* (Oxford: Oxford University Press)

——1986. *Middlemarch* (Oxford: Clarendon Press)

——1991. *Middlemarch* (New York, London, and Toronto: Everyman)

——1993. *Romola* (Oxford: Clarendon Press)

——1994. *Impressions of Theophrastus Such* (London: Pickering)

——1996. *Silas Marner* (Oxford: Clarendon Press)

——1999. *The Lifted Veil; Brother Jacob* (Oxford: Oxford University Press)

——2005. *The Complete Shorter Poetry of George Eliot* (London: Pickering and Chatto)

ELLIS, DAVID, MARK KINKEAD-WEEKES, and JOHN WORTHEN. 1998. *D. H. Lawrence, 1885–1930: The Cambridge Biography* (Cambridge: Cambridge University Press)

ELLIS, ROGER MAY, and OTHERS. 2005. *The Oxford History of Literary Translation in English* (Oxford: Oxford University Press)

EMERSON, CARYL. 2006. 'Answering for Central and Eastern Europe', in *Comparative Literature in the Age of Globalization*, ed. by Haun Saussy (Baltimore: Johns Hopkins University Press), pp. 203–11

EMPSON, WILLIAM. 1950. 'Double Plots: Heroic and Pastoral in the Main Plot and Sub-Plot', in *Some Versions of Pastoral* (London: Chatto and Windus), pp. 27–88

ENGELHARDT, DORTHE G.A. 1996. *L. N. Tolstoy and D. H. Lawrence: Cross-Currents and Influence* (Frankfurt am Main: Peter Lang)

EOYANG, EUGENE. 1998. 'The Genial and Congenial Art of Comparison', *Comparative Literature*, 50.3: v–xiii.

ERMARTH, ELIZABETH DEEDS. 1983. *Realism and Consensus in the English Novel* (Princeton: Princeton University Press)

—— 1997. *The English Novel in History 1840–1895* (London: Routledge)

ÉTIEMBLE, RENÉ. 1963. *Comparaison n'est pas raison: la crise de la littérature comparée* (Paris: Gallimard)

EVANS, MARY. 1989. *Mary Evans Reflecting on 'Anna Karenina'* (London: Routledge)

FERNIHOUGH, ANNE. 1993. *D. H. Lawrence: Aesthetics and Ideology* (Oxford: Clarendon Press)

—— (ed.). 2001. *The Cambridge Companion to D. H. Lawrence* (Cambridge: Cambridge University Press)

FERRAN, PASCALE. 2006. *Lady Chatterley et l'homme des bois*. France: Maïa Films

FERRIS, DAVID. 2006. 'Indiscipline', in *Comparative Literature in the Age of Globalization*, ed. by Haun Saussy (Baltimore: Johns Hopkins University Press), pp. 78–99

FIGES, ORLANDO. 2002. *Natasha's Dance: A Cultural History of Russia* (London: Penguin)

FINKELSTEIN, NORMAN G. 2003. *The Holocaust Industry: Reflections on the Exploitation of Jewish Suffering*, 2nd edn (London and New York: Verso)

FISCHE, HAROLD. 1965. 'Daniel Deronda or Gwendolen Harleth?', *Nineteenth Century Fiction* 19.4: 345–56

FITZGERALD, F. SCOTT. 1965. *'The Crack-up', with Other Pieces and Stories* (Harmondsworth: Penguin Books)

FITZLYON, APRIL and MICHELLE FERDINANDE PAULINE VIARDOT-GARCIA. 1964. *The Price of Genius: A Life of Pauline Viardot* (London: John Calder)

FJÅGESUND, PETER. 2008. 'D. H. Lawrence's Women in Love: Gerald Crich and Captain Scott', *English Studies*, 89.2: 182–94

FLEETWOOD, JANET RYE. 1980. *The Spider and the Beehive: A Study of Multiplicity in George Eliot's 'Middlemarch' and Tolstoy's 'Anna Karenina'* (Indiana: Indiana University Press)

FLEISCHMAN, AVROM. 2008. 'George Eliot's Reading: A Chronological List', *George Eliot-George Henry Lewes Studies*, 54–55: 1–106

FONTENELLE, BERNARD DE. 1955. *Entretiens sur la pluralité des mondes* (Oxford: Clarendon Press)

FORD, GEORGE H. 1963. 'An Introductory Note to D. H. Lawrence's Prologue to *Women in Love*', *Texas Quarterly*, 6.1: 92–97

FREUD, SIGMUND. 1930. *Das Unbehagen in der Kultur* (Vienna: Internationaler Psycho-analytischer Verlag)

FRYE, NORTHROP. 2006. *Anatomy of Criticism: Four Essays* (Toronto: University of Toronto Press)

GARETH JONES, W. (ed.). 1995. *Tolstoi and Britain* (Oxford: Berg)

GARNETT, EDWARD. 1914. *Tolstoi: His Life and Writings* (London: n.pub.)

GARNETT, RICHARD (1835–1906). 1899. *The International Library of Famous Literature* (London: The Standard)

GARNETT, RICHARD (1923–). 1991. *Constance Garnett: A Heroic Life* (London: Sinclair-Stevenson)

GARRETT, PETER K. 1980. *The Victorian Multiplot Novel: Studies in Dialogical Form* (New Haven and London: Yale University Press)

GENETTE, GÉRARD. 1980. *Narrative Discourse*, trans. by Jane E. Lewin (Oxford: Blackwell)

—— 2007. *Discours du récit* (Paris: Seuil)

GIFFORD, HENRY. 1959. 'Anna, Lawrence and "The Law"'. *Critical Quarterly*, 1 (3), 203–20

—— 1960. 'Further Notes on *Anna Karenina*', *Critical Quarterly*, 2 (2), 158–60

—— 1969. *Comparative Literature* (London: Routledge & Kegan Paul)

—— 1978. 'On Translating Tolstoy', in *New Essays on Tolstoy*, ed. by Malcolm Jones (Cambridge: Cambridge University Press), pp. 17–38

—— 1982. *Tolstoy* (Oxford: Oxford University Press)

GILES, PETER. 1901. *A Short Manual of Comparative Philology for Classical Students*, 2nd edn (London: Macmillan)

GIRARD, RENÉ. 1961. *Mensonge romantique et vérité romanesque* (Paris: Bernard Grasset)

—— 1965. *Deceit, Desire and the Novel: Self and Other in Literary Structure*, trans. by Yvonne Freccero (Baltimore: The Johns Hopkins University Press)

—— 1982. *Le Bouc émissaire* (Paris: Bernard Grasset)

—— 1986. *The Scapegoat*, trans. by Yvonne Freccero (Baltimore: The Johns Hopkins University Press)

GOETHE, JOHANN WOLFGANG. 1967. *Werke*, III: *Dramatische Dichtungen Erster Band* (Hamburg: Christian Wegner Verlag)

—— 1972. *Werke I: Gedichte, West-Östlicher Divan, Epen* (Munich: Winkler)

GORKY, MAXIM. 1920. *Reminiscences of Leo Nicolayevitch Tolstoi*, trans. by S. S. Koteliansky and Leonard Woolf (Richmond: Leonard and Virginia Woolf)

GRAY, RONALD. 1969. '*Women in Love* and the German Tradition in Literature', in *D. H. Lawrence: 'The Rainbow' and 'Women in Love'*, ed. by Colin Clarke (London: MacMillan), pp. 188–202

GROVE, GEORGE and ERIC BLOM. 1954. *Grove's Dictionary of Music and Musicians*, 5th edn (London: Macmillan)

GUÉRARD, ALBERT. 1958. 'Comparative Literature?', *Yearbook of Comparative and General Literature*, 7: 1–6

GUILLÉN, CLAUDIO. 1993. *The Challenge of Comparative Literature*, trans. by Cola Franzen (Cambridge, Mass.: Harvard University Press)

GUTHKE, KARL S. 2002. 'Destination Goethe: Travelling Englishmen in Weimar', in *Goethe and the English-Speaking World*, ed. by Nicholas and John Guthrie Boyle (New York: Camden House), pp. 111–44.

HABERER, ERICH. 1995. *Jews and Revolution in Nineteenth-Century Russia* (Cambridge: Cambridge University Press)

HAIGHT, GORDON S. 1968. *George Eliot: A Biography* (New York and Oxford: Oxford University Press)

HARDY, BARBARA. 1963. *The Novels of George Eliot: A Study in Form* (London: The Athlone Press)

—— 1971. 'Form and Freedom: Tolstoy's *Anna Karenina*', in *The Appropriate Form: An Essay on the Novel*, 2nd edn (London: Athlone Press)

—— 1982. *Particularities: Readings in George Eliot* (London: Peter Owen)

—— 1997. 'The Miserable Marriages in *Middlemarch*, *Anna Karenina*, and *Effi Briest*', in *George Eliot and Europe*, ed. by John Rignall (Aldershot and Vermont: Scolar Press), pp. 64–83

HAZLITT, WILLIAM. 1998. *Table Talk* (London: Pickering and Chatto)

HEYNS, MICHIEL. 1994. *Expulsion and the Nineteenth-Century Novel: The Scapegoat in English Realist Fiction* (Oxford: Clarendon Press)

HIRAI, MASAKO. 1998. *Sisters in Literature: Female Sexuality in 'Antigone', 'Middlemarch', 'Howards End' and 'Women in Love'* (London: Macmillan)

HIRST, DAVID L. 1984. *Tragicomedy* (London and New York: Methuen)

HOBBES, THOMAS. 1971. 'Hobbes's Answer to the Preface', in *Sir William Davenant's Gondibert*, ed. by David F. Gladish (Oxford: Clarendon Press)

HOWELLS, WILLIAM DEAN (ed.). 1958. *Howells and James: A Double Billing: Novel-Writing and Novel-Reading, an Impersonal Explanation* (New York: New York Public Library)

HYDE, WILLIAM J. 1957. 'George Eliot and the Climate of Realism', *PMLA*, 72: 147–64

IRWIN, JANE (ed.). 1996. *George Eliot's 'Daniel Deronda' Notebooks* (Cambridge: Cambridge University Press)

JAMES, HENRY. 1962. *The Art of the Novel: Critical Prefaces* (New York: Charles Scribner's Sons)

——1964. 'Daniel Deronda: A Conversation, 1876', in *Henry James: Selected Literary Criticism*, ed. by Morris Shapira (Harmondsworth: Penguin), pp. 32–48

——1978. *Letters of Henry James* (London: Macmillan)

JANSOHN, CHRISTA and DIETER MEHL (ed.). 2007. *The Reception of D. H. Lawrence in Europe* (London: Continuum)

JAUSS, HANS. 1982. *Toward an Aesthetic of Reception*, trans. by Timothy Bahti (Brighton: Harvester)

JELLIFFE, R. A. 1947. 'An Experiment in Comparative Literature', *College English* 9.2: 85–87

JEUNE, SIMON. 1968. *Littérature générale et littérature comparée: essai d'orientation* (Paris: Lettres Modernes)

JOHNSTON, MARGARET HARRIS and JUDITH (ed.). 1998. *The Journals of George Eliot* (Cambridge: Cambridge University Press)

JONES, PETER. 1975. *Philosophy and the Novel: Philosophical Aspects of 'Middlemarch', 'Anna Karenina', 'The Brothers Karamazov', 'A la recherche du temps perdu' and of the Methods of Criticism* (Oxford: Clarendon Press)

KARL, FREDERICK. 1995. *George Eliot: A Biography* (London: HarperCollins)

KAUFMANN, DAVID. 1877. *George Eliot and Judaism: An Attempt to Appreciate 'Daniel Deronda'*, trans. by James Walter Ferrier (Edinburgh and London)

KAYE, PETER. 1999. *Dostoevsky and English Modernism 1900–1930* (Cambridge: Cambridge University Press)

KERMODE, FRANK. 1967. *The Sense of an Ending: Studies in the Theory of Fiction* (New York: Oxford University Press)

KING, JEANETTE. 1978. *Tragedy in the Victorian Novel: Theory and Practice in the Novels of George Eliot, Thomas Hardy and Henry James* (Cambridge: Cambridge University Press)

KINKEAD-WEEKES, MARK. 1996. *D. H. Lawrence: Triumph to Exile, 1912–1922* (Cambridge: Cambridge University Press)

KNAPP, SHOSHANA. 1983. 'Tolstoj's Reading of George Eliot: Visions and Revisions', *Slavic and East European Journal*, 27: 318–26

——1997. '"Too Intensely French for My Taste": Victor Hugo as Read by George Eliot and George Henry Lewes', in *George Eliot and Europe*, ed. by John Rignall (Aldershot: Scolar Press), pp. 190–209

KNOEPFELMACHER, U. C. 1968. *George Eliot's Early Novels: The Limits of Realism* (Berkeley: University of California Press)

KNOWLES, A. V. (ed.). 1978. *Tolstoy: The Critical Heritage* (London: Routledge and Kegan Paul)

KOELB, CLAYTON (ed.). 1984. *Thomas Mann's 'Goethe and Tolstoy': Notes and Sources,* (University, Alabama: University of Alabama Press)

——and SUSAN NOAKES. 1988. *The Comparative Perspective on Literature: Approaches to Theory and Practice* (Ithaca and London: Cornell University Press)

KOVALEVSKAYA, SOFIA. 1978. 'A Russian View of George Eliot', *Nineteenth Century Fiction*, 33.3: 348–65

KROCKEL, KARL. 2007. *D. H. Lawrence and Germany* (Amsterdam: Rodopi)

KROPOTKIN, PETR. 1916. *Russian Literature: Ideals and Realities* (London: Duckworth)

LAWRENCE, D. H. 1961. *Phoenix: The Posthumous Papers of D. H. Lawrence* (London: Heinemann)

—— 1968. *Phoenix II: Uncollected, Unpublished and Other Prose Works by D. H. Lawrence* (London: Heinemann)

—— 1979–. *The Cambridge Edition of the Letters and Works of D. H. Lawrence* (Cambridge: Cambridge University Press)

—— 1980. *La serpiente emplumada*, trans. by Pilar Giralt (Barcelona: Braguera)

—— 1981. *The Trespasser*, ed. by Elizabeth Mansfield (Cambridge: Cambridge University Press)

—— 1983. *The Prussian Officer and Other Stories*, ed. by John Worthen (Cambridge: Cambridge University Press)

—— 1984. *Mr Noon*, ed. by Lindeth Vasey (Cambridge: Cambridge University Press)

—— 1985. *Study of Thomas Hardy and Other Essays*, ed. by Bruce Steele (Cambridge: Cambridge University Press)

—— 1987a. *Love among the Haystacks and Other Stories*, ed. by John Worthen (Cambridge: Cambridge University Press)

—— 1987b. *Women in Love*, ed. by David Farmer, Lindeth Vasey, and John Worthen (Cambridge: Cambridge University Press)

—— 1988a. *Aaron's Rod*, ed. by Mara Kalnins (Cambridge: Cambridge University Press)

—— 1988b. *Reflections on the Death of a Porcupine and Other Essays*, ed. by Michael Herbert (Cambridge: Cambridge University Press)

—— 1989. *The Rainbow*, ed. by Mark Kinkead-Weekes (Cambridge: Cambridge University Press)

—— 1992a. *Sketches of Etruscan Places and Other Italian Essays*, ed. by Simonette de Philippis (Cambridge: Cambridge University Press)

—— 1992b. *The Fox; The Ladybird; The Captain's Doll*, ed. by Dieter Mehl (Cambridge: Cambridge University Press)

—— 1993. *Lady Chatterley's Lover*, ed. by Michael Squires (Cambridge: Cambridge University Press)

—— 1994a. *Kangaroo*, ed. by Bruce Steele (Cambridge: Cambridge University Press)

—— 1994b. *Twilight in Italy and Other Essays*, ed. by Paul Eggert (Cambridge: Cambridge University Press)

—— 1995a. *The Plumed Serpent* (Ware: Wordsworth Editions)

—— 1995b. *Quetzalcoatl*, ed. by Louis L. Martz (New York: New Directions Publishing Corporation)

—— 1995c. *The Woman Who Rode Away and Other Stories*, ed. by Dieter Mehl and Christa Jansohn (Cambridge: Cambridge University Press)

—— 1998. *The First 'Women in Love'*, ed. by John Worthen and Lindeth Vasey (Cambridge: Cambridge University Press)

—— 1999. *D. H. Lawrence: The Plays*, ed. by Hans-Wilhelm Schwartze and John Worthen (Cambridge: Cambridge University Press)

—— 2000. *The Selected Letters of D. H. Lawrence*, ed. by James T. Boulton (Cambridge: Cambridge University Press)

—— 2004. *Psychoanalysis and the Unconscious and Fantasia of the Unconscious*, ed. by Bruce Steele (Cambridge: Cambridge University Press)

—— 2005. *Introductions and Reviews*, ed. by N. H. Reeve and John Worthen (Cambridge: Cambridge University Press)

—— 2008. *D. H. Lawrence Selected Poems*, ed. by James Fenton (London: Penguin)

LAWRENCE, FRIEDA. 1983. *Not I, but the Wind* (London: Granada Publishing)

Leavis, F. R. 1948. *The Great Tradition* (London: Chatto and Windus)

—— 1955. *D. H. Lawrence, Novelist* (London: Chatto and Windus)

—— 1967. *'Anna Karenina' and Other Essays* (London: Chatto and Windus)

—— 1976. *Thought, Words, and Creativity: Art and Thought in Lawrence* (London: Chatto and Windus)

—— 1986. *Valuation in Criticism and Other Essays* (Cambridge: Cambridge University Press)

Leskov, Nikolai S. 1986. *The Jews in Russia: Some Notes on the Jewish Question*, trans. by Harold Klassel Schefski (Princeton: The Kingston Press)

Levin, Harry. 1966. *Refractions: Essays in Comparative Literature* (New York and Oxford University Press)

—— 1972. *Grounds for Comparison* (Cambridge, Mass.: Harvard University Press)

Levine, George (ed.). 2001. *The Cambridge Companion to George Eliot* (Cambridge, Cambridge University Press)

Levitt, Ruth. 1975. *George Eliot: The Jewish Connection* (Jerusalem: Massada)

Lewes, George Henry. 1875. *On Actors and the Art of Acting* (London: Smith, Elder, & Co.)

—— 1911. *The Life and Works of Goethe: With Sketches of His Age and Contemporaries* (London: J. M. Dent)

Lonnqvist, Barbara. 2002. 'Anna Karenina', in *The Cambridge Companion to Tolstoy*, ed. by Donna Tussing Orwin (Cambridge: Cambridge University Press), pp. 80–95

Lukács, Georg. 1955. *Der historische Roman* (Neuwied and Berlin: Luchterhand)

—— 1962. *The Historical Novel*, trans. by Hannah and Stanley Mitchell (London: Merlin Press)

Makins, Marian. 1994. *Collins English Dictionary*, 3rd edn (Glasgow: Harper Collins)

Mandelker, Amy. 1993. *Framing 'Anna Karenina': Tolstoy, the Woman Question, and the Victorian Novel* (Ohio: Ohio State University Press)

Mann, Thomas. 1923. *Goethe und Tolstoi* (Aachen: Die Kuppel)

Mansell, Darrell, Jr. 1967. 'George Eliot's Conception of Tragedy', *Nineteenth Century Fiction*, 22.2: 155–71

—— 1985. 'Ruskin and George Eliot's "Realism"', *Criticism*, 7: 203–16

Martin, Graham. 1999. 'Lawrence and Modernism', in *D. H. Lawrence in Italy and England*, ed. by George Donaldson and Mara Kalnins (Basingstoke: Macmillan), pp. 135–53

Marx, Karl and Friedrich Engels. [1848] 1918. *Das kommunistische Manifest* (Berlin: Vorwärts Paul Ginger)

—— 1996. *The Communist Manifesto*, trans. by Samuel Moore (London and Chicago: Pluto)

Masson-Oursel, Paul. 1926. *Comparative Philosophy* (London: Kegan Paul)

Mckay, Brenda. 2003. *George Eliot and Victorian Attitudes to Racial Diversity, Colonialism, Darwinism, Class, Gender, and Jewish Culture and Prophecy* (Lampeter: Edwin Mellen Press)

Mckeon, Michael (ed.). 2000. *Theory of the Novel: A Historical Approach* (Baltimore and London: The Johns Hopkins University Press)

Mehl, Dieter and Christa Jansohn. 2007. 'The Reception of D. H. Lawrence in the German-Speaking Countries, 1922–1945' and 'After 1945', in *The Reception of D. H. Lawrence in Europe*, ed. by Elinor Shaffer (London: Continuum), pp. 23–52, 53–78

Meyers, Jeffrey. 1990. *D. H. Lawrence: A Biography* (London: Macmillan)

Miller, J. Hillis. 1975. 'Optic and Semiotic in *Middlemarch*', in *The Worlds of Victorian Fiction*, ed. by J.H. Buckley (Cambridge, Mass.: Harvard University Press), pp. 137–60

Miller, Malcolm V. Jones and Robin Feuer. 1998. *The Classic Russian Novel* (Cambridge: Cambridge University Press)

Mills, Howard. 1996. 'Mischief or Merriment, Amazement and Amusement — and Malice: Women in Love', in *Lawrence and Comedy*, ed. by Paul Eggert and John Worthen (Cambridge: Cambridge University Press), pp. 45–69

MILNE, DREW. 2001. 'Lawrence and the Politics of Sexual Politics', in *The Cambridge Companion to D. H. Lawrence*, ed. by Anne Fernihough (Cambridge: Cambridge University Press), pp. 197–216

MINER, EARL. 1987. 'Some Theoretical and Methodological Topics for Comparative Literature', *Poetics Today*, 8.1: 123–40

MITRY, JEAN. 1998. *The Aesthetics and Psychology of the Cinema*, trans. by Christopher King (London: Athlone Press)

MORETTI, FRANCO. 1996. *Modern Epic: The World-System from Goethe to García Marquez* (London: Verso)

——2007. *Graphs, Maps, Trees: Abstract Models for a Literary History* (London: Verso)

MORSON, GARY SAUL. 1987. *Hidden in Plain View: Narrative and Creative Potentials in 'War and Peace'* (Stanford: Stanford University Press)

——2007. *Anna Karenina in Our Time: Seeing More Wisely* (New Haven: Yale University Press)

MURRY, JOHN MIDDLETON. 1931. *Son of Woman: The Story of D. H. Lawrence* (London: Jonathan Cape)

——1916. *Fyodor Dostoevsky: A Critical Study* (London: n.p.)

MYERS, WILLIAM. 1984. *The Teaching of George Eliot* (Leicester: Leicester University Press)

NABOKOV, VLADIMIR. 1981. *Lectures on Russian Literature* (London: Weidenfeld and Nicolson)

NEHLS, EDWARD. 1957–79. *D. H. Lawrence: A Composite Biography* (Madison: University of Wisconsin Press), 3 vols

NEWMAN, JOHN HENRY. 1976. *The Idea of a University* (Oxford: Clarendon Press)

NEWTON, K. M. 1981. *George Eliot: Romantic Humanity: A Study of the Philosophical Structure of her Novels* (London: Macmillan)

——1986. *In Defence of Literary Interpretation: Theory and Practice* (London: Macmillan)

——1998. '*Daniel Deronda* by George Eliot 1876', in *Encyclopaedia of the Novel*, ed. by Paul Schellinger (Chicago: Fitzroy Dearborn), pp. 279–80

——2005. 'Revisions of Scott, Austen and Dickens in Daniel Deronda', *Dickens Studies Annual*, 35: 241–66

OLIPHANT, LAURENCE. 1854. *The Russian Shores of the Black Sea in the Autumn of 1852* (Edinburgh: Blackwood and Sons)

ORWIN, DONNA TUSSING. 1993. *Tolstoy's Art and Thought 1847–1880* (Princeton: Princeton University Press)

——(ed.). 2002. *The Cambridge Companion to Tolstoy* (Cambridge, Cambridge University Press)

PARIS, BERNARD J. 1965. *Experiments in Life: George Eliot's Quest for Values* (Detroit: Wayne State University Press)

PHELPS, GILBERT. 1956. *The Russian Novel in English Fiction* (London: Hutchinson)

PINKNEY, TONY. 1990. *D. H. Lawrence* (London: Harvester Wheatsheaf)

PINNEY, THOMAS (ed.). 1968. *Essays of George Eliot* (London, Routledge and Kegan Paul)

POLIAKOV, LEON. 1985. *The History of Anti-Semitism: Suicidal Europe, 1870–1933*, trans. by George Klin (Oxford: Oxford University Press)

POLONSKY, RACHEL. 1998. *English Literature and the Russian Aesthetic Renaissance* (Cambridge: Cambridge University Press)

POLOWETZKY, MICHAEL. 1995. *Jerusalem Recovered: Victorian Intellectuals and the Birth of Modern Zionism* (London: Praeger)

POOLE, ADRIAN. 1983. 'Hidden Affinities in *Daniel Deronda*', *Essays in Criticism*, 33.4: 294–311

POPE, REBECCA A. 1994. 'The Diva Doesn't Die: George Eliot's *Armgart*', in *Embodied Voices: Representing Female Vocality in Western Culture*, ed. by Nancy A. Jones and Leslie C. Dunn (Cambridge: Cambridge University Press), pp. 138–51

POSNETT, H. M. 1886. *Comparative Literature* (London: Kegan Paul)

—— 1901. 'The Science of Comparative Literature', *Contemporary Review*, 79: 864–65

PRAWER, SIEGBERT SALOMAN. 1973. *Comparative Literary Studies: An Introduction* (London: Duckworth)

PRAZ, MARIO. 1956. *The Hero in Eclipse in Victorian Fiction*, trans. by Angus Davidson (London: Oxford University Press)

PRESTON, PETER. 1988. 'Mr Noon and Lawrence's Quarrel with Tolstoy', *Études Lawrenciennes* 3: 109–23

QIAN, ZHONGSHU and RONALD C. EGAN. 1998. *Limited Views: Essays on Ideas and Letters* (Cambridge, Mass.: Harvard University Asia Center)

READER, A. 1890. *Russia and the Jews: A Brief Sketch of Russian History and the Condition of its Jewish Subjects* (London: Digby & Long)

REINHOLD, NATALYA. 2007. 'Russian Culture and the Work of D. H. Lawrence: An Eighty-Year Appropriation', in *The Reception of D. H. Lawrence in Europe*, ed. by Christa Jansohn and Dieter Mehl (London: Continuum), pp. 187–98

REMAK, HENRY FESTSCHRIFT 1961. 'Comparative Literature, its Definition and Function', in *Comparative Literature: Method and Perspective*, ed. by Newton Phelps Stallknecht and Horst Frenz (Carbondale: Southern Illinois University Press), pp. 3–37

— and RIESZ, JA NOS (ed.). 1986. *Sensus Communis: Contemporary Trends in Comparative Literature: Panorama de la situation actuelle en littérature comparée* (Tübingen: Narr)

RIGNALL, JOHN (ed.). 1997. *George Eliot and Europe* (Aldershot, Scolar Press)

— (ed.). 2000. *Oxford Reader's Companion to George Eliot* (Oxford, Oxford University Press)

RÖDER-BOLTON, GERLINDE. 1998. *George Eliot and Goethe: An Elective Affinity* (Amsterdam: Rodopi)

RORTY, RICHARD. 2006. 'Looking Back At "Literary Theory"', in *Comparative Literature in the Age of Globalization*, ed. by Haun Saussy (Baltimore: Johns Hopkins University Press), pp. 63–67

ROTH, JOHN K. 1995. *International Encyclopedia of Ethics* (London and Chicago: Fitzroy Dearborn)

ROUTH, H. V. 1913. 'The Future of Comparative Literature', *MLR*, 8.1: 1–14

RUSSELL, KEN. 1969. *Women in Love*. UK, MGM

SAGAR, KEITH. 1982. *A D. H. Lawrence Handbook* (Manchester: Manchester University Press)

—— 2008. 'A Note on the "Shame" Chapter of *the Rainbow*', *Journal of the D. H. Lawrence Society*, 1.3: 29–32

SANKOVITCH, NATASHA. 1998. *Creating and Recovering Experience: Repetition in Tolstoy* (Stanford: Stanford University Press)

SAUSSY, HAUN. 2003. 'Comparative Literature?', *PMLA*, 118.2: 336–41

—— (ed.). 2006. *Comparative Literature in an Age of Globalization* (Baltimore: Johns Hopkins University Press)

SCHERR, BARRY J. 1996. *D. H. Lawrence's Response to Plato: A Bloomian Interpretation* (New York: P. Lang)

SCHERR, BARRY J. 2004. *D. H. Lawrence Today: Literature, Culture, Politics* (New York: Peter Lang)

—— 2008. *Love and Death in Lawrence and Foucault* (New York: Peter Lang)

SCHOPENHAUER, ARTHUR. 1969. *The World as Will and Representation*, trans. by E. F. J. Payne (New York: Dover)

—— 1987. *Die Welt als Wille und Vorstellung* (Frankfurt am Main: Insel Verlag)

SCHULTZE, SIDNEY. 1982. *The Structure of 'Anna Karenina'* (Ann Arbor: Ardis)

SEYMOUR, BRUCE. 1996. *Lola Montez: A Life* (London: Yale University Press)

SHAFFER, ELINOR. 1975. *'Kubla Khan' and 'The Fall of Jerusalem': The Mythological School in Biblical Criticism and Secular Literature 1770–1880* (Cambridge: Cambridge University Press)

——(ed.). 1979–2004. *Comparative Criticism: A Yearbook* (Cambridge: Cambridge University Press)

——1996. 'George Eliot and Goethe: "Hearing the Grass Grow" ', *Publications of the English Goethe Society*, 66: 3–22

SHAKESPEARE, WILLIAM. 1986. *The Complete Works* (Oxford: Oxford University Press)

SHESTOV, LEV. 1907. *Добро в учении Гр. Толстого и Ф. Нитше* (Санкт Петербург: Издание М. В. Пирожкова)

——1969. *Good in the Teaching of Tolstoy and Nietzsche: Philosophy and Preaching*, trans. by Bernard Martin (Ohio: Ohio University Press)

SHKLOVSKII, VIKTOR. 1967. *Лев Толстой* (Москва: Издательство Ц К ВЛКСМ)

——1978. *Lev Tolstoy*, trans. by Olga Shartse (Moscow: Progress Publications)

SHUTTLEWORTH, SALLY. 1984. *George Eliot and Nineteenth Century Science* (Cambridge: Cambridge University Press)

SIMMONS, ERNEST J. 1935. *English Literature and Culture in Russia (1553–1840)* (Cambridge: Harvard University Press)

SKLENICKA, CAROL. 1991. *D. H. Lawrence and the Child* (Missouri: University of Missouri Press)

SMILES, SAMUEL. 1996. *Self-Help* (London: The IEA Health and Welfare Unit)

SMITH, ANTHONY D. 1986. *The Ethnic Origins of Nations* (Oxford: Blackwell)

SMITH, DOUGLAS. 2008. *The Pearl: A True Tale of Forbidden Love in Catherine the Great's Russia* (New Haven: Yale University Press)

SMITH, G. GREGORY. 1905. 'Some Notes on the Comparative Study of Literature', *MLR*, 1.1: 1–8

SOUSA CORREA, DELIA DA. 2002. *George Eliot, Music and Victorian Culture* (Basingstoke: Palgrave Macmillan)

SPEIRS, LOGAN. 1971. *Tolstoy and Chekhov* (London: Cambridge University Press)

SPIVAK, GAYATRI CHAKRAVORTY. 2003. *Death of a Discipline* (New York: Columbia University Press)

STALLKNECHT, NEWTON PHELPS and HORST FRENZ (eds). 1961. *Comparative Literature: Method and Perspective* (Carbondale: Southern Illinois University Press)

STARK, SUZANNE. 1997. 'Marian Evans, the Translator', in *Translating Literature*, ed. by Susan Barnett (Cambridge: The English Association Collection), pp. 119–40

STEINER, GEORGE. 1967. *Tolstoy or Dostoevsky* (London: Penguin)

——1975. *After Babel: Aspects of Language and Translation* (Oxford: Oxford University Press)

——1996. 'What Is Comparative Literature?', *Comparative Criticism*, 18: 157–71

STENBOCK-FERMOR, E. 1967. *The Architecture of 'Anna Karenina': A History of Its Writing, Structure, and Message* (Lisse: Peter de Ridder Press)

STOKES, JOHN. 1984. 'Rachel's "Terrible Beauty": An Actress among the Novelists', *English Literary History*, 51: 771–93

STRICH, FRITZ. 1949. *Goethe and World Literature*, trans. by C. A. M. Sym (London: Butler & Tanner)

——1957. *Goethe und die Weltliteratur* (Bern: Francke Verlag)

SWALES, MARTIN. 1979. 'The German *Bildungsroman* and '*The Great Tradition*', *Comparative Criticism*, 1.1: 91–105

SZONDI, PETER. 1967. *Hölderlin-Studien: mit einem Traktet über philologische Erkenntnis* (Frankfurt am Main: Insel Verlag)

TEXTE, JOSEPH. 1900. 'Introduction', in *La Littérature comparée*, ed. by Louis-P. Betz (Strasbourg: Trüebner), pp. xix–xxiv

THORLBY, ANTHONY. 1987. *Tolstoy: 'Anna Karenina'* (Cambridge: Cambridge University Press)

TODOROV, TZVETAN. 1978. *Les Genres du discours* (Paris: Seuil)

TOLSTOI, ILIA. 1914. *Reminiscences of Tolstoi*, trans. by George Calderon (London: Chapman and Hall)

TOLSTOI, LEV. 1896. *Anna Karénina*, trans. by Nathan Haskell Dole (London: Walter Scott)

—— 1898. *Что такое искусство?* (Москва: n.pub.)

—— 1901. *Anna Karenin*, trans. by Constance Garnett (London: Heinemann)

—— 1904. *War and Peace*, trans. by Constance Garnett (London: Heinemann)

—— 1910. *Письма Л. Н. Толстого 1848–1910 гг*, ed. by P. A. Sergienko (Москва: Книга)

—— 1921. *A Confession, What I Believe*, trans. by Aylmer Maude (London: Oxford University Press)

—— 1931. *Люцерн* in *Польное собрание сочинении* (Москва: Государственное издательство художественной литературы), v, 3–26

—— 1939. *Anna Karenina*, trans. by Constance Garnett (New York: Random House)

—— 1950. 'О Шекспире и о драме', in *Л. Н. Толстои, Польное собрание сочинении* (Москва: Государственной издательство художественной литературы) xxxv, 216–72

—— 1952. *Анна Каренина: роман в восьми частях*, in *Л. Н. Толстои, Собрание сочинении в четырнадсати томах* (Москва: Государственное издательство художественной литературы) VIII, IX

—— 1955. *О литературе* (Москва: Государственное издательство художественной литературы)

—— 1956. *Anna Karenin*, trans. by Rosemary Edmonds (London: Penguin)

—— 1957. *'Ivan Ilych' and 'Hadji Murad' and Other Stories*, trans. by Louise and Aylmer Maude (London: Oxford University Press)

—— 1963. *Что такое искусство?* (Letchworth: Bradda Books)

—— 1963. *Исповедь* (London: Bradda Books)

—— 1978. *Tolstoy's Letters*, trans. by R. F. Christian (London: Athlone Press)

—— 1983. *The Kreutzer Sonata and Other Stories*, trans. by David Mcduff (London: Penguin)

—— 1985. *Tolstoy's Diaries*, trans. by R. F. Christian, 2 vols (London: Athlone Press)

—— 1989. *I Cannot Be Silent: Writings on Politics, Art and Religion by Leo Tolstoy*, trans. by W. Gareth Jones (Bristol: Bristol Press)

—— 1993. *'How Much Land Does a Man Need?' and Other Stories*, trans. by Ronald Wilks (London: Penguin)

—— 1995. *Anna Karenina*, trans. by Louise and Aylmer Maude (Hertfordshire: Wordsworth Editions)

—— 1997. *The Kreutzer Sonata and Other Stories*, trans. by Louise and Aylmer Maude and J. D. Duff (Oxford Oxford University Press)

—— 2000. *Anna Karenina*, trans. by Richard Pevear and Larissa Volokhonsky (London: Penguin)

—— 2004. *Resurrection*, trans. by Louise Maude (New York: Dover Publications)

—— 2005. *War and Peace*, trans. by Anthony Briggs (London: Penguin)

TÖTÖSY DE ZEPETNEK, STEVEN. 1998. *Comparative Literature: Theory, Method, Application* (Amsterdam: Rodopi)

TROLLOPE, ANTHONY. 1964. *Phineas Redux* (London: Oxford University Press)

TROTTER, DAVID. 1993. *The English Novel in History 1895–1920* (London and New York: Routledge)

TROYAT, HENRI. 1965. *Tolstoi* (Paris: Fayard)

—— 1968. *Tolstoy*, trans. by Nancy Amphoux (London: W. H. Allen)

TUCKER, IRENE. 2000. *A Probable State: The Novel, the Contract, and the Jews* (Chicago and London: University of Chicago Press)

TURGENEV, IVAN. 1961. *Собрание сочинении* (Москва: Государственное издательство художественной литературы)

TURNER, C. J. G. 1993. *A Karenina Companion* (Ontario: Wilfrid Laurier University Press)

VERGA, GIOVANNI. 1928. *'Cavalleria Rusticana' and Other Stories*, trans. by D. H. Lawrence (London: Cape)

VOGÜE, E. MELCHIOR DE LE VICOMTE. 1892. *Le Roman russe*, 3rd edn (Paris: Plon, Nourrit)

WASIOLEK, EDWARD. 1978. *Tolstoy's Major Fiction* (Chicago: The University of Chicago Press)

WATT, IAN. 1957. *The Rise of the Novel: Studies in Defoe, Richardson and Fielding* (London: Chatto and Windus)

WEISSTEIN, ULRICH. 1968. *Einführung in die vergleichende Literaturwissenschaft* (Stuttgart: W. Kohlhammer Verlag)

——and WILLIAM RIGGAN. 1973. *Comparative Literature and Literary Theory: Survey and Introduction* (Bloomington: Indiana University Press)

WELLEK, RENÉ. 1963. 'The Crisis of Comparative Literature', in *Concepts of Criticism*, ed. by Stephen G. Nichols (New Haven and London: Yale University Press), pp. 282–95

——and AUSTIN WARREN. 1949. *Theory of Literature* (London: Jonathan Cape)

WENINGER, ROBERT. 2006. 'Comparative Literature at a Crossroads?', *Comparative Critical Studies*, 3.1–2: xi–xix

WERSES, SHMUEL. 1976. 'The Jewish Reception of Daniel Deronda', in *'Daniel Deronda': A Centenary Symposium*, ed. by Alice Shalvi (Jerusalem: Jerusalem Academic Press), pp. 11–47

WILDE, OSCAR. 2006. *The Importance of Being Earnest* (New York and London: Norton)

WILLIAMS, BERNARD. 1993. 'Moral Luck', in *Moral Luck*, ed. by Daniel Statman (New York: State University of New York), pp. 35–56

WILLIAMS, RAYMOND. 1960. 'Lawrence and Tolstoi', *Critical Quarterly*, 2: 33–39

——1963. 'Tolstoi, Lawrence and Tragedy', *Kenyon Review*, 25: 633–50

——1966. *Modern Tragedy* (London: Chatto and Windus)

——1971. *The English Novel: From Dickens to Lawrence* (London: Chatto and Windus)

WILSON, A. N. 1988. *Tolstoy* (London: Penguin)

WITEMEYER, HUGH (ed.). 1992. *George Eliot's Originals and Contemporaries: Essays in Victorian Literary History and Biography* (Basingstoke: Macmillan)

WOOD, ELLEN. 2000. *East Lynne* (Ontario: Broadview)

WOOLF, VIRGINIA. 1957. 'The Russian Point of View', in *The Common Reader* (London: The Hogarth Press), pp. 219–31

——1988. 'George Eliot (1819–1880)', in *The Essays of Virginia Woolf* (III) (London: Hogarth Press), pp. 293–94

WORTHEN, JOHN. 2005. *D. H. Lawrence: The Life of an Outsider* (London: Penguin)

WRIGHT, T. R. 2000. *D. H. Lawrence and the Bible* (Cambridge: Cambridge University Press)

ZARKHI, ALEXANDR. 1967. *Анна Каренина*. Советский союз: Мосфильм

ZYTARUK, GEORGE J. 1971. *D. H. Lawrence's Response to Russian Literature* (The Hague: Mouton)

INDEX